PERGAMON INTERNATIONAL LIBRARY
of Science, Technology, Engineering and Social Studies

*The 1000-volume original paperback library in aid of education,
industrial training and the enjoyment of leisure*

Publisher: Robert Maxwell, M.C.

Stopping Rape

THE PERGAMON TEXTBOOK
INSPECTION COPY SERVICE

An inspection copy of any book published in the Pergamon International Library
will gladly be sent to academic staff without obligation for their consideration for
course adoption or recommendation. Copies may be retained for a period of 60 days
from receipt and returned if not suitable. When a particular title is adopted or
recommended for adoption for class use and the recommendation results in a sale
of 12 or more copies the inspection copy may be retained with our compliments.
The Publishers will be pleased to receive suggestions for revised editions and new
titles to be published in this important international Library.

THE ATHENE SERIES

An International Collection of Feminist Books
General Editors: Gloria Bowles and Renate Duelli-Klein
Consulting Editor: Dale Spender

The ATHENE SERIES assumes that all those who are concerned with formulating explanations of the way the world works need to know and appreciate the significance of basic feminist principles.

The growth of feminist research has challenged almost all aspects of social organization in our culture. The ATHENE SERIES focuses on the construction of knowledge and the exclusion of women from the process — both as theorists and subjects of study—and offers innovative studies that challenge established theories and research.

ON ATHENE — When Metis, goddess of wisdom who presided over all knowledge was pregnant with ATHENE, she was swallowed up by Zeus who then gave birth to ATHENE from his head. The original ATHENE is thus the parthenogenetic daughter of a strong mother and as the feminist myth goes, at the "third birth" of ATHENE she stops being Zeus' obedient mouthpiece and returns to her real source: the science and wisdom of womankind

---

Volumes in the Series
MEN'S STUDIES MODIFIED The Impact of Feminism
on the Academic Disciplines
edited by Dale Spender

MACHINA EX DEA Feminist Perspectives on Technology
edited by Joan Rothschild

WOMAN'S NATURE Rationalizations of Inequality
edited by Marian Lowe and Ruth Hubbard

SCIENCE AND GENDER A Critique of Biology and Its Theories on Women
Ruth Bleier

WOMAN IN THE MUSLIM UNCONSCIOUS
Fatna A. Sabbah

MEN'S IDEAS/WOMEN'S REALITIES *Popular Science*, 1870-1915
edited by Louise Michele Newman

BLACK FEMINIST CRITICISM Perspectives on Black Women Writers
Barbara Christian

THE SISTER BOND A Feminist View of a Timeless Connection
edited by Toni A.H. McNaron

EDUCATING FOR PEACE A Feminist Perspective
Birgit Brock-Utne

STOPPING RAPE Successful Survival Strategies
Pauline B. Bart and Patricia H. O'Brien

NOTICE TO READERS

May we suggest that your library places a standing/continuation order to receive all future volumes in the Athene Series immediately on publication?
Your order can be cancelled at any time.

Also of Interest

WOMEN'S STUDIES INTERNATIONAL FORUM*
Editor: Dale Spender
Free sample copy available on request

Stopping Rape

Successful Survival Strategies

Pauline B. Bart
UCLA
Patricia H. O'Brien
St. Xavier College

Pergamon Press

New York • Oxford • Toronto • Sydney • Frankfurt

Pergamon Press Offices:

U.S.A.   Pergamon Press Inc., Maxwell House, Fairview Park,
                       Elmsford, New York 10523, U.S.A.

U.K.   Pergamon Press Ltd., Headington Hill Hall,
                       Oxford OX3 0BW, England

CANADA   Pergamon Press Canada Ltd., Suite 104, 150 Consumers Road,
                       Willowdale, Ontario M2J 1P9, Canada

AUSTRALIA   Pergamon Press (Aust.) Pty. Ltd., P.O. Box 544,
                       Potts Point, NSW 2011, Australia

FEDERAL REPUBLIC   Pergamon Press GmbH, Hammerweg 6,
OF GERMANY   D-6242 Kronberg-Taunus, Federal Republic of Germany

Copyright © 1985 Pergamon Press Inc.

Library of Congress Cataloging in Publication Data

Bart, Pauline.
    Stopping rape.

    (The Athene series)
    1. Rape--United States. 2. Rape--United States--
Prevention. I. O'Brien, Patricia H. (Patricia Helen),
1949-   . II. Title. III. Series.
HV6561.B367   1985   362.8'83   85-6589
ISBN 0-08-032814-8
ISBN 0-08-032813-X (pbk.)

Printed in Great Britain by A. Wheaton & Co. Ltd., Exeter

We dedicate this book to the women who shared their experiences with us, some of them enduring nightmares and anxiety at the thought of being interviewed and having to speak once more about their assaults. They did so because they wanted to give their suffering purpose by helping other women avoid sexual assault.

We also dedicate this book to Maura and Jake, Pat's children, and Rebecca, Pauline's granddaughter, with the fervent hope, but not the expectation, that they will be able to live in a rape-free society.

Contents

continued

Preface

We became concerned about sexual assault long before writing this book, for fear of rape lies within the hearts of all women. We are warned to be wary of rapists at an early age (Griffin, 1971), and we are advised on how to avoid rape by family, friends, schools, legal institutions, and the media.

This is not a recent trend. In 1857, the Macon Missouri *Gazette* presented women with the following cautionary note:

> A young lady of California recently broke her neck while resisting an attempt of a young man to kiss her; this furnished a fearful warning to young ladies. (State Historical Society of Missouri)

We all know women who have been raped and who have avoided rape though they may not have told us. In 1973, one of us (Bart) was awakened by the telephone at seven o'clock one morning. It was a friend in tears. I had never heard her cry before; she was a tough woman. She told me that she'd been raped, that the police were there and that they were taking her to a nearby hospital. My roommate and I went to the hospital to meet her. She was in the examining room, legs up in stirrups, but we couldn't be with her. She was kept in that vulnerable position for what seemed to her an interminable length of time. After that, I was able to go with her to x-ray; had I not gone with her, she would have been by herself. She was treated very much as if she had suffered a sprained ankle, rather than having been violated for several hours in danger of being murdered.

Later, her landlord refused to refund her apartment deposit when she wanted to move, as is common with women who are raped at home in their beds. He also warned her not to tell her experience to other women in the building. But a group of feminists said that they would picket the building unless he returned the deposit, so he relented. After the hospital experience she talked with my roommate, a feminist therapist. The next time I saw her, several hours later, was outside the Women and Health class that I was teaching. She said, "Pauline, do you think that it would be good for the class if I would talk about what happened?" I said, "It would be good for the class, but I don't know if it would be good for you, which is the most important thing." She thought it would be, so she decided to talk about it.

It bonded the class, which became like a Greek chorus, validating her perceptions and giving her support. She is continuing to study rape because, as she told me, "I have to find out why he did that to me," but she says she now feels more in control. It had taken her eight years to reach this point.

After that incident, two men tried to force their way into her car while she was starting it. She thought, "NEVER AGAIN!" and pushed and kicked them and managed to get away. So, it is clear that the same woman could on one occasion be raped and on another avoid it.

The next year Pauline Bart received the following letter from her mother who was in her seventies about a young man who tried to pull her into his car to "show her a good time." She had not only freed herself from his grasp, but memorized the license number of his car.

> Dear Pauline,
> . . . . When I reported to the police in order to remove him from further activity by bringing charges against him, I went through an ordeal at police headquarters which I will always remember. It seems that *I* was the criminal who attempted to attack him. I was suspect 100% and they tried to dissuade me from bringing charges by all psychological means. Of course, I had my say and gave them plenty. They jailed him . . . and released him on bail. He skipped town, forfeiting his bail. Any time I read of a rape and murder, I think of this young man.
>
> If I were in the leadership of women's organizations, I would attempt to change this medieval procedure, 100 years old. It must be taken out of the hands of men—police, judges, photographers. They must be banned and kept out of all laws regarding rape. I am convinced that each one of them, thinking of his indiscretions past, present, and future, identifies with the rapist, having the mortal fear that some woman may "frame him."

These are just two of the experiences which served as the catalysts for this study and book. These experiences resound with the pain women have experienced since the beginning of time: the pain of male violence.

Acknowledgments

Pauline B. Bart

This book is based on research funded by the Center for the Prevention and Control of Rape of the National Institute of Mental Health, Grant #MH 29311, awarded in 1977.

Joyce Lazare of the National Institute of Mental Health, Marlene Drescher, Pat Miller, Rae L. Blumberg and Ellen Perlmutter helped with the grant preparation. The staff of the University of Illinois, particularly Elaine Engstrom, Pat Kratochwill, Luberta Shirley, and Cynthia Baines, helped with the manuscript preparation. Miki Tomaschewski and Patricia O'Brien were Project Directors for the study. Elaine Sciolino, formerly of *Newsweek* and now with *The New York Times*, and Carol Kleiman of *Ms.* and the *Chicago Tribune* helped publicize the study, and Carol as well as Denise Rondini skillfully edited our work. Letitia Keller edited the revised version of the manuscript and performed the various tasks, both psychological and editorial, necessary to bring the manuscript up to date when it was revised in 1983–84. Dr. Marlyn Grossman interviewed 19 of the 94 women we studied, and Nancy Cygan did the computer work. Pat Miller, our methods consultant, was always available to insure the rigor of our analysis as well as giving us data analysis methods that facilitated our work. Kim Scheppele co-authored with Bart the paper on which Chapter 2 was based, "There Ought to Be a Law: Self Perceptions and Legal Perceptions of Rape," presented at the meeting of the American Sociological Association in 1980 and which appears in the *Journal of Social Issues*, in a somewhat different form. Scheppele also drafted several appendices. Penelope Seator returned to Chicago from California to help us finish the book, particularly revisions of Chapter 4. Lee McMahon facilitated the writing of Chapter 7 and spent her long holiday weekend proofreading and preparing the manuscript for submission so it could be sent out in time to meet the deadline. Diana Russell read the manuscript and made valuable suggestions.

My agent, Sandra Elkin, was always confident of the importance of this book and that confidence helped us over some rough times. Louis Shapiro, M.D. was a constant source of support and encouragement.

I also thank my son, Bill Bart, and daughter, Melinda Bart Schlesinger. When I returned to school to obtain my PhD they endured the stress of my life on overload. In fact, they helped me code and collate my dissertation on depression in middle-aged women, "Portnoy's Mother's Complaint." Bill has used his skill as a lawyer to help victims of sex discrimination, and Melinda has used her skill as a social worker to direct a program for children in a battered women's shelter and to work with sexually abused children and their families.

Patricia O'Brien

Thanks to Vince and Maura Vizza for their patience in living with me while I worked on this book and all the concessions in "normalcy" that meant. Thanks to Kathy McDonough, Marge O'Brien, and Barb Kramer for keeping Maura out of trouble while this book was being written. Thanks to Marge Jozsa and Dan Sheridan for their skilled advice as well as their moral support.

1 Why Study Women Who Avoided Rape?

This is a study of women who were attacked and avoided being raped. Although psychoanalysts say a gun is a substitute phallus, in the case of rape, the reverse is true—a phallus is a substitute gun.[1]

We know that violence against women and the threat of such violence, of which rape is paradigmatic, is widespread, underreported and trivialized. Violence, and the threat of violence functions as a means of social control, subordinating women. Rapists, as Susan Brownmiller says, are "The shock troops of male supremacy, batterers are the home guard" (Jones, 1980, p. 82).

We know that rapes by men that the women know are especially under-reported, and we know that those rapes frequently cause more harm than the stereotyped stranger-in-the-alley rape (Bart, 1975).

We know that women reporting such violence are commonly labelled deviant (Schur, 1984).

We know that child rape, mistakenly called seduction, particularly father-daughter incest, is widespread and probably the most underreported crime (Finkelhor, 1979; Herman, 1981; Rush, 1980).

We know that every female from nine months to ninety years is at risk, but certain categories of women, especially young, single women living alone, women who come home late, and women who use public transportation, are particularly at risk for rape by strangers.

We know that the myths about rape (e.g., that you can't rape a woman against her will, that virtuous women are not attacked, that women enjoy being raped) are lies that function to maintain the inequality between the sexes.

We know that advice about how to behave when attacked, advice telling women to act in traditionally feminine ways, is wrong.

Rape analysts, such as Susan Brownmiller (1975), Diana Russell (1975),

---

[1]See MacKinnon, 1979, *Sexual Harassment*, p. 298, for a critique of the idea that rape has nothing to do with sex. Also see discussion of the "intercourse in rape" and the "rape in intercourse" later in this chapter. See also Catharine A. MacKinnon, in-class lecture, Stanford University Law School, 1981.

and Susan Griffin (1971) have stated that women have a trained inability to avoid rape because of the female socialization to be victims. Women are taught to equate physical fighting with unfeminine behavior and to believe that men will protect them. Thus many women believe that they do not need to learn to take care of themselves because a man will. But from whom will men protect them? From other men, of course. This is the biggest protection racket in the world, according to the philosopher Susan Rae Peterson (1977).

Historically women have been advised to avoid rape by restricting their behavior; thus the Israeli parliament suggested a curfew on women when the rape rate increased. However, Prime Minister Golda Meir suggested a curfew on men because they were the ones doing the raping. Women are advised not to hitchhike, not to go out at night, not to dress provocatively. Researchers Riger and Gordon (1981) have shown that this fear of rape and the subsequent restriction of behavior act as a form of social control over women. Frederick Storaska (1975), claiming data that he will not make public, charges huge fees to tell women how to say no to a rapist and survive. Police departments put out leaflets, and rape crisis centers and self-defense groups produce pamphlets and offer courses. Holly Near, a feminist, sings "Fight Back" (1978). Hanmer and Saunders (1984) discuss the "Well Founded Fear."

But, until recently, there was no available data-based advice (e.g., based on systematically talking to women who had been raped and women who avoided being raped) that could be given to schools, hospitals, police, courts, or individuals, stating how rape could be avoided. This lack of data left unanswered the question of "What do I do if someone tries to rape me?"

This book was written to help women answer that question. It will focus on the differences between women who were raped and women who avoided being raped.

HOW THE BOOK IS ORGANIZED

Starting with Chapter 2, how the women define their situation (whether they consider themselves raped or avoiding rape), we follow the women through the rape situation, noting the factors in the situation, such as the presence of a weapon and the location of the attack, that are associated with rape avoidance. We then arrive at Chapter 4, the raison d'être of the book, "How Accosted Women Prevented Rape." In this chapter we list the kinds of strategies, the number of different strategies, and the combination of strategies that are effective in stopping attacks. We also show that what the women were thinking about, whether they focused on not being raped or not being killed or mutilated, was associated with the outcome of the assault. We demonstrate the inadequacy of traditional advice to women on how to prevent rape, notably attempts to humanize the situation, although we note the valuable function that can be played by negotiation with the rapist. Next in Chapters 5 and 6 we turn to factors in the women's backgrounds that are associated with stopping an attack. We learn about the importance of independence training, of having women in their lives whom they admire as role models, and we learn that women who know self defense, first aid, and how to deal with common emergencies are also women who are more likely to avoid rape.

Since there are tendencies for different ethnic groups to have differences in ratio of rape to rape avoidance, relevant data are discussed in Chapter 6. Based on the data we collected, Chapter 7 addresses the important issue of why men rape. We give the women's answers to that question, their description of what their assailants said, and integrate these data into existing research on rapists and "normal" men. The concept of entitlement is introduced here — the male ideology that they are entitled to goods and services from women as a class. This belief system can in part account for men's raping, battering, and committing incest and child sexual assault.

In the concluding chapter, after summarizing the findings, we draw out the policy implications with the hope that our society can be changed so that it will no longer be a rape culture.

METHODS

The Interviews

This book is based on an analysis of 94 interviews with women 18 or older who had been attacked and avoided being raped ($n = 51$) or had been raped ($n = 43$) in the two years prior to the interview.

It should be noted that we limited the sample to women who experienced either force or the threat of force in their experience, so that the experience would approximate the standard definition of rape or rape avoidance. The interview consisted of a self-report section dealing with demographic variables and unstructured and semi-structured questions dealing with situational and background variables. Because of the exploratory nature of the research, questions were added when unanticipated patterns emerged; e.g., regarding incest and child sexual assault and other violence in the woman's life, and whether the women were primarily concerned with being killed or mutilated or primarily concerned with not being raped. The first part of the schedule addressed situational variables, such as the presence of a weapon, the number of assailants, the response of the woman, the acts that occurred during the assault, and the degree of acquaintance with the assailant. The second part dealt with background variables, such as childhood and adult socialization experiences, issues of competence, autonomy, and socialization into a traditional female role. Additional questions dealt with the raped woman and her significant others' (e.g., parents, spouse, lover) response to the assault, as well as her interaction with institutions such as the police, hospitals, and therapists. We also examined the negotiation process between the woman and her assailant(s) if such negotiation took place.

Eighty percent of the interviews were conducted by the principal investigator (Bart) and 20 percent by a female clinical psychologist (Grossman). The interviews lasted from one and a half to six hours, depending on the subject's desire to talk, as well as her history of violence. These interviews were transcribed.

The Sample

A random sample was not feasible because of the nature of the major research question of this study. Therefore, following a pretest, a campaign to recruit respondents was launched. A total of 94 women were recruited through various sources: (a) 25 women responded to newspaper ads (including major Black and Hispanic papers), (b) 20 women were reached through press releases, (c) 8 women were reached through public service announcements (the radio announcements were in both English and Spanish), and (d) appearances on radio and T.V., (e) 5 women were reached through flyers, (f) 24 women participated because of contacts initiated through friendship networks of the project staff and other subjects.

The resulting purposive (i.e., nonrandom) sample, as compared to the female population of the Chicago SMSA (standard metropolitan statistical area—including DuPage, Kane Lake, McHenry and Will Counties), was disproportionately white, young, unmarried (i.e., both single and divorced),[2] and either economically active or students (i.e., none of the women who responded were only engaged in domestic labor at the time of the interview). However, while the sample is not representative of women in the Chicago SMSA, it is not very different from the population of raped women and rape avoiders in the "victimization" data (McDermott, 1979), except for an overrepresentation of Caucasian females. See Tables 1.1 and 1.2.

In addition to the assumed demographic bias, the sample is shaped by the use of volunteers.[3]

---

[2]May 3, 1982. Channel 2, CBS News, Chicago. The manager of an apartment house in Lincoln Park West was killed chasing a man who had attacked a woman in the lobby of the building and whose screams drew him in. Police said that it is a high crime area because there are many single women there who are stalked by men.

[3]We attempted to illuminate this phenomenon in two ways: (a) we first asked women why they volunteered (the two primary motives proved to be "altruism" and "catharsis," often in combination); and (b) we then questioned them as to where they learned about the study so we could tell what the pathways to the study were.

Table 1.1. Comparison of Data on Sexually Assaulted Women

Variable	Percentage of Women in Study			
	Bart and O'Brien ($n = 94$)	McIntyre ($n = 32$)	Queen's Bench ($n = 108$)	National Victimization Surveys[a] ($n =$ approx. 22,000)
Age:				
Under 25	36	66[b]	71	59
Over 35	10	—	7	15
Race:				
White	81	75	79	69
Nonwhite	19	—	21	31
Marital status:				
Single	57	68	80	58
Married	16	—	10	22
Separated or divorced	27	—	11	17
Widowed	—	—	—	3
Work status:				
Employed full-time	62	46	39	46
Employed part-time	13	—	—	—
Student	12	35	37	15
Unemployed	8	—	13	6
Homemaker	4	—	1	33
Missing information	1	—	—	—
Attacked by stranger	78[c]	77	81	82
Rape completed	46	60	63	33
Weapon present	46	—	33	40
Attacked by multiple assailants	13	14	15	16
Reported attack to police	66	—	—	56

Sources — Jennie J. McIntyre, "Victim Response to Rape: Alternative Outcomes" (final report to National Institute of Mental Health, grant R01MH29045); Queen's Bench Foundation, "Rape: Prevention and Resistance" (Queen's Bench Organization, 1255 Post St., San Francisco, California, 1976); Joan McDermott, "Rape Victimization in 26 American Cities" (Washington, D.C.: Department of Justice, Law Enforcement Assistance Administration, Government Printing Office, 1979).

[a] All percentages (except for the percent attacked by strangers) are calculated for attacks by strangers only.

[b] Percentage calculated for women under 26, not 25.

[c] Includes 71 percent raped by total strangers and 7 percent raped by men known by sight or met on a casual first encounter.

A final source of possible bias in our sample was the very high proportion of women who had been raped by strangers (approximately 71 percent). An additional 7 percent were attacked by men they had met for the first time just prior to the assault. The high proportion of rape by strangers can account for the relatively high rate of reporting to the police that was found — 66 percent (see Russell, 1982 — only 8 percent of her sample reported rape; see also Bart, 1975, where only one third reported).

Actually, we currently have no way of knowing what the "real" population of women who were sexually assaulted looks like. On the one hand, rapes reported to the police are known to be gross undercounts of total

Table 1.2. Demographics of the Victims in This Study ($n = 94$)

Variable	Percentage	(n)
Age		
Range: 18–72 years		
Mean: 28.14 years		
Race		
Caucasian	81	(76)
Black	15	(14)
Hispanic	4	(4)
Religion		
Catholic	35	(33)
Protestant	37	(35)
Jewish	19	(18)
Other	2	(2)
No religion	7	(6)
Marital status at Time of Attack		
Never married	58	(54)
Married, living with husband	15	(14)
Married, not living with husband	6	(6)
Divorcing or divorced	20	(19)
Missing information	1	(1)
Education		
High school or less	12	(11)
Some college	44	(41)
Four-year degree	19	(18)
Post-graduate work	25	(24)
Occupation		
Dependency	2	(2)
Housewife	2	(2)
Blue collar	10	(9)
Clerical	33	(32)
Professional	31	(29)
Student	9	(8)
Interim job (usually student)	12	(11)
Degree of Acquaintance with Assailant		
Stranger	71	(67)
Knew by sight/casual first encounter	7	(7)
Known assailant including husband	22	(20)

rapes and disproportionately involve rapes by strangers (Bart, 1975). On the other hand, victimization researchers have found that some respondents have failed to tell the interviewer about rapes actually reported to the police (McDermott, 1979). Further clouding the nature of the universe is the problem of defining rape; many women who agree that they have been forced to have sex do not label it rape (Frieze et al., 1979).

When examining the methodology it should be recalled that our purpose is not to describe who gets raped, but to learn what strategies are effective in avoiding rape, as well as the background and situational variables that differentiate raped women from rape avoiders. Were this study unique in concluding that the use of active strategies including physical resistance is effective in rape avoidance we would hesitate to make inferences from the data. However since, as we will show, there are four other studies that arrive at similar conclusions, even though we worked independently of one another, we feel more confident about our findings. As will be shown in Chapter 4, we did not find that degree of acquaintance was substantially related to the effectiveness or use of any particular strategy. Nonetheless, we do want the reader to bear in mind that, particularly in the more elaborate analyses, we are dealing with relatively few individuals.

The women were paid $25 for their time; moreover, all their expenses, including travel from outside Chicago and babysitting, were reimbursed. When the women called, they were told they would be paid for their time.

During the initial telephone call, we asked them for their own definition of the situation. Specifically, we asked them to tell us whether they had been raped or had been attacked but avoided being raped. In this way, *the women defined themselves* into two parts of the sample: rape avoiders versus raped women.

Before exploring what we found, we will briefly review other works on rape avoidance. William B. Sanders (1980) studied 481 women in southern California (261 raped women and 220 attempted rape victims). He classified their responses into various categories including struggling, screaming, fighting, running, and so on. Analysis of the women's responses indicate that just about any form of resistance had some effectiveness. Doing nothing increased the likelihood of rape.

The Queen's Bench Study (1976) conducted in San Francisco included 108 women (68 raped women and 40 women who had undergone attempted rape). The researchers found that women who avoided rape used more types of resistance measures, both physical and/or verbal strategies, and their resistance was more forceful. In addition, the women who avoided rape tended to be more suspicious and to respond in a rude or hostile manner to the rapist prior to the onset of the actual sexual assault. Furthermore, women who avoided rape were more likely to resist immediately and appeared more determined to deter the rape at any cost. These findings contradict directly Storaska's advice (1975).

The third study, conducted by Jennie McIntyre (1980) in the Washington, D.C. area, consisted of interviews with 320 women (192 raped women and 128 women who avoided rape when attacked). McIntyre included screaming, running, strong verbal aggression, and physical fighting among the responses categorized as aggressive behaviors. McIntyre found that if a woman acted aggressively she was less likely to be raped and that the earlier her aggressiveness, the more effective were her efforts. McIntyre acknowledged the role of situational factors, including the location of the attack, but stressed the importance of prompt action. Hesitation increased the likelihood of rape.

A fourth study (Block and Skogan, 1982), based on a random sample drawn by the National Crime Survey and limited to stranger-to-stranger crimes, comes to similar conclusions. When Block and Skogan analyzed the 550 rapes in the survey they found that forceful resistance by the "target" was associated with rape avoidance, while nonforceful resistance was associated with rape. Eighty-three percent of rape "targets" resisted. Nonforceful resistance included reasoning, verbally threatening the assailant, yelling for help, or running away. Forceful resistance included physical attack with or without a weapon. Women were less likely to forcefully resist when attacked at home and when the offender was armed. Fifty-six percent of the rape "targets" suffered an injury in addition to the rape, but less than 10 percent were seriously injured enough to be hospitalized overnight. Slightly over half of the women who used forceful resistance were injured, compared with 30 percent of those who did not resist. When the assailant had a gun, 54 percent of those who forcefully resisted were injured, 29 percent of those who nonforcefully resisted were injured, and 41 percent of those who did not resist were injured.

The latter three studies also concluded that most victims of rape or attempted rape were not seriously injured. The myth that resistance only excites the man and thus leads to severe injury or death was voiced by many of the women.

In an effort to learn the number of deaths in an assault, we obtained homicide rates from the Statistical Analysis Center edition of the Illinois Crime Report Data (1981) for the Chicago area. From 1976 to 1980, there were 9,766 reported incidents of sexual assault (8,391 rapes and 1,375 attempted rapes). In the same period there were 78 rape/attempted rape homicides in the Chicago area. During that time less than 1 percent (.8%)[4] of the women assaulted were killed. The statistics do not support the myth about lack of resistance: It does not increase women's chances of avoiding rape. Five women we interviewed used no resistance strategies, and all were raped. In fact, two of these women were severely beaten, despite their lack of struggle.

After reading our report (1980) and the McIntyre report (1980), Tacie Dejanikus (1981) interviewed police rape prevention units in six areas of the United States to find out what they were telling women about resisting attacks. Almost all the police officers said that their department encouraged women to use passive resistance before or instead of active resistance.

---

[4]The 78 homicides are not included in the 9,766 total for two reasons: (a) Given procedure, the type of crime is upgraded and classified according to its severity; homicide is a more serious crime than rape, therefore, is included in the homicide statistics; and (b) the 78 homicides included both rape and attempted rape victims. Differentiation between the two types of victims is currently impossible.

A sergeant in the Portland, Maine police department said that he advised women to use tricks, such as saying she had her period[5] or playing along with the rapist in an attempt to gain time to escape. He said, "We recommend physical resistance as a last resort." A Houston officer said, "There is no sound advice you can give for all the time. We recommend passive resistance like getting a person's confidence by talking and doing what you were taught to do as girls growing up, to help resist attack." The officers stated that attackers "will probably become angrier or even sexually aroused if women resist," thus increasing her chances of being injured. However, the advice currently being given by the Chicago law enforcement agencies indicates that they advocate active rather than passive strategies. A pamphlet called "Rape Be Aware," compiled through the efforts of numerous public and private sources, including the Chicago Police Department, lists six steps to take if attacked. All are active and involve use of multiple strategies. These include running, yelling fire, screaming, physically resisting (pointing out vulnerable spots such as knees, instep, throat, eyes; nowhere is the groin area mentioned), using techniques mastered in self-defense courses, including the use of items a person would normally carry (e.g., a lighted cigarette, keys, a comb, an umbrella, a book) as a weapon.

If it appears as though escape is impossible, the pamphlet next advocates attempting to show no fear and using verbal strategies, such as telling the rapist you are pregnant, mentally ill, or have a disease, with emphasis on the believability of the story. Given the findings of this study and others, using active resistance and multiple strategies would seem more likely to improve a woman's chance of avoiding rape. Although this book focuses primarily on what is associated with a woman successfully resisting an attempted rape, certain other findings emerged that are both interesting and relevant to our understanding of sexual assault.

One finding from the women we interviewed was the apparently subjective nature of the definition of rape and avoidance. What was one woman's rape seemed to be another woman's avoidance. We did discover after analyzing the relationship between self-definition and acts that occurred (see Chapter 2) that women define rape as what is done with a penis, not what is done to a vagina. While there may be some differences in women's definitions of rape avoidance, women appear to have no problem distinguishing between rape and "seduction."

Our findings also demonstrate that men and women often live in different worlds. A man may interpret a woman's behavior as implying that she is willing to have intercourse, while a woman simply thinks she is being

---

[5]Although about one quarter of the women in this study were menstruating at the time of the attack, in no instance did that fact deter the assailant, whether the woman mentioned it or not.

human and friendly. Sometimes after hours of physical struggling, he realizes that she is not playing a game and apologizes. Such was the case of one of the women interviewed (case 67). The woman was hitchhiking and accepted a ride from a fairly safe-looking older man. Before taking her to her destination, the man said he had to drop off a passenger at his home and pick something up. Naively she entered his home. Initially nothing happened, but then he began sexually assaulting her after luring her into his bedroom to "see the pool from the window." She protested, but he persisted, confessing after the fact that he thought she was teasing and playing hard to get. It was only after a long physical and verbal struggle that he stopped the attempted rape. He apologized to her and gave her some jewelry he had made. The woman defined her actions as being human, while the man defined her actions as a kinky type of foreplay. He was a former motorcycle gang member and claimed that former sexual partners enjoyed feigning protest.

Perceptual differences between men and women were not limited to this case. These incidents can be viewed as exaggerated versions of normal interactions.

One assailant told his victim (case 51) that there was no such thing as rape and that "a man is doing a woman a favor." Another assailant told a woman (case 31) who was fighting back and yelling that he was not going to rape her, that he wasn't trying to rape her. "I only want to screw you," he said.

The difficulty some men have differentiating heterosexual intercourse from rape has been addressed by law professor Catharine A. MacKinnon (1981), who noted that the woman has a rape script, the man has a date script, and the evidentiary rules (the rules that say what evidence can be brought up in court) state which part of those scripts can be used in the trial. Women see the rape in intercourse, while judges see the intercourse in rape. This is just one of the problems women experience when attempting to deal with the criminal justice system after an assault.

Another important finding concerns the pervasive nature of violence in women's lives, from incest through molestation and other forms of child sexual abuse, through battering culminating in at least one rape or avoidance. Indeed 40 percent (51) of the 94 women had multiple experiences: either they were raped twice in their lives, had avoided rape at least twice, or had both experiences. One woman (case 31) began her interview by saying, "You're not going to believe me, but I was raped twice in the same day." The first rape occurred after she left her mother's home with a man she knew from the neighborhood. He promised to give her a ride to the apartment she shared with her boyfriend and his male cousin. Instead of the ride, he raped her. When she arrived at her apartment she took a bath;

while she was in the bathroom, her boyfriend's cousin tried to rape her. She attempted to stop him by telling him that she had her period, and pleaded with him not to force her to endure another rape. He raped her anyway.

The women in this study often described the frustrations they experienced in their efforts to obtain justice. Although we did not originally plan to study the responses of the judges, we recorded the statements made by women whose cases were heard in court. In one case (48) a judge in a bench trial (no jury) stated that rape is a charge easily made and—following a 200-year-old dictum—"hard to be defended by the party accused, tho' never so innocent."[6] He then found the two adolescents who raped the woman innocent, crossing age, race, and class lines but not gender lines to do so. Another judge (case 14) dismissed charges of rape of a 17-year-old virgin, merely charging the defendants with robbing the woman of 13 cents. This woman was on her way to a track meet practice when abducted and raped seven times by two men. She escaped by jumping out of the bathroom window in the apartment to which they had taken her. As if the multiple assaults and courtroom nightmare were not enough, the jump injured the woman's ankle, and she was unable to accept the athletic scholarship in track which she had been offered. The police officers on the case, who were Black, told the woman's father (who was Black) that if it were their daughter in this situation, they would not bring charges because "there is only law, not justice." Again, although we did not originally intend to study the responses of the police, we recorded their treatment of the women. In other instances, the police responded differently. A Black woman (case 13) had been badly battered but managed to escape by yanking hard on the assailant's penis. When she was talking to the police she realized by their shocked silence and then grimaces and groans that they identified with the assailant's injured organ, not her battered body. In addition, when she went to the police station to report the attempted rape and murder she was asked the rapist's social security number, since she knew him from her church. She was also sent back and forth between the misdemeanor and felony sections, since the police could not decide if her case were a battery (misdemeanor) or attempted rape (a felony). It was only when she learned from her own investigation that the man was a child molester and reported this information to the police that they arrested him. When the case came to trial a year later, the white public defender asked the Black raped woman

---

[6] This phrase (called Hale's Dictum, after Lord Chief Justice Hale who stated it in 1778) incorrectly assumes that women make false charges which are difficult to defend against. It has been widely quoted in legal writings on rape and was, until recently, presented to California jurors as part of their instructions (LeGrand, 1973).

what she would settle for in plea bargaining. She told him one year. He replied, "A year is a long time for a man to stay in Cook County jail. Do you know what you're saying?" She recounted what she had endured. He said, "Yeah, you know, you have your freedom." The white public defender identified with the assailant despite the fact that he was Black, an alcoholic, unemployed, on public aid, and a known sex offender.

The data in this study, as well as a reading of the data on incest, woman abuse, and sexual harassment suggest that in issues of violence against women, gender is the most important factor. Men identify with men.

Although we did not originally plan to study the responses of the hospitals and doctors, we observed that not one woman was given the proper warnings before being given the morning after pill, diethylstilbestrol (DES), a cancer-causing drug. A doctor in the emergency room of a suburban hospital said to a young woman who had been raped by two men after her high school graduation party, "Were you really raped or are you just trying to make trouble for someone?" Another doctor responded to a woman who was bleeding rectally after having been sodomized by her husband (case 90) by saying, "Have you been stimulating yourself anally?"

We will end this chapter with another case study that exemplifies many of the concepts we have discussed or will discuss. This woman had been gang raped as an adolescent. As an adult, she avoided being raped by two strangers in an alley. Not long after this avoidance, her husband, who also had been battering her, raped her. He felt entitled to sex because she was his wife (case 80).

The rape avoidance began late one evening, as the woman and her husband were arguing in their car. He jumped out of the car, and she followed. While chasing him she passed a vacant lot and noticed two men leaving their car and heading for her. She sensed something was wrong, and one of the men grabbed her and put his hand over her mouth. He said, "You don't have to be chasin' after a man, honey, I'm here." The other man tore her pantyhose, her dress, and then dragged her behind a building. She yelled, fought, and bit one man's hand all the way to the bone. Although she was frightened and had no conscious plan of action, she made use of the bottles and rocks in the alley. A police officer who was passing heard her screams, stopped, and chased the men as they fled. The woman later reported that "... The policeman ... he says, what are you doing in an alley this time of night? Like he thought I was asking for it." He advised her not to make a police report since it would be "so embarrassing" and because "nothing really happened to you." Despite his invalidating her experience, she called him a "nice guy" because he bought her coffee after the incident.

In recounting the rape avoidance, this woman remembered her prior attack when she was gang raped at 13 and wondered how this could have happened again, since "lightning is not supposed to strike twice in the same place." She was angry at being in a similar situation, but angrier still at her husband's actions. He failed to intervene, even though he heard her scream. She said that as she was fighting off her assailants, she was thinking of her husband and saying to herself, "Boy, as soon as I kill you, I'm gonna kill him . . . I knew I was gonna win. I had to win . . . I think if I was lying there bleeding to death I'd still feel like, boy, I'm gonna kill you . . ."

Because her husband did not intervene though he heard her scream, she would no longer have sex with him. He had begun to beat her shortly after their marriage, two years before the incident. When she was pregnant with his child, she was beaten because he claimed she was being unfaithful to him and the unborn child was not his. Even in these instances, she fought back. One evening several months after the rape attempt she reported that her husband awoke her, saying, "'Well, you're my wife and you'll have sex with me if I want' . . . and he tore my clothes off and me and him went round and round and he ended up doing it to me on the floor . . . I mean he did worse to me than the guy in the alley." During their struggle her husband said to her, "Maybe you liked those guys the other night. Maybe you didn't tell me the truth." Ultimately she submitted to the rape "to get rid of him." She had no plan of action in this situation for a number of reasons. First, "I always just thought your husband's not supposed to rape you . . . and if he does, what am I gonna do about it anyway? . . . what are you gonna say, "my husband raped me.' People are gonna say you're crazy." Second, the rape took place in a hallway in which there were no items present that could have been used as weapons.

Third, her response to the situation was one of disbelief and she found herself laughing hysterically because, "You know this is . . . first in my thought, you know . . . husbands can't really rape you, but I felt like he was raping me, you know what I mean." In response to her laughing hysterically, he became angrier and "he just got a weird look about him, like he could really kill ya. He grabbed me around the neck . . . cut my wind off." She continued talking about the violence in her marriage and recounted how he had choked her several times till she blacked out when she was pregnant. That made her angry because it could have hurt her baby. (Some women have been brought up to believe that it is only permissible to be angry in defense of their children and other people.)

It is clear that her husband's view of her as his possession angered her, since she had learned at some feminist meetings that women were not property. She considered her husband's assault, rape (though she said at one time in her life she would not have) because when she saw the ad for subjects in the newspaper, she thought of her husband rather than the event in the alley. But when she called to make an appointment, she spoke about the avoidance in the alley and only spoke about her husband in the interview. She was in the process of divorcing him when she was last contacted.

CONCLUSION

Women need and want to know what to do if they are assaulted. Since we are feminists as well as sociologists, we believe in using our skills and resources to demystify the world for women, to answer questions women want answered. Therefore, we felt compelled to search for the answer to that age old problem. We found that the best overall advice we could offer women to increase the probability of avoiding rape is "Don't be a nice girl."

We hope other people will continue where we left off so that women everywhere will not only be able to take back the night (i.e., be able to go anywhere at anytime, including the night), but to take back the control of our lives which has been relinquished to men in our quest for survival.

In our society "survival is an act of resistance" (Kaye and Uccella, 1981). We are entitled to more than survival.

REFERENCES

Bart, Pauline. 1975. Rape doesn't end with a kiss. *Viva* 11(9):39–41, 100–101.

———. 1976. From those wonderful people that brought you the vaginal orgasm: Sex education for medical students. Unpublished paper presented at the meeting of the American Sociological Association.

———. 1981. A study of women who were both raped and avoided rape. *Journal of Social Issues* 37(4):123–137.

Block, Richard, and Wesley C. Skogan. 1982. Resistance and outcome in robbery and rape: Nonfatal stranger to stranger violence. Unpublished paper, Center for Urban Affairs and Policy Research, Northwestern University.

Brownmiller, Susan. 1975. *Against our will: Men, women and rape.* New York: Simon and Schuster.

Chicago/Cook County Criminal Justice Commission. Date not mentioned. *Rape be aware.* A pamphlet distributed by numerous Cook County agencies.

Dejanikus, Tacie. 1981. New studies support active resistance to rape. *Off Our Backs* (February): 9–23.

Finkelhor, David. 1979. *Sexually victimized children.* New York: The Free Press.

Frieze, Irene Hanson, Jaime Knoble, Carol Washburn, and Gretchen Zomnir. 1979. Psychological factors in violent marriages. Unpublished paper.

Giarrusso, R., Johnson, P., Goodchilds, J., and Zellman, G. 1979. *Adolescents' cues and signals: Sex and assault.* Paper presented at the Annual Meetings of the Western Psychological Association, San Diego, California.

Griffin, Susan. 1971. Rape: the all-American crime. *Ramparts* 10:26–35.

Herman, Judith Lewis with Lisa Herschman. 1981. *Father-daughter incest.* Cambridge, MA: Harvard University Press.

Jones, Ann. 1980. *Women who kill.* New York: Fawcett Columbine.

Kaye, Melanie, and Michaela Uccella. 1981. Survival as an act of resistance. In *Fight Back*, edited by Frederique Delacoste and Felice Newman. 14–25. Minneapolis, MN: Cleis Press.

LeGrand, Camille E. 1973. Rape and rape laws: Sexism in society and law. *California Law Review* 61:919–941.

MacKinnon, Catharine A. 1979. *Sexual harassment and working women*. New Haven, CT: Yale University Press.

——. 1981. In-class lecture at Stanford (California) University Law School.

Malamuth, N. 1981. Rape proclivity among males. *Journal of Social Issues* 37(4):138–157.

McDermott, Joan. 1979. *Rape victimization in 26 American cities*. Washington, DC: U.S. Department of Justice.

McIntyre, Jennie J. 1980. Victim response to rape: Alternative outcomes. Final report to Grant #MH 29045 NIMH.

Near, Holly. 1978. "Fight Back." On *Imagine My Surprise* album, Redwood Records, Oakland, California.

Peterson, Susan Rae. 1977. Coercion and rape: The state as a male protection racket. In Queen's Bench Foundation. 1976. *Rape prevention and resistance*. San Francisco, California.

Riger, S. and M. Gordon. 1981. The fear of rape: A study in social control. *Journal of Social Issues* 37(4):71–92.

Rush, Florence. 1980. *The best kept secret: Sexual abuse of children*. Englewood Cliffs, NJ: Prentice-Hall.

Russell, Diana E. H. 1975. *The politics of rape*. New York: Stein and Day.

——. 1982. *Rape in marriage*. New York: Macmillan.

Sanders, William B. 1980. *Rape and woman's identity*. Beverly Hills, CA: Sage Publication.

Schur, Edwin M. 1984. *Labelling women deviant: Gender, stigma and social control*. New York: Random House.

Scully, Diana, and Pauline Bart. 1973. A funny thing happened on the way to the orifice: Women in gynecology texts. *American Journal of Sociology* 78:1045–1051.

Statistical Analysis Version of Department of Law Enforcement Supplementary Homicide Report. 1981. Table: Total Rape Homicide Offenses in Chicago Standard Metropolitan Statistical Area: 1976–1980 by victim and offender race.

Statistical Analysis Center Edition of the Illinois Crime Report Data. 1981. Table: Rape and Attempted Rape Offenses in Chicago Standard Metropolitan Statistical Area: 1972–1980.

Storaska, Frederick. 1975. *How to say no to a rapist and survive*. New York: Random House.

Vetterling-Bragin, Mary, Frederick A. Elliston, and Jane English (Eds.). 1977. *Feminism and philosophy*, Totowa, NJ: Littlefield, Adams & Company.

2 What Constitutes Rape? How the Women Defined Their Situations*

By the time a report of sexual assault makes it into the newspapers, onto the television, or into the courtroom, the event has already been labeled as a rape or other crime. But the relationship between the label and what occurred is not always clear. Women in their daily experience encounter men constantly and are continuously interpreting the actions of these men as friendly or hostile, well-intended or wicked, platonic or sexual. When do women begin to define the actions of men as sexual assault?

The 94 women in this book considered themselves sexually assaulted. Some of the women defined themselves as having been raped, while others defined themselves as having been attacked but avoiding rape. How did these women arrive at these definitions? What was it about the situation that led a woman to think of herself as having been raped or having avoided rape? Before coming to the interview women were asked whether they considered themselves raped women or avoiders. Once they arrived, they were asked to describe the assault in great detail. Comparing the actions that occurred with the woman's definition of the situation, we can begin to arrive at some idea of how these definitional processes work.

Some of the women said that they had a feeling that "something was wrong" before the attacks occurred. Many had noticed their attackers acting "suspiciously," although it was often difficult for the women to say exactly what these men were doing to arouse such suspicion. Although a woman often noticed the attacker and he made her uncomfortable before he made any specific move, she ignored her feelings, labeling them "paranoid" or "oversensitive." There was a tendency for women to give men the benefit of the doubt. This means that even though there might have been

---

*Some of these data were included in "There Ought to be a Law: Self Definitions and Legal Definitions of Sexual Assault," by Pauline B. Bart and Kim L. Scheppele, presented at the annual meeting of the American Sociological Association, 1981. Some of that paper was incorporated in "Through Woman's Eyes: Defining Danger in the Wake of Sexual Assault," Kim Lane Scheppele and Pauline B. Bart, *Journal of Social Issues.*

some clue that the situation was one of potential sexual assault, women distrusted their own feelings.[1]

Almost all the incidents involved physical contact between the attacker and the woman. Generally the woman indicated to the man that she did not want this contact. Originally this physical contact was separated into various categories of sexual acts. For example, we first thought that the assailant putting his fingers into the woman's vagina was different from his putting a foreign object into her vagina; we thought forced fellatio was different from other ways the woman could be forced to masturbate the man. It became clear, however, that certain acts, for example forced fellatio, were associated with the woman's self-perception as a raped woman. Other acts, such as cunnilingus or the assailant's placing his finger(s) into the woman's vagina, led to the woman's believing she had avoided rape (see Table 2.1).

When we studied what happened, it turned out that there were three broad categories:

1. Sexual acts using a penis (phallic sex). This included all those acts that involved vaginal penetration; anal sex; the woman being forced to perform oral sex on the man; the attacker placing his penis between the woman's thighs and using them to masturbate himself; and the assailant forcing the woman to masturbate him.
2. Sexual acts not involving the penis (nonphallic acts). This included other specifically sexual acts that did not involve the penis: the assailant digitally masturbating the woman; the assailant placing his finger(s) in the woman's vagina or anus; cunnilingus; kissing, fondling the woman. We also included the instances in which vaginal intercourse was impossible because the assailant was impotent (case 76) or the woman had a physical condition that prevented him from doing so. For example, a clerical worker (case 2) who was attacked while waiting for a bus could not be penetrated because the radiation she had received for cancer closed her vagina.
3. "Other." This category included beating, threatening with a weapon, ripping off clothes, verbal threatening, restricting or forcing the woman's movement, and other threats or actions. See Table 2.1.

Ninety-eight percent ($n = 42$) of the 43 women who said they were raped had experienced one or more acts of phallic sex, while only 6 percent ($n = 3$) of the 51 women who said they avoided had phallic sex. Thirty-eight of these 42 women were forced to have traditional sexual intercourse,

---

[1]According to Kidder and Harvey (1979), taking a personal self-defense course enables a woman to recognize and label a situation as dangerous earlier than she would have if she had not taken such a course.

Table 2.1. Relation Between Self-Definition of the Woman as Having Been Raped or Having Avoided Rape and the Acts that Occurred

	Acts							
	Phallic Sex[a]		Nonphallic Sex[b]		Other[c]		Total	
Self-Definition	%	(n)	%	(n)	%	(n)	%	(n)
Raped	98	(42)	2	(1)	0	(0)	100	(43)
Avoided	6	(3)	45	(23)	49	(25)	100	(51)

[a]Phallic sex includes vaginal penetration with penis, sodomy, fellatio, female masturbating male, interfemeral penetration.

[b]Nonphallic sex includes vaginal penetration with finger or object other than penis, cunnilingus, fondling and touching sexual parts, kissing, and lack of vaginal penetration with penis due to loss of erection or inability to penetrate.

[c]Other includes all other actions or threats which are not listed above.

often along with other sexual acts. The four other women who defined themselves as having been raped were forced to engage in other forms of phallic sex. Two were anally raped; two others were forced to perform fellatio.

The one woman who did not have phallic sex, but who said that she was raped (case 26), was taken at knife point to a park where all her clothes were ripped off and the man kissed and fondled her. At one point he actually stuck a knife between her legs. (In this case, genital intercourse did not take place because a dog came over to "investigate" during the attack. When the woman suggested that the dog's owner might follow and find them, the attacker was thrown off guard long enough for the woman to take the "crocheted shawl my arthritic mother had made," throw it over the hand holding the knife, and run "like a gazelle.")

For the avoiders, a more complicated definitional pattern emerges. While 6 percent ($n = 3$) of the 51 avoiders engaged in phallic sex, 45 percent ($n = 23$) were forced into nonphallic sex, and 49 percent ($n = 25$) managed to avoid specifically sexual acts (although sexual acts have been very narrowly defined). By looking at these cases more closely, we can see the way in which these definitional processes work.

Two of the three avoiders who engaged in phallic sex actually had, for brief moments, the assailant's penis in their vaginas. In both cases, however, the women responded quickly and through their own actions were able to make the attackers stop. Both women were able to prevent their attackers from finishing what they had started, and these women called themselves avoiders. The third case in this category involved a woman who was attacked along with a friend, by two male strangers on a train platform (case 24). Although she was badly beaten, digitally penetrated, robbed, and forced to orally stimulate one man's penis, she chased her attackers after a train's arrival scared them away. They were caught.

Most of the 23 avoiders were *forced* into nonphallic sex. These acts were primarily kissing and fondling. A number of more extreme cases indicate how the definitions of sexual assault work, however. Three of the avoiders were attacked by men who tore off the women's clothes and positioned themselves for traditional sexual intercourse. In each of these cases, the men either lost their erections or could not penetrate the woman, and the women defined themselves as avoiders. In four more cases, the assailant put his finger(s) into the woman's vagina, and in one other case, the attacker performed cunnilingus. One case involved a woman who was forced at gun point to perform oral sex on her roommate after her roommate had been raped by the attacker. All of these women defined themselves as avoiders.

The 25 women who considered themselves avoiders when no specifically sexual acts occurred were by no means free from terrible experiences. Ten of these women were threatened with weapons (four with guns, five with knives, and one with a razor); fourteen of these women were beaten or grabbed; six had their clothes ripped (two were stripped entirely); four were specifically informed that the attackers intended to have sex with them (in addition, these women were grabbed or beaten); six were either forced to move to another place or were held against their will where they were attacked (only including cases that did not involve beating), and two had their residences invaded. Only one of the 25 women did not have at least one of these experiences, and in that case, the police said, the man fit the description of a rapist operating in the area. This man ran directly at the woman as if to attack her, but her screams scared him away.

The fact that these 25 women had no specific sexual acts performed on them does not mean that the attacks were free from sexual overtones. All of these cases had sexual components. One woman, for example, who arrived at the train station to go to a job interview in New York, took a jitney (non-licensed) cab. The driver stopped the car, jumped in the back seat with her, sat on her head to pin her down, ripped off all her clothes, and when he was removing his own she managed to open the door and flee naked down the street (case 20).

Common sense would lead one to think that women who have been forced to have traditional vaginal intercourse would consider themselves raped and that those who were "merely" forcibly fondled and kissed would consider themselves avoiding rape. But what about the cases that fall in between?

Most women distinguish between phallic acts and nonphallic acts and nonphallic penetration. Most women feel differently about cunnilingus than about fellatio. When cunnilingus occurs, the woman considers herself an avoider, but when fellatio occurs she defines herself as having been raped. The former is not phallic, and the latter is.

How do acts involving a penis differ from those that don't? Aside from the greatly increased possibility of pregnancy and venereal disease when the penis is used, the man also has a much greater likelihood of achieving orgasm. It may be that if the man can have an orgasm at the woman's expense, she feels raped. Thus these women define rape as something done with a penis, not something done to a vagina.

LEGAL DEFINITIONS OF SEXUAL ASSAULT

When the assault is reported, the police and prosecuting attorneys may define it as a "real rape" or a "bullshit rape." They examine the woman's report of what happened. Their judgments are affected by written law and whether they think they can win the case. (If you are interested in how situations are legally defined, see Appendix C.)

Legal definitions have the advantage of being precise and explicitly spelled out; this does not mean they are easy to apply. When the definition of attempted rape includes a requirement that there be a "substantial step" on the part of the attacker toward an actual rape, what does this mean? Is it enough that the attacker grab the woman's breasts or does he have to rip all of her clothes off? In fact, in Cook County (until July 1, 1984 when the new Sexual Assault Law went into effect), both the assailant and the woman had to be at least partially unclothed (Anderson, 1980).

There is quite a bit of agreement between the women's experiences (the acts) and the assailants' breaking the law: Those incidents that the women felt were sexual attacks but would not have been able to "hold up" in court were those which were part of an ongoing relationship (e.g., an assault by a boyfriend, husband, etc.).

REPORTING OF RAPE AND ATTEMPTED RAPE

Some women experienced sexual assaults that met legal criteria. In other situations the woman did not have a legal case. Given these differences, to what extent did women use the legal system? In 20 percent of the rape incidents, over half of the cases of deviate sexual assault and one third of the attempted rapes were not reported. The reason most often cited by these women was that they didn't think that the report would do any good. This means that some women still distrust the legal system, and for good reason. In many instances, the police did a good job, but in other cases, they were insensitive and actually harassed the women. In case 13, a Black woman was asked to provide the rapist's social security number after she gave the police his name and address. In another case, the police failed to make an arrest for five days after the rape, even though the rapist left his wallet with his name and address at the scene and threatened the raped woman on the day following the rape. In *no case* did a woman report an incident where no legally defined crime had taken place.[2]

CONCLUSION

This study was conducted in Illinois, a state where if someone entered your hallway without your permission it was called home invasion, a Class X Felony, in the same category as the most serious crimes such as premeditated murder. However, if someone enters your vagina with fingers or an object it is only a misdemeanor — battery. This study was also conducted in a state where there was no legal penalty for a man who raped his wife. While this book was being written the legislature revised this law so that penetration with an object and marital rape, under certain conditions, are considered criminal sexual assault.[3]

Legal scholars and feminists note there is a long tradition of women being treated as property. Ironically, if indeed women were treated as property, we would be better off, since Illinois law generally considers crimes against property more seriously than crimes against women. (See MacKinnon, 1983 for another analysis of why considering women as property is an inadequate analysis.)

Even when a woman uses the legal system, it doesn't mean that the charges filed against her attacker reflect the kind of injury she feels. All the women we talked with defined their attack as sexual. But the legal system erases the sexual part of the crime by labeling it assault, aggravated assault, battery, aggravated battery, unlawful restraint, attempted kidnapping, burglary or robbery.[4]

---

[2] This conclusion must be tempered by our assumption that all the women who came to us had sufficient evidence to support their stories. In many instances this is not legally true. Our data suggest, however, that these women are more likely *not* to file valid claims than they are to report nonjustifiable ones.

[3] This revised sexual assault bill has been in effect since July, 1984, but we have been told that the law's constitutionality will be challenged. To date, however, it has not been challenged.

[4] The only current legal category that seems to cover many of these instances is battery. Battery is a Class A misdemeanor, which means that the attacker can get a maximum of up to one year in prison. The typical battery case is quite different from the sorts of cases we encountered in our study in that the encounter is not generally of a sexual nature. But the women in our study do not equate being punched with having their breasts grabbed, and they do not equate nonsexual physical fighting with being jumped and thrown to the ground while their attacker attempts to remove their clothes. The sexual component of these crimes makes them more serious to the women in this study.

When men violate women sexually but are convicted of some nonsexual offense, they have no record showing a history of attacking women. This means that if they sexually attack another woman, and many rapists are repeaters, the court would not know either during the trial or when the man is sentenced that they had such records. Judges could give rapists more appropriate sentences with such knowledge.

The law should reflect women's reality as well as men's. Sexual violation should be called sexual violation. Those states that do not call attacks short of rape and attempted rape sexual crimes should change their legal code to include sexual battery as a felony.

There ought to be a law!

REFERENCES

Anderson, Mary Pennington. 1980. Personal communication.

Kidder, Louise H., Joanne L. Boell, and Marilyn M. Moyer. 1983. Rights consciousness and victimization prevention: Personal defense and assertiveness training. *Journal of Social Issues* 39(2):155–170.

MacKinnon, Catharine A. 1983. Feminism, Marxism, method, and the state: Toward feminist jurisprudence. *Signs* 8(4):635–658.

3 The Rape Situation

I tended to see the whole experience politically too, you know, in terms of guerilla warfare on the streets. And women . . . women being the victims of the guerilla warfare. (Subject 26, raped)

The police said: "Men prey on women living in areas where there are a lot of young single women." (The manager of an apartment house, drawn by the woman's screams in response to an attempted rape, was shot when he pursued the fleeing rapist down the street.) (CBS Morning News, May 3, 1982)

We all know the standard rape scenario, the "real" rapes in contrast to what police call the "bullshit" rapes: The woman is out alone at night, is suddenly pounced upon by an armed, large stranger who looks like a criminal. She is dragged into an alley, raped, and beaten, lucky to escape with her life. In this section, we will describe the actual situations the women were in and how these situations were related to the outcome—rape or avoidance.

SITUATIONAL FACTORS

Physical Characteristics of the Assailant

Men who assault women come in all sizes, builds, and colors. The assailants in this study ran the gamut of sizes (from 5′5″ and under to 6′2″), builds, races, and ethnicities (whites, Blacks, and Hispanics). You would expect the size of the assailant to affect the outcome of the attack, but there was no relationship between an assailant's perceived build and whether or not the women were raped. However, it is important to note that in many instances, the information on the size of the assailant was based on the woman's description. If the assailants were not taken into custody, or known by the woman prior to the assault, size could not be verified.

In this study 61 percent (71) of the assailants were Black, 29 percent (33) were white, and 10 percent (11) Hispanic. There were a total of 116 assailants in the 94 assaults presented in this study. In 11 assaults there was more than one assailant. When the assailant was Black[1], 27 women were raped, and 27 avoided rape; when the assailant was white, 11 women were raped and 17 avoided rape; when the assailant was Hispanic, 2 women were raped and 7 avoided rape[2]. Overall, the physical characteristics of the assailant were not associated with rape or avoidance. The next section will clarify this point.

Ethnicity of the Assailant(s)

Although it first appeared as if the race of the assailants was associated with rape or avoidance, this finding was true only if the assailants were armed. Nine women were assaulted by Hispanic men, but only two of these men were armed. In neither instance was the assailant able to rape the woman. Twenty-eight women were assaulted by white men. Seven of these men (25 percent) were armed. In these assault situations, five women were able to avoid rape, and two women were raped. Fifty-four women were assaulted by Black men. Twenty-six of these assailants were armed. When faced with an armed Black assailant, 17 women were raped, while only 9 women avoided rape. However, when the assailant was unarmed, the results were reversed. Twenty-eight women were assaulted by Black unarmed assailants. Of these, 20 women avoided rape, while 9 women were raped. Twenty-one women were assaulted by a white unarmed assailant. Of these, 11 women avoided rape, while 10 women were raped (see Table 3.1).

Time of the Attack

Twenty-six women were attacked between 6 A.M. and 6 P.M. (The time of the assault was not identified in eight instances. In these eight assaults, five of the women were raped, and three avoided rape.) Women were more likely to stop their rapes if they were assaulted during the day: 7 women

---

[1]This study focuses on factors associated with rape or the avoidance of rape. We are thus not devoting space to factors not relevant to this issue, such as the high proportion of Black assailants in this study. When presence of a weapon was controlled for, the race of the assailant is not associated with the outcome — rape or rape avoidance. One might hypothesize that the overrepresentation of Black assailants reflects the demography of Chicago itself. It might also reflect the greater willingness of white women to disclose rapes by Black men, since that follows the stereotype about rape. Finally, this finding reflects our belief that were we to have more data on marital rape in this study, there would be a higher proportion of white assailants. LaFree (1980), summarizing 23 other studies of rape, finds a very low percent of white on Black rape. The rates fluctuate between 0.0 and 6.7 percent.

[2]The residual information is unavailable. For various reasons three subjects were unable to identify the race of their assailants.

Table 3.1. Outcome by Race of Assailant and Whether He was Armed

Assailant	Number of Raped Women	Number of Rape Avoiders
Black		
Armed	17	9
Unarmed	8	20
White		
Armed	2	5
Unarmed	10	11
Hispanic		
Armed	—	2
Unarmed	3	4

were raped, while 19 women avoided rape. After 6 P.M. more women were assaulted, but fewer were able to stop their rapes. Thus, at night 31 women were raped, while 29 women avoided being raped. During the daytime more women are likely to be outside, and there is a greater possibility of environmental intervention, both factors that increase the woman's chances of avoidance. In spite of these factors, almost half of the women assaulted at night were able to stop their rapes.

Whether Women Were Asleep or Awake

While most women were awake when assaulted ($n = 82$), ten women were asleep when attacked[3]. Being assaulted while asleep at home has the most long lasting effect on women and seems the most difficult to escape (Burgess and Holmstrum, 1979). Although four of the ten sleeping women were able to stop their rapes, and six were raped, there are too few sleeping women to state that being asleep when attacked is associated with being raped.

Whether Women Were Inside or Outside

Avoidance was more probable if the assault occurred outside, but more assaults took place inside than outside. Half of the women who were attacked inside were raped. When the assault occurred outside, 16 of the women were raped, and 23 of the women avoided rape.[4]

---

[3] In one case, the woman was drugged and unconscious. In another the woman had been knocked unconscious. Technically, neither of these women was asleep and so neither is computed here.

[4] Information on location of assault was unavailable for one woman, who avoided being raped.

Attack Style: Blitz or Con

The two most frequently described assailant approaches were the attack style called a "blitz" and the verbally manipulative style called a "con."[5] One victim explains the con approach:

> I learned from the minute one, he was doing this whole trip. . . . He was a mastermind at seeing my weak spots, or my vulnerable spots . . . it was such an intense thing . . . he was talking and just slowly peeling away my layers of who I am. . . . He raped me emotionally so he could get to me physically. (case 46)

Another woman who experienced a blitz approach explains:

> I was walking down the street spacing into all the beautiful windows and then all of a sudden there was no oxygen and there was cement. And it took several seconds to just realize what was going on, that you've been jumped. (case 28)

A total of 78 cases could be classified blitz or con: Of these 55 were blitz attacks, and 23 were con. Women were somewhat more likely to avoid con than blitz attacks. The ratio of victimization to avoidance for blitz attacks was 28 to 27, while for con attacks it was 9 to 14.

Sexual Assault Plus Another Crime

In 27 of the 94 cases other crimes were committed in addition to sexual assault or attempted sexual assault. In two instances, the additional criminal act involved sexual assault of other persons. The most frequent crime was robbery (15 cases). The second most frequent crime was burglary (four cases). Five women experienced two or more crimes in addition to sexual assault, and one woman had her car stolen.

The woman was more likely to be raped when another crime was committed, especially in the case of burglary. All four of the women who were burglarized were raped.

Multiple Assailants and Multiple Victims

Women were as likely to stop the rape of multiple assailants as of one assailant. However, this finding held only if there were also more than one potential victim. Seven of the women were assaulted when there was another woman present. Five of these women stopped the rape; in the other

---

[5]Additionally seven women were harassed by their assailants; two of these were raped, and five avoided rape. Nine other women had "normal" interactions with their assailants prior to the attack. Of these nine women, four were raped, and five avoided rape.

two, the woman was raped. A heartening finding was that the women frequently were sisterly to each other, trying to help the other woman avoid rape.

In one instance (case 4), the woman diverted the assailant from assaulting her friend to assaulting her. She noted that her friend

> was pushing the knife away and he was pressing it in. And it [her neck] wasn't bleeding but I sensed that her life was really in danger . . . she was a person and my friend and I had to save her life . . . I was feeling very protective towards her, plus my thinking at that time was 'Well I've been raped, I can handle this. I can be a victim, right?' So I turned to him again fiercely and I said "Leave her alone!" So he turned to me. Came to me . . . Sally [not real name] was sitting there in shock . . . she couldn't come to my aid. I think maybe she patted me on the shoulder but that's all that she could do.

Both she and her friend were able to avoid being raped.

In another instance (case 87), two roommates were assaulted in their apartment by a man who offered to help one of them carry heavy shopping bags into the apartment. The woman recalled:

> My roommate and I were holding each other, in our fear. . . . When we saw that the other one was about to start crying one of us would assume some kind of a strong facade or something.

After the assailant raped her roommate, he brought the bound and gagged woman from a closet in which he had confined her. When he said "Now it's your turn," her roommate screamed at him, "Haven't you had enough? Come on. Get the hell out of here!" Her roommate's protest worked: She was not raped.

Use of Force

The use of force can take many forms, ranging from threat of force to the use of a weapon. The rapist can physically attack the woman, slapping, punching, or choking her; he can use some ordinary object as a weapon; or he can actually have a knife or gun. Since men are typically stronger than women, face-to-face confrontation can be threatening. However, the use of force by an assailant makes this confrontation even more threatening.

A weapon was present in 43 of the scenarios. In 16 scenarios there was a gun; in approximately 21 there was a knife, and in 5 there was an object such as a rat tailed comb that was used as a weapon. Five assailants said they had a weapon, but the women didn't believe them. Some women thought their assailants had a weapon even though they did not threaten them with one. In 51 of the cases, there was no weapon used or threatened. It is not surprising that the absence of a weapon is associated with avoidance, but some women avoided rape even when there was a weapon. Three women were wounded with a weapon; two of these women were raped and one avoided. Eleven men tried to choke or smother the women. Eight of these women were raped, and three avoided rape.

Only 16 of the assailants used *no* physical force. However, 62 of the assailants were "rough." They pushed, shoved, or slapped the woman. More raped women than avoiders were treated roughly, and as we would expect, more avoiders were in situations where physical force was not used. Eleven women were beaten, and nine of these were women who stopped their rapes. Out of the five women who were beaten brutally, three were raped.

WOMEN WHO HAD PREVIOUS EXPERIENCES: RAPE AND RAPE AVOIDANCE WHEN ATTACKED

What happens to a woman when she is attacked by a man who wants to rape her depends on many background factors (see also Chapter 5), including:

1. Her training to be "feminine"
2. Her height.
3. Her ordinal (birth) position
4. Her image of the future when she was growing up
5. Her role models
6. Her knowledge of survival and competency skills from how to put out a grease fire when cooking to self-defense

The outcome of sexual assault depends on situational factors:

1. The assailants' use of force and threat of force
2. The location (indoors or out)
3. The time of day
4. Whether the subject was asleep or awake
5. Whether or not there were multiple assailants and/or victims

In order to tease out the relative importance of the situation compared with the women's background, we looked at 13 women, each of whom had been raped one time and had avoided rape another time.[6] These women had both experiences when they were adults, not in school, but in the labor force or managing a household. Because these women had the same background for each of the assaults — a logic something like the use of identical twins who are used to study the effects of environment since heredity is held

---

[6]A more technical analysis of these women can be found in Pauline B. Bart, "A Study of Women Who Both Were Raped and Avoided Rape," *Journal of Social Issues* 37 no. 4 (1981):123–137.

constant — we can see what situational factors led to the same woman being raped on one occasion and avoiding rape on another.

A natural question to ask is "Were they raped the first time and then avoided rape the second?"

Unfortunately, that's not how it works. Eight women who had previously been raped avoided rape in their second assault. But five women who had first avoided rape were then raped at a later date. This doesn't mean that prior experience is irrelevant. For example, one woman fought back in her second assault because she had not in her first when she was raped. She said that she felt bad about herself because she had not fought back the first time. Another, knowing the damage the rape had done to her life, said that "it would not happen again." A third learned judo after her rape and subsequently avoided the next attack because of the automatic response-to-danger pattern she had developed as a result of her self-defense training.

Scenarios

Women were more likely to avoid rape when they were attacked by a stranger and more likely to be raped when attacked by a man they knew. Although the possession of a weapon by the rapist was not in itself associated with rape, force or threat of force was. Most men are stronger than women and have more experience with physical force. They do not need weapons to intimidate. Many men who "only" beat women with their fists inflict substantial injury.

Use of Strategies

Analysis of the strategies used by women revealed that physical response (i.e., fighting/struggling and yelling/screaming) along with the use of more than one defense strategy were associated with avoiding rape. Talking, including pleading, as the sole strategy (which many women feel is their best defense) was the most frequently used strategy when the woman was raped. (See Chapter 4 for elaboration of these data for the entire sample.)

Primary Concerns

Women who were primarily concerned with avoiding murder and/or mutilations were more likely to be raped. The media reinforce this attitude. One study (Heath et al., 1979) shows that newspapers report 13 completed rapes for every one attempted rape and that the media will present only accounts of rapes which will grab the reader's interest. These women's fears could be grounded in the media coverage. Analysis of crime statistics (see Chapter 1) indicates that murder is rarely a result of resistance to rape.

SR-B*

Rape and Rape Avoidance: One Woman's Story

One woman (case 62) avoided rape twice and was raped once. She came to us with her second successful avoidance (see Chapter 4).

She first avoided rape on the 4th of July a few years before her interview when she was riding her bicycle. An adolescent male appeared from nowhere, jumped in front of the bike, and stopped it by grabbing the handlebars. He then reached out and started grabbing for her breasts. She started smacking him, which did not stop his assault, and simultaneously began yelling to attract some of the people who were out enjoying the holiday. No one helped, and her shouts had no effect on her assailant. Finally, she "jammed the bike into his crotch . . . he fell to the ground in pain," and she rode away.

The second time she was raped she was living in a commune. One evening as she lay sleeping in her "usually locked room," a fellow commune mem-

Table 3.2. Effect of Situational Variables

Avoiders	Raped Women	No Difference
Day (6:00 A.M.–6:00 P.M.)	Night (6:00 P.M.–6:00 A.M.)	Height and weight of assailant were not associated with outcome
Attack outside	Attack inside	
"Con" approach	Another crime was committed (e.g., burglary in addition to the rape)	
Absence of a weapon or an object used as a weapon	Presence of gun, knife or other object	
No physical force used	Nonlinear relationship between degree of force and victimization	Previous attack
		Race/ethnicity no relationship when control for presence of weapon

For 13 women who were either raped or avoided rape at the same life cycle stage:

Avoiders	Raped Women
Stranger	Acquaintance
Primary concern: not being raped	Primary concern: not being killed
Multiple strategies	One strategy
Physical strategies	Pleading/talking
Yelling/screaming	

ber came in and raped her. She asked him to stop but without success. In this incident there seemed neither the time nor the opportunity to stop the rape.

However, in her third assault, she was determined to stop her rape. She wrestled with the assailant and screamed until he ran away.

CONCLUSION

We conceptualize the occurrence of rape as the result of both situational and background variables. This chapter focuses on factors in the situation itself and how they relate to the outcome — rape or rape avoidance. In addition we studied a subsample of thirteen women who both were raped and avoided rape. Investigating this group enabled us to learn the effect of situational variables, since background factors, by definition, were held constant. Table 3.2 summarizes our findings.

REFERENCES

Burgess, Ann Wolbert and Lynda Lytle Holmstrum. 1979. Rape: Sexual disruption and recovery. *Journal of Orthopsychiatry* 49:648–657.

Heath, Linda, Margaret T. Gordon, Stephanie R. Riger, and Robert LeBailey. 1979. What newspapers tell us (and don't tell us) about rape. Paper presented at the meetings of the American Psychological Association, New York.

LaFree, Gary. 1980. The effect of sexual stratification by race on official reactions to rape. *American Sociological Review* 45:824–854.

4 How Accosted Women Prevented* Rape

> Try and fight him . . . it's more natural to be angry, if you let yourself feel the anger, maybe that'll give you strength. . . . I used to think you could give him some kind of Jesus rap . . . I used to think you could reason 'em out of it. And talk to him like a human being, say, "OK, you don't want to do this, what are you doing?". . . . He seemed to listen to anger, yelling.

PB: What methods do you think would be ineffective, once a man tries to accost a woman?

A: Crying and pleading and begging. (case 88)

Women are in a double bind. On the one hand, we are told that fighting back will only excite a rapist or make him angry. This assumes he is not already angry and that fighting back immediately is the most dangerous strategy. We are also warned that resistance will result in serious injury if not mutilation and death, with parts of our bodies turning up in garbage cans and under park benches.

On the other hand, rape has traditionally been legally defined as carnal knowledge of a woman not his wife by a man over 14 *by force and against her will*. This definition means that it is not enough for a man to use or threaten to use force for it to be considered rape. Under traditional law, a man can force a woman to have sex *with* her will. Therefore, in order to legally prove rape, the woman has to prove it was against her will, and the best way to prove that she is not willing is *not* by saying "please don't," or "I have my period." The best way to prove that the sexual act is not consensual is by physical resistance.

In this chapter we will describe what strategies worked in preventing rape and the conditions under which they were effective. We will deal with the

---

*There are many terms that can be substituted for *prevented*, each of which describes certain cases accurately, but none of which is universally appropriate. We can use *stopped*, *avoided*, *eluded*, *escaped*, or *obstructed*. Each describes certain cases accurately.

central issue of the book — how women thwarted their rapists. We will compare the strategies of women who avoided being raped with those of women who were raped. First, we can report, as the Queen's Bench study did (1976), that women who avoided rape used more defense techniques than raped women.

When the women described their assaults, distinct types of defense techniques emerged:

1. Fleeing or trying to flee from the attacker(s)
2. Screaming, yelling or talking loudly, usually in an effort to attract attention
3. Using "affective verbal" techniques, including begging and pleading with the assailant, trying to gain his sympathy
4. Using "cognitive verbal" techniques, including attempting to reason with the assailant, conning him, making him "see her as a person," stalling, etc.
5. Experiencing environmental intervention: someone or something in the surroundings that intruded on the scene and either caused the assailant to stop the assault and/or gave the woman an opportunity to escape
6. Using physical force, ranging from the woman pushing back the assailant to self-defense techniques.

In addition to using more different *kinds* of strategies, women who stopped their rapes were most likely to yell, scream, or use physical force. There was also more likely to be environmental intervention (i.e., other people such as the police intruding).

Women who were raped were more likely to plead or cry. About four fifths of the women in our study tried to talk their way out of the rape. This was rarely effective by itself, but no more characteristic of raped women than of women who were not raped. The most effective combination of strategies was physical force and yelling[1] (see Table 4.1).

Two warnings, however, must be noted. First, the group of women who spoke to us were obviously those who had survived attacks, and were not permanently, totally, or nearly totally incapacitated. The women whose horrible deaths are reported with relish in lurid media accounts are not in our sample (see Chapter 1).

---

[1]For those interested, the correlation between the two for avoiders is .42, a high correlation for the behavioral sciences. Nash and Krulewitz (1977) found that male subjects attributed more intelligence and less fault to women who were raped if they resisted more forcefully. Some of the imprisoned rapists that Diana Scully interviewed believed that, even if a woman's assailant were armed, she implied consent to sex if she did not physically resist.

Table 4.1. Strategies of Rape Avoidance

Strategy	Raped Women		Avoider		Total n
	%	(n)	%	(n)	
Flee or try to flee	9	(4)	33	(17)	21
Scream/Yell	35	(15)	49	(25)	40
Physical Force	33	(14)	59	(30)	44
Cognitive Verbal (reasoning, using wiles, etc.)	72	(31)	67	(36)	67
Affective Verbal (pleading, etc.)	33	(14)	22	(11)	25
Environmental Intervention	5	(2)	20	(10)	12
No Strategy	12	(5)	—	—	5
Total	100	(43)	100	(51)	94

Note: Percentages are based on the raped women (43) and the avoiders (51) respectively. Thus, for the first column, 4 of the 43 raped women fled, while 17 of the 51 avoiders fled. The numbers add up to greater than 100% because some women used more than one strategy.

Second, because these 51 women successfully used certain defense strategies to avoid rape does not mean women can always successfully defend themselves against rape by simply using the correct type and number of strategies. The situation, including the attacker's behavior, how the women were brought up, and their ethnicity, also determined the woman's likelihood of avoiding rape when attacked (see Chapter 5). The kind of situation in which a woman finds herself (whether the attack is indoors or outdoors; whether there is more than one assailant, etc.) also affects the kinds of strategies women use (see Chapter 3).

It is necessary to understand the context of these women's behavior in order to comprehend fully how and why they avoided rape or were raped. Therefore, we are presenting more of their stories than we have in other chapters.

STRATEGIES

One of the most important findings was that when a woman used physical force as a defense technique together with another technique, her chances of avoiding increased (no women in our study used physical force alone). In fact, the more additional strategies she used, the greater her chances. Of the 13 women who used physical force plus one additional strategy, 6 avoided rape and 7 were raped. Nine women who used physical force and two additional strategies avoided rape. None of the 13 women who used three or four strategies in addition to physical force was raped.

The way in which women used these physical strategies varied. The question becomes, what is the *sequence* of events in rape avoidance? Because we interviewed the women instead of using questionnaires or other methods, we can answer this question.

Patterns of Physical Resistance

Women Who Physically Responded Immediately

Six women were able to stop their rapes by an *immediate* physical response, plus yelling or screaming. Yelling or screaming together with using force was the most effective combination to avoid rape. Effectiveness in this context was measured in terms of the amount of abuse, whether physical or verbal, that women had to endure prior to her avoidance.

How did these methods actually work? Four women were attacked outside where it is easier to escape, and the other two were attacked as they were entering the foyers of their apartment buildings (cases 62, 73). None of the assailants were armed; in only one case was there more than one attacker (case 82). In that one case, the woman fought and yelled curses at them and then escaped in a cab driven by her friend, which happened to pull up to the bus stop where she was waiting (an instance of environmental intervention). There were people present in two other cases (cases 62, 84), though they did not actually intervene. These are examples of factors that are beyond the woman's control, factors present in the situation itself.

Another interesting phenomenon was the anger that some of these women recalled feeling at the time of the assault. These women were not only angry but *enraged* at their attacker for daring to intrude on their space. They believed that he did not have a right to assault them. Unfortunately, not all women in this society have enough self-esteem to feel *entitled* to their space and to feel that unwanted touching is "just not permissible" (case 84). (See Chapter 7 for an elaboration of the male sense of entitlement.)

The angry women recognized danger early, at the first unwanted approach. This early recognition helped them avoid rape. Women in self-defense classes learn the necessity of constant awareness and the early recognition of danger (Cohn, Kidder and Harvey, 1978). The women who were more likely to be raped did not realize they were in danger until they were attacked. Women who avoided were able to pick up on more general cues (e.g., "this man is getting too close to me," etc.) and used defense techniques sooner.

One such woman (case 83) said: "There was just something about him that just made me feel very suspicious. I'm just wary of everybody in the street." This is an example of the basic mistrust women have to develop. Another woman (case 82) said that she first sensed danger because of "subtle kinds of mannerisms."

> He came too close to my body. There was no reason for him to keep advancing on me and to get that . . . you know, you just don't assault people like that. That's an insult, almost, for him to get right up on me. And that . . . immediately provokes a negative response in you.

Still another woman was assaulted as she was entering her apartment building. She simultaneously screamed, pushed the man who had grabbed her breast and buttocks, and kicked him in the groin. He "hobbled away." In two cases, the woman chased her attacker as he fled. Some of these women were incensed that the men attacked them. They did not try to make excuses for their assailants. The woman who was knocked from her bicycle by her assailant (case 83) said:

> He seemed to be sort of a physically weak enough person, I felt like I could do something to him, you know, really physical. I was so violently angry at this point, I think I would have killed him . . . he really . . . fought me hard. I was really pissed off he would not give me back my bicycle. . . . I mean, I just thought he had no right to do that, and he surely had no right to take my bicycle.

Another woman (case 62), who had been hassled by men on the street during the day and was feeling angry, said:

> I have to admit, that once we were fighting, I actually felt a release in the fighting. I mean, I felt like, I want to fight. I want to kill this guy. I want to really do this . . . you know. So, what I'm saying is, I was enraged. And this, this ambitious, stupid young guy, ambitious because he's so small and I'm so large—happened to get into my thing at that moment, and he got bruised.

Some of these women said they were determined not to be raped. One woman who had been raped previously (case 80) said that her plan was:

> Just resist, resist. You know, do anything. After I had been raped I vowed that it would never happen to me again, you know, that I would just do anything to avoid it. So I was really into resisting however I could.

With their early recognition of danger, strong determination to resist rape, sense of indignation that a man should assault them, and immediate angry and forceful response, these women were able to stop their rapes immediately in situations that were conducive to avoidance.

Women Who Were Overpowered

Five women were simply overpowered. Nothing they could have done would have stopped their rapes. One (case 17) was walking in an isolated area when a man grabbed her and dragged her toward a cornfield. When she screamed and started to hit him, he threatened her with a knife. He knocked her unconscious by hitting her twice with his fist.

A young woman (case 56) was raped in the elevator of a housing project by five men, one with a gun. (Rape is epidemic in the housing projects, particularly in elevators.) The woman fought with one of the men. Because she successfully fought him off, one of the men gave him the gun. He put the gun to the woman's head and said, "You gonna be my lady?" When she said no, the men forced her into an elevator. She refused to take off her clothes when one of the men, while holding the gun to her head, told her to do so. She also refused to lie down when the men told her to. They undressed her and knocked her to the floor, and all five of them raped her.

Another woman (case 14), who was 17 and a virgin when attacked, was assaulted by two men. She screamed and struggled. When she broke free and tried to flee, she fell on the icy pavement. These men were armed with a knife and a gun. They repeatedly threatened to kill the woman and may have done so if she had not jumped from a second story bathroom window and escaped after the men brutally and repeatedly raped her.

Another woman (case 50) was attacked as she was entering her apartment building by a man who grabbed her from behind and put an icepick to her throat. The woman immediately began to scream and fight with the man, kicking and hitting him. The man knocked her to the ground. She told him to leave her alone, but he pounded her head on the floor, hit her, forced her to her knees, and shoved his penis into her mouth. The woman continued to fight and bit his penis. This woman was attacked under circumstances similar to and reacted in much the same way as the three women who were attacked as they were entering their apartment buildings and who stopped their rapes immediately. This woman, nevertheless, was brutally and violently raped. Her armed assailant was not deterred by her physical resistance. She was simply overpowered.

Two women who used physical force and were still raped were attacked by men who invaded their homes while they slept. Both began to struggle. One (case 25) stopped when the man smothered her with a blanket; in the other case (52) the woman stopped struggling when the man put his hand on her throat.

Women Who Physically Struggled and Stopped Their Rapes

In five cases the women avoided rape after a somewhat prolonged and, in two cases, brutal struggle. Two men had knives: In two other brutal and violent attacks the assailants threatened to kill the women. In three of these cases, the woman knew the man who attacked her. Two of the attacks took place inside, two outside, and one in a boxcar in which the woman and man were working together.

The assault of one of these five women (case 13) was described in Chapter 1. The struggle between this woman and her assailant was brutal and continued for an extended period. After having been nearly strangled the woman was limp, her energy nearly spent from the struggle. She said:

> He started trying to insert his penis, and . . . warned me if I screamed
> he would choke me. . . . And then I felt his penis against my body and
> I just convulsed. I couldn't handle it, I mean I was just so horrified.
> Um . . . and I said to myself, "If he's going to kill me he'll just have to
> kill me. I will not let this happen to me." And I grabbed him by his
> penis, I was trying to break it, and he was beating me all over the head
> with his fists, I mean, just as hard as he could. I couldn't let go. I was
> just determined I was going to yank it out of the socket. And then he
> lost his erection . . . pushed me away and grabbed his coat and ran.

Another man preceded his assault with a day and a half of sexual harassment (case 53). The woman and man had been working together for two
days loading a boxcar. During that time the man had been grabbing the
woman and putting his arms around her. She had told him to stop harassing her. She said she "kind of took it," sometimes getting angry at him and
sometimes laughing about it. The second day he grabbed her and pushed
her into a corner of the boxcar. At first, she thought that this was just additional harassment. But when he started pulling down her pants, she realized
he was serious, and she began to get violent. After struggling with him to
free herself, she fled from the boxcar and avoided being raped.

Women Who Physically Struggled and Were Raped

Two women who engaged in relatively prolonged struggle with their
assailants were raped. One of these women (case 80) was assaulted by her
husband. Another woman (case 77) was grabbed from behind as she
walked along the street one night. The man put an arm around her neck
and a foot on her sandal. He told her in a low, indistinct voice that he had
something at her neck and that if she would behave he would not injure
her. She began to struggle with him and told him to put her down. She continued to fight and talk to him as he dragged her between two buildings.
When she saw that he had a knife, she quit struggling because she feared he
would kill her. He blindfolded and raped her.

Women Who Talked and Then Used Physical Force

Six women followed traditional rape avoidance advice and tried to talk
to the assailant; they used physical force when this method proved ineffective. In three of these cases, the men approached the woman sexually
because they apparently thought the women were sexually available. (See
Giarusso et al. in Chapter 7 for a discussion of men attributing sexual
meanings to behaviors that women do not.) These women told the men they
did not want sex and tried to talk them out of the assault. When that didn't
work, the women used physical force to escape. In the other three cases in
which the woman stopped the attack by first talking to her assailant and

then using physical force, the man who assaulted her was armed. These women talked to their rapists, not to talk the men out of the attack, but to avoid injury in addition to sexual assault. In one case, these strategies enabled the woman to get the knife and stop the rape.

One woman (case 34) went to her landlord's office in her apartment building to have a drink with him and a male acquaintance. After the other man left, the landlord made sexual advances. When she told him she was not interested in sex with him, he became more forceful. She still believed she could "talk him down," but he continued to act more forcefully. She kicked him in the groin, got up, and ran to the door, screaming that she had to get out. After letting her "quiet down," the landlord unlocked the door and told the woman he would like to take her to dinner sometime.

In one case (10) the woman went for a beer to the apartment of a man she met at a neighborhood bar. She went because she was trying to drum up support for a tenant's union in the neighborhood and felt safe because she thought the man was gay. When he approached her sexually, she tried to talk him out of it. He was using some force, though not enough for the woman to feel justified in using self-defense strategies. When it became apparent that talking was getting her nowhere, she threatened to hurt him if he did not stop. When he didn't, she bent his little finger back (a standard self-defense strategy) enough that it surprised and hurt him badly, though not enough to break the finger. She grabbed her things and hurriedly left. When she discovered she had left her expensive winter gloves she ran back up, retrieved them, and left again.

Women Who Used Physical Force and Then Talked

In the sixth category are those women who initially used force against their assailants, then threatened or otherwise talked to them. Four of these women fought with their assailants, but they did not stop the attack until they threatened the men. One stopped the attack in part by convincing the assailant that she was a karate expert. The sixth avoider, unable to escape by the use of force, convinced the man who was trying to rape her that she wanted to get to know him better before they had sex (case 92) and talked him into going to a restaurant for a milkshake. In another instance (case 39), described in Chapter 6, the woman said:

> It was a really long struggle. . . . He didn't have a weapon. . . . I knew that I could fight him. . . . I was just really very clear that I would not get raped again. . . . I actually thought about killing him. There was, at one point, when I took my hands off his testicles, and I put both my hands around his throat, I remember thinking I could kill him, and then realizing that I didn't want to actually try to kill him . . . then I stopped, suddenly, all my screaming. And I just said, in a real low, authoritative voice, real, real full of anger, that I was gonna get him,

and I knew who he was, and put him in the penitentiary. And I'd salt
him away for years, and I could do it . . . and I'd get him. I just said
it real threateningly, real deep and nasty.

This man had said to the woman several times, "I don't want to rape you,
I just want to screw." When she stopped screaming and threatened him, he
said, "Just get outta here, just get your purse and go."

Not all women who used physical resistance first and then tried to talk
the man out of the raping were able to avoid rape. One case (case 15) was
tackled from behind as she crossed a cornfield with her bicycle. At first, she
screamed and fought, but when the man smothered her by sitting on her
head, she stopped fighting. He forced her to get up, take her clothes off,
then he led her across the field. She again began to fight and scream, but
fearing he would kill her (he threatened to knock her unconscious), she
stopped fighting and tried to talk him out of raping her. After he had raped
her, she got up, saying she needed to stretch her legs, and fled.

Another woman (case 89) was attacked by her boss after he talked her
into going with him to a motel room. She fought at first, but stopped fighting and tried to talk him out of the assault.

He hit me, you know, we just went through a struggle as he took my
clothes off. And . . . by this time he had me on the bed, and I realized . . . that he was gonna rape me. Then all of the things you hear
about rape and what to do in that situation kind of flooded my mind.
And, at first I was struggling, I was fighting back, and then I . . . I
stopped, and I said, "Well maybe, I know that I've heard that if you
fight back, that . . . you know, gives them added spirit." And . . . it
was like a real effort to calm myself down. . . . Then I talked to
him . . . I tried to calm him down.

After he had raped her and she started to leave, he blocked the doorway
and asked her if she were planning to go to work the next day, either unaware of the harm he had done or attempting to normalize the situation.

Physical Strategies and Injury

Physical Injury

We are told that if we fight back, if we physically resist, we will pay the
price of severe injury or death. Not only is this admonition not supported
by our findings, it is also unsupported in the work of McIntyre (1980),
Queen's Bench (1976), Sanders (1980), and Block and Skogan (1982). Furthermore, advising women to either comply or risk injury assumes that rape
in itself does not result in injury, physical as well as mental. Several women
who talked to us reported serious injury from the rape. One woman (case
60) had a psychotic break that required hospitalization. Her rapist had
torn the area between her vagina and her anus, which had to be surgically

repaired. In addition she became pregnant and had to have an abortion. Since she was not conscious during the attack, the injury did not stem from her resistance. Another woman (case 14), a virgin, was raped seven times by her two armed assailants. Not only did she injure her ankle in her successful escape jumping out of a window after the rape, but she started hemorrhaging in school, and her vagina required surgical repair. A third woman (case 63) contracted venereal disease, which led to pelvic inflammatory disease, and is now permanently sterile. She screamed and tried to reason with her assailant but did not resist physically. We know that women who resisted physically were more likely to avoid rape. But we also know that there was no relationship between the women's use of physical resistance and the rapist's use of additional physical force over and above the rape attempt. When we examine the relationship between outcome and additional physical and verbal abuse by the assailant, we find that 25 raped women and 19 avoiders suffered physical violence in addition to the rape. We also know that sexual assault does not usually result in serious physical injury and that physical resistance often results in minor injury such as bruises and scratches. But some women who used physical force were moderately or seriously injured. One such woman (case 42) argued with her assailant, who was trying to enter her apartment, and was punched in the eye and pushed into her apartment, where she continued to struggle. Her screams alerted the neighbors, who called the police. They arrived in time to avert the rape. A second woman (case 17) screamed while being attacked in a cornfield and tried to strike her assailant. He pulled a knife, hit her twice with his fist, knocked her unconscious, and raped her. A woman (case 13) who had decided to submit to her rape, rather than be choked to death with a telephone cord, couldn't yield "because he was so dirty." Although she was beaten, she was able to yank at his penis and stop her rape.

Women who fought back sustained the following kinds of injuries: bruises and bite marks on the neck (case 34); soreness for a few days (case 77); strained muscles, bruises, and minor cuts (case 57); cut elbow on glass, which required stitches (case 62); cut arm and back injury (case 53); and aching the next morning (case 15).

Although we asked the women about the assailants' tactics including physical abuse, we did not systematically ask about their injuries, so there may have been minor injuries that were not reported. It is likely that all the women who had serious injuries told us.

We can examine the problem of injury as a result of fighting back by looking at the interviews of the five women who were brutally beaten or suffered serious injury. Three were raped, and two avoided their attacks. One avoider's injury (case 13) resulted from fighting back. Another avoider was injured (case 24) because of her physical resistance. However, the resistance delayed the rape long enough for a train to pull into the platform where the assault took place, causing the assailants to flee. A third woman who was raped fought back even though her assailant had an ice pick as a weapon. It is unclear whether her beating was in response to her fighting back or to her screams (case 50). A raped virgin (case 14), attacked by two armed assailants, fought back and was seriously injured. But the injury was not a result of her struggle but of her seven rapes and her escape method. The last woman (case 63) screamed and reasoned but did not fight her armed assailant. She was torn vaginally and became permanently sterile.

In the following section, on women who used no strategies, you'll see that several were seriously injured, although they used no defense techniques at all. Because of this we can state that fighting back significantly increases the woman's chances of rape avoidance and somewhat increases her chance of rough treatment. However, not resisting is not a guarantee that no injury will occur. The choice, of course, is the woman's.

However, let's look at the psychological results of fighting back for the woman, so that we can understand fully the advantages and disadvantages of the strategies. Some women have said that resisting the attack in every way possible made them feel better about themselves afterward. Is this true? We'll find out in the next section.

Psychological Injury

Even if people are willing to admit that fighting back is useful in avoiding rape, they are still concerned about its effect. What if the woman is injured physically or traumatized psychologically? We have just seen that the probability of serious injury is about the same if you fight back or if you offer no resistance whatsoever. Let us now look at the psychological aftereffects for women who fought back compared with those who didn't. The women who said they were depressed after the rape or who had symptoms of depression such as insomnia and weight loss were those who were raped but had *not* used physical strategies. Sixteen such women were depressed compared with the nine who were raped and had *used* physical resistance. Additionally, women who did not fight back were twice as likely to have sexual problems after their rapes as the women who fought back (the numbers are small though — ten to five).

There was no difference in frequency of depression between women who avoided their rapes by fighting back and those who avoided their rapes without using physical strategies. So it seems as if one of the most important functions of physical resistance is to keep women from feeling depressed even if they have been raped.

Surprisingly the effects of rape are not wholly negative. Twelve of the raped women who did not fight back felt that the experience toughened or strengthened them. Women who stopped their rapes and who used physical force were also likely to feel toughened and/or strengthened. Both groups learned basic mistrust and were less likely to be "nice girls" and "ladies" (Fox, 1977).

What about the rapists? Were they injured? The purpose of self-defense is not necessarily to overpower the assailant but to get away. In a number of cases (e.g., 39 and 10) when the woman could have seriously injured the man, she decided not to. The karate expert (case 94) who threatened her assailant with spilling his blood and guts on the floor only put her fist into his throat to keep him at arms length while she was verbally assertive. When the police mocked her knowledge of self-defense and asked her why she didn't use it, she said, "I did!" Using minimal force while stopping the unwanted behavior is the best defense of all.

Fleeing As a Strategy

Fleeing or trying to flee was the single most effective strategy that the women used. However, it was also the least frequently used of all five strategies. The small number of women who fled or attempted to flee may be accounted for in part by the situations in which they found themselves; some women also considered fleeing, especially fleeing their own homes, as an admission of defeat. Seventeen of the 20 women who fled or attempted to flee avoided rape. Two of the three women who were raped despite fleeing or attempting to flee fled after they were raped (cases 14, 15, and 16).

In one case (3), the woman fled immediately upon being attacked. She was standing at a bus stop at about 6:00 P.M. when a man walked up behind her and stuck a pointed object in her back. He said that if she didn't move or try to put up a fight she would be all right and that she should do what he said. This woman, whose mother and sister had been raped, was able to avoid rape by immediately fleeing.

Another woman (case 5), who had previously been brutally raped, fled immediately when confronted by a man with a gun who attempted to force her into an abandoned building.

Number of Strategies

Another way of looking at the ways in which women were able to avoid rape is by the number of different defense techniques they used.

No Strategies (Five Rapes; No Avoidances)

All of the five women who used no strategies were raped, although their rape scenarios differed. In no case did the lack of response cause the rapist to lose interest and find a black belt in karate to rape.

One such woman (case 64) experienced a brutal rape. Late one evening after her husband had gone to bed, she went to her basement to complete the laundry. Soon after her arrival, she was "grabbed from behind by my assailant . . . he had one hand over my mouth and . . . the other hand, which had a knife in it . . . to my throat . . . he then took some electrical tape and put it over my mouth and eyes." He demanded that she undress, which she did. She noted that he had "tied my hands behind my back . . . wrists together . . . [he] made me lie on my back on the floor." Because "it hurt to lie on my wrists," she recalled moaning. She said that he "moved me and retied my hands in front of me." Before penetrating he "proceeded to carve up my chest and my stomach with his knife. . . . he wrote 'Pig' across my abdomen and did sort of a tic-tac-toe across my chest . . . I didn't know that he was doing it with the knife . . . it just felt like something cold crossing my body." Furthermore "he was talking the whole time, making crude sexual remarks or other really horrible statements." Although this woman was unable to use any strategies, she had two dogs who attempted to assist her. The "dogs . . . followed me down in the basement . . . they started harassing the rapist . . . [he] got up [and chased them] . . . one of the dogs came back . . . biting at his legs or something . . . he seemed to be trying to hit her [the dog] with the knife . . . [he] got sick and tired of the whole thing and tied my ankles up . . . and tied my wrists to my ankles and left."

One Strategy (Thirteen Rapes; Nine Avoidances)

Using one strategy was better than using no strategies but did not result in rape avoidance as often as using two strategies. Thirteen women who used one strategy were raped, and nine avoided. Most (ten) of the women using one strategy who were raped used a verbal strategy, reasoning and talking with the assailant. Two women fled, and one screamed. About half (five) of the women using one strategy who avoided rape used rational verbal strategies, one fled, one screamed, and two pleaded.

Using one strategy improved a woman's chances of avoiding rape. Of the women who used only one strategy, 30 percent (13 women) were raped and 18 percent (9 women) avoided rape. The type of strategy used varied with both the women and the situation. The most effective single strategy was fleeing (Table 4.1). Only one woman (case 3) used this single strategy, and she avoided rape (see Chapter 7).

Women who were raped. Rapists don't observe holidays. This lesson was dramatically learned by one woman (case 16), a virgin, as she was attempting to travel to the home of friends with whom she planned on spending Christmas. She was a Pentacostal seminary student, living on campus. Her foster parents, a Pentacostal minister and his wife, had left the country to spend six weeks in Kenya. The woman was to spend Christmas on campus but "when it got close to Christmas time I had decided I didn't want to be alone . . . when everyone had left." Since she had no money she decided that she "was gonna hitchhike to Wisconsin to see some friends." She was "almost in Illinois" when the assault occurred. Having been out in the bitter cold for six hours, she decided to get in a van that had stopped. She saw only one person, the driver, who "looked like a college student," a gentle hippy. The seemingly safe odds, and the fact that it was Christmas Eve, made the ride "seem okay." After she had gotten into the van she noticed this other guy in the back of the van. "First they just talked to me and stuff . . . then this guy started trying to rip off my clothes . . . by that time they had pulled the car over to the side or to a rest stop and something . . . they were stronger than me and also I was really freaked out . . . I couldn't really do anything . . . couldn't even move." During the assault she asked them, "Why are you doing this?" and asked them "to stop" but they didn't. After the assault, "they dumped me on the side of the road . . . they didn't give me back my knapsack which contained my money, identifications, etc." Ironically she had "bounced around" numerous foster homes before moving in with the minister and his family and "converting." She recalled that when she was a kid, "I didn't take anything from anybody . . . I was really into fighting. . . . Five years ago if this woulda happened to me . . . there's no way it woulda ever happened to me . . . there's no way it woulda even happened. . . . I'm sure I woulda put up an awfully good fight. I'm sure I woulda done something. . . . I used to carry a switchblade too when I was a kid . . . if this happened 4 or 5 years ago, I would have killed the guy." Her religious convictions, which said she should love her assailants, as well as her seminary life, diminished her street smarts and contributed to the immense difficulty she had both in living through the rape and pulling herself together afterward. She told her parents about the rape after her interview, since the interviewer (PB) gave her emotional support, telling her it was unreasonable to demand of herself that she love her rapist and that a Christian attitude toward her should not be rejection. But her foster parents blamed her for the rape and for her lost virginity, since she shouldn't have been hitchhiking, and told her that no one would marry a woman who wasn't a virgin. Most women felt better after their interviews, but in this case the catharsis she felt and the validation she experienced led to unfortunate results. She called and talked with Bart one afternoon, and the Women's Ecumenical Center tried to find a fundamentalist minister to talk to her father, but she left town and lost touch before the connection between the minister and her father could be made.

Were it not for this case, it would have been difficult to understand another case of rape, one that received worldwide publicity in May 1985. Cathleen Crowell Webb (whose testimony about her brutal rape, and the supporting evidence the prosecution presented at the trial, resulted in Gary Dotson being found guilty and sent to prison for an exceptionally long sentence—25 to 50 years) claimed that since she was now a born-again Christian, on the advice of her pastor and his wife, she needed to confess that she had lied in 1979, and that the rape never occurred. Governor Thompson of Illinois, a former prosecutor, examined the evidence and cross-examined Mrs. Webb. He concluded that the trial transcript and the inconsistencies in her current account demonstrated to his satisfaction that she was telling the truth in 1979 and was not telling the truth in her recantation (Press, 1985).

The only factor that still puzzled people was her motivation in falsely recanting. However, an examination of the case above (case 16) shows that a born-again Christian woman may feel morally compelled to love her rapist(s) and feel guilty if she does not. Loving your enemy of course implies that you do not want him to be punished for what he did.

Since Dotson was in prison, the only way Mrs. Webb could affirm her Christian spirit (or, at least the best way), could demonstrate her transformation, was by becoming a martyr—again in the Christian tradition. She could lie for his sins (as Jesus is said to have died for our sins). In her bad old days when she fornicated and was "selfish" enough to believe that women might have careers, she said she had lied, injuring herself to appear raped. My (PB) analysis has not been proven, but it does shed light on an apparently puzzling case.

Women who were not raped. Another woman (case 36) was working as an auditor and was on her way to the auditing of a brokerage house when her assault occurred. She was pushing the button for the elevator when her assailant grabbed her from behind, saying, "if you don't cooperate, bitch, I'm gonna stab you." She said she "never saw the knife, which [was] about the only thing that kept [me] calm." He had his hand over her mouth, and

> I couldn't breathe very well. And he was trying to get my coat off of me . . . he was fumbling with it at the top though, which to me, seemed rather strange . . . if he's really trying to attempt a rape . . . he was going at it . . . the wrong way . . . trying to get my coat off of me at the top . . . When he removed his hand I said, "Why don't you just take my purse, that's all I've got." . . . All of a sudden [he just] stopped, and let go of me and he stood up. I got my purse with its contents back except for the paper money. I think he was nervous with what he was doing. Either that or he has never done it before or not done it too often before. It didn't seem like he was really going about it the right way . . . it was like he knew what he was wanting to do and he had his mind made up to do it . . . but I changed his plans for him,

like right in the middle. Before he left, he kissed me on the cheek, saying "You're an all right chick."

Two Strategies (Twelve Rapes; Fifteen Avoidances)

Twenty-seven women used two strategies. Of these 12 were raped, and 15 avoided rape. While seven of the raped women used physical force, only one used the most effective combination of strategies – physical force and screaming or yelling. All others (five) except one, used physical force and some type of verbal technique: reasoning, conning, and flattering. One woman used physical force and pleading. In contrast, eight of the fifteen avoiders used physical force, but four used it together with screaming, and one used it along with fleeing. Only three used physical force in combination with cognitive strategies and were able to avoid rape.

Women who were raped. Spending time with her seven children was so important to one woman (case 11) that she worked nights. Being aware of her vulnerability, she took some precautions, such as "usually having one of the men from work walk me to the subway to see that I got on the train safely." However, one night, about two o'clock in the morning as she was going home, she was assaulted. She had been reading on the bus, oblivious to her surroundings. But, she recalled "as I got off the bus, I heard someone get off after me. I didn't pay any attention. And I stood there and the bus driver, instead of going right away, he sat there and he looked at me, kind of a funny look, and he kept the door open . . . but then he just closed the doors and drove off . . . " She was perplexed at his behavior but began her walk home. She "heard footsteps across the street . . . looked across . . . saw this young, Black man." Fearing trouble she quickly planned to go "to the first apartment house and walk into it. And I'm going to be safe . . . I was walking quickly. And I didn't walk any faster. I didn't want him to think that I was afraid of him . . . got into the apartment building and pressed myself against the outer door. My intention was to reach over and start pressing doorbells. . . . The vestibule was a large one and in order to hold against the door and reach the [doorbells] it was impossible . . . thought I had some time to get to the doorbells [but] he was there." He came into the vestibule, "grabbed me . . . he had a knife . . . open." She froze. "I couldn't scream. I couldn't move. I was paralyzed . . . like a rag doll. And he dragged me out of the hallway . . . I was only thinking about he might kill me . . . " She told him, "Look, I have seven children . . . you're a young man . . . you're nice looking. You can get someone else . . . you're as scared as I am." He responded, "Just be quiet and I won't hurt you." After they walked down the street, he pulled her into another hallway, a vestibule, pushed her down on the floor. And he kept saying very quietly, "Don't make a sound. I'll kill you if you make a sound." She recollected that he began the assault by "going down on me" (cunnilingus), which she found "completely insane." She said, "this is something that I've had performed on me, but only in a very close and loving relationship." He then penetrated her genitally. After the assault, he "picked up the knife, closed it . . . waited for me to get dressed." He then took her arm and walked her to the apartment building from which he had abducted her. She noted that he apparently "thought it was my door . . . he patted me on the cheek and walked away." Neither pleading nor trying to reason with this rapist prevented rape.

Women who were not raped. Another woman (case 84) was walking home alone, around midnight when she was attacked:

> I was upset . . . I had a disagreement with my boyfriend and left his apartment to return to my own. Ordinarily I had a habit of being very wary when I walk down the street but I was not in the frame of mind at the time.

She noticed a man waiting on the lawn of an apartment building. As she passed him he said, "Come here, I want to fuck you."

> As I proceeded to walk under the viaduct towards my apartment . . . he grabbed me, put his arms between my legs from the front and back . . . I tensed up . . . used my energy to become strong . . . I shoved him away . . . started running through the streets screaming . . . afterwards he was just standing there yelling at me and being somewhat upset that he didn't get his thing accomplished. . . . He was running after me yelling for a short time and then gave up the chase.

She stopped the assault because she used physical force to break out of his grip and then screamed to scare him off by attracting other people.

Three Strategies (Nine Rapes; Seventeen Avoidances)

Twenty-six women used three types of defense techniques. Nine women were raped, while seventeen avoided rape. Six of the nine raped women pleaded as one of their three strategies, while four used physical force as one of their strategies. In contrast, only four of the eighteen women who avoided rape pleaded, while twelve used physical force. In four cases of avoidance there was environmental intervention. There was no environmental intervention for the nine raped women.

Women who were raped. Looking for a job is seldom easy. After an interview, one woman (case 23) "decided to go to a lounge and visit some friends" with another woman, who met someone she knew who joined them. About 1:30 A.M. she became tired and told her friend she was ready to leave. Her friend agreed and went about "her goodbyes." To speed up the process, the woman said she would wait in the car. "I sat in the car with my feet up on the seat . . . I stayed out there about ten minutes . . . two men came out that I knew and I spoke to them . . . it was getting too late for my friend to come right out . . . I decided to go back in and see what was keeping her so long." A bus pulled up behind her and while looking in the rear view mirror at the bus, she "saw this man walking toward the car . . . but didn't pay any attention to him." She recalled that her car window was not even halfway down despite the summer heat, and the doors were locked. She felt very safe being locked in a car that was parked on a busy corner. The man she had seen "came up on the driver's side . . . and asked me for a match." When she told him that she didn't have one he walked on.

> But before I knew it, he was back . . . he reached inside the car and grabbed me by my neck. . . . He said if I screamed he'd kill me . . . he had a gun . . . he said it was a gun . . . but I didn't know . . . he had something in his hand but he had it covered with a bag or scarf or something . . . he unlocked the door, got in pushed me over to the passenger's side.

He took off, driving very crazily, "going through a lot of red lights . . . he was all over the yellow line . . . going down a lot of alleys, a lot of side streets." She was convinced this was a robbery, and told him he could have whatever he wanted, he could have the money, he could have the car. He said 'No' and just kept telling me to shut up . . ." When she finally asked him what he wanted, he didn't answer. "But he kept telling me to shut up or he'd kill me. . . . When we got to this lot [a deserted church schoolyard] it came to my mind that I was gonna be attacked. He forcibly undressed me (evidently I wasn't taking off my clothes fast enough)." He vaginally raped her and forced her to suck his penis. She recalled, "I was crying and he told me to shut up . . ." She noted that at one point she "started to refuse and then thought about this thing he had to my head . . ." After the oral sex, she "started to scream . . . and that was when he changed his mind. He decided he was going to put on his clothes and leave." Before leaving, he took her purse and discovered that she didn't have any money. He got out of the car and apologized. "He said he was sorry, he never meant to rape me, he never meant to hurt me." She screamed, reasoned, and fled.

Women who were not raped. Life is full of surprises, even for a rapist. One woman (case 9) was assaulted when she got off a bus and was walking under a viaduct:

> I didn't know how he knew [I] was a girl . . . [I] had three pair of army pants on, long underwear, a parka . . . I told myself, you're being paranoid . . . it seemed almost obvious . . . so obvious it can't

> be . . . about a block later I was pretty sure [of the possible assault],
> but still had two blocks to go . . . I kept walking. . . . I took out my
> keys and had them in my hand.

She went into the building vestibule, hoping he wouldn't follow.

> I started to open my door and he came in, threw me on the ground
> . . . started putting his hands down my pants . . . I was fighting with
> him . . . fighting hard . . . I didn't let up at all.

She recalled thinking:

> . . . if the fighting wasn't working out, I was gonna try something else
> . . . I was screaming at him. . . . All of a sudden he stopped and we
> both stood up. . . . And he started yelling all those things at me – "you
> filthy whore, you filthy bitch" . . . I started yelling at him "You crazy
> moron, get out of here," . . . when I got up . . . he was still in the ves-
> tibule and I started ringing all the bells . . . he began acting as though
> the assault was over . . . when he was leaving he continued saying all
> those things to me . . . I was saying, "You filthy nerd, can't you get it
> any other way?"

In retrospect she stated that she really felt he was surprised at her resistance. "I felt that he expected me to lie down and open my legs."

It is interesting to compare case 11 with this case. Both women were
working nights and took public transportation home. Both were assaulted
as they were walking from their buses. They both tried to find safety in a
vestibule of a house. However, the woman who was raped used cognitive
verbal strategies and pleaded, while the woman who avoided rape was very
angry, screamed, fought, and cursed her assailant. She was prepared for an
attack, holding her keys when she became suspicious. The raped woman
froze and couldn't scream or move ("I was paralyzed like a rag doll"),
although she tried to flatter and reason with the assailant as well as plead
with him. She attributed her inability to fight back to her long history as a
battered woman, systematically abused by her husband. Although she
divorced him the effect remained.

Four Strategies (Four Raped; Ten Avoidances)

All the avoiders and three of the raped women used physical force. Out
of the four raped women, only three of the ten avoiders used pleading.
However, because the numbers are so small, we should be cautious about
interpretations. One of the four women who defined herself as raped was
an exception to the model of rape presented in Chapter 2 as involving a
penis. There were no phallic acts, but she defined herself as raped because
she *would have been raped* had a dog not appeared, enabling her to flee.

Women who were raped. While returning from work late one evening, another woman (case 15) was raped. On the evening of the assault she was "working a shift for another girl . . . I was working two jobs so I was really tired and I was off my guard." She had biked to work and in order to get home,

> I had to go across the cornfields . . . it was kind of a pastoral setting and I didn't expect anyone to be in those cornfields. I thought I knew my way but I lost my way and so I was going back and forth . . . looking for a particular break in the hedge . . . I saw this man out there . . . I thought he was just looking at the fields. . . . I made the mistake of asking him if he knew where the break in the hedge was . . . I was a little freaked out he was there but he seemed to answer normally . . . and I relaxed a little bit and then I heard these steps, thudding steps and I thought 'He must be after me' and then I tried to push the bike further and I was only about 10 feet from the parking lot . . . I had seen the break in the hedge . . . he knocked me down from behind . . . he practically smothered me . . . he told me to get my clothes off and then I said, "Are you going to rape me?" and he said "Yes" and I said "Have you ever raped a woman before?" and he said "No." I said "Well, why are you doing this now?" and then I tried to talk him out of it. . . . I pretty much screamed and fought kind of instinctively and then when nobody came, when nothing happened after all that screaming, I must have screamed for a good 10, 15 minutes. . . . I did try at least twice after that to get away and scream again and he threw me back down on the ground and started smothering me . . . took my face and shoved it into the dirt and sat on my head. . . . I couldn't breathe, I couldn't get any air at all.

After he had forced her to remove her clothes he took her to the middle of the cornfield, about eight blocks from the starting point. The site of the assault was fairly isolated.

> At one point I said, "Are you really enjoying this?" And he said, "No". . . . I kept on trying to ask him, "Why are you doing this?" and I kept also asking him, "Are you gonna kill me?" I was talking to the guy who raped me trying to get him to see me as a person . . . when I got too close to making him see me as a person he told me to shut up . . . and kept talking about how he was good at knocking people out.

After he had raped her vaginally she noted that "when he started to get his clothes up . . . I got up . . . he said 'Why did you get up?' and I said 'Well I just have to stretch my legs. They're cramped.' And then I took off . . . I ran across the fields and then I stood on this big highway naked. . . . And I was screaming 'Help.'" Eventually a man, working in his yard, came to her assistance. Despite her use of physical force, and screaming, as well as her attempts to reason with the rapist and flee, she was unable to avoid being raped.

Women who were not raped. The literature on violence against women is full of stories of attacks by estranged husbands and boyfriends. One case (78) is an example of such an assault. The woman had left her husband three weeks earlier and was living in the apartment of friends who were out of town. She had been taking the phone off the hook because her husband had been making harassing phone calls in the middle of the night since she left him.

On the day of the assault, as she was starting to get "ready to go to work, he came over with my son (age 3) . . . they both looked a mess." She did not want to answer the door but was afraid he would cause a disturbance if she refused. He wanted to know whether she planned on returning to him. She recalled that "I didn't want to give him a final yes or no because I thought it would precipitate some kind of incident." She had not been able to get dressed before they arrived and said that although she "had on a nightgown" it was "long" and "not suggestive." She recalled:

> I was sitting on the bed Indian style and he came over and said "You better call in, 'cause you're not going anywhere" . . . when I got my bearings I quickly turned around and tried to go to the end of the bed . . . my husband said 'I'm gonna get this one way or another.' And he pulled his penis out of his pants . . . grabbed me . . . fell on top of me . . . I was so conscious of the fact that my son was there. I didn't want to hit my husband because I didn't want my son to see that . . . all I could say was "How could you do this in front of your son?" . . . I started to cry . . . he started pumping . . . there was no penetration. . . . I started getting hysterical . . . I said "Goddamn you get off me." And I started hitting him . . . then my son started getting hysterical. And I think when he started hitting my husband saying, "You leave my Mommy alone" it got to my husband. He got up and left the room.

This woman tried to reason with her husband (cognitive strategy), cried, and physically fought with him. When her son intervened (environmental intervention) the assault ended, and she was able to avoid rape.

ADDITIONAL RESPONSES

Fear of Death or Fear of Rape

Two principal patterns of the woman's dominant fear or concern at the moment of attack are fear of being murdered and/or mutilated or fear of being raped.

When women were most afraid of being murdered or mutilated they were more likely to be raped. Often a woman who had this fear said that she hoped that by going along with the rapist she would deter him from further and more horrible violence. One such woman (case 11) said:

I was only thinking about he might kill me, and I was really afraid of that. That was my main worry. To put it quite bluntly, I wasn't afraid of his raping me. There wasn't fear there. There was a revulsion. I didn't want that to happen, but primarily I was afraid of being killed.

Women who were most afraid of being raped were more likely to avoid rape. They spoke of their *determination* not to be raped as well as their refusal to think about the possibility of death. Under these circumstances, a woman was likely to put up a more vigorous and successful defense. One avoider (case 57) said: "I knew I didn't want to get raped. I decided I'd rather risk getting cut than raped."

Not all women mentioned either of these fears. It is significant that of those who did, over half the women who stopped their rapes said that fear of rape and determination not to be raped was their main concern. Almost all the raped women said their primary concern was fear of death or mutilation (see Table 4.2).

Depersonalization

Many women used depersonalization to cope when faced with assault, making statements such as:

- "I felt as if it wasn't happening to me."
- "I didn't believe it was happening."
- "I wasn't there."

A dramatic instance of such a mechanism in operation was one woman who said that while she was being raped in her car she felt as if she were on the roof of the car observing the assault. Raped women were much more likely to cope this way than women who were not raped.

Negotiations Between the Women and Their Attackers

A great deal of what occurred in the assault depended on how the woman interacted with her assailant. We discovered that women were able to negotiate parts of the scenario.

Table 4.2. Primary Fears of Attacked Women

	Raped	Avoided Rape	Total
Fear of death, mutilation, beating	28	19	47
Fear of rape; determination not to be raped	3	26	29
Unclear or missing information	10	6	16

Although it was difficult to negotiate out of genital intercourse itself, some women were able to negotiate their way out of other sexual acts after vaginal rape was completed. Thus, several women negotiated their way out of sodomy and/or fellatio afterwards. One woman who had been sodomized and forced to perform fellatio was able to avoid subsequent vaginal intercourse. In one of the more unusual "sexual" negotiations, a woman (case 40) said she was a "good girl living with her mother."

> I tried using as much naivete as I could. . . . I told him that I was really frightened of getting pregnant and I would have to tell my mother if I was pregnant . . . have to tell my boyfriend . . . he said . . . "It's all right honey we aren't going to make any babies tonight" . . . and then he withdrew before ejaculation.

This man was no amateur rapist. That very afternoon he had been acquitted of a rape charge, and the following night he was arrested by police in the act of beating and raping another woman.

A second related area of negotiation concerned the place in which the assault occurred. For example, a woman who avoided rape (case 7) noted:

> I was telling him I'd be happy to have sex with him, but not in the alley. . . . I suggested . . . a bar around the corner . . . there I felt like I'd have more options or more control.

Women also negotiated about money or credit cards. One woman who was raped (case 49) described her negotiation in the following way:

> He went for my credit cards. I said, "Don't take my credit cards! . . . Because they're not gonna do you any good at all . . . Because I'm gonna put a 'Stop' on them."

Women were also able to negotiate some conditions of their assaults, from being tied up in a more comfortable position to being assisted in walking from one place to another. One woman, a mental health technician (case 58) we call "The Super Negotiator," superbly illustrates the range of individual negotiations. Although she was awakened by an armed assailant straddling her, she was able to persuade him to: (a) put his knife in a different room, because she said the sight of it made her nervous; (b) permit her to go to the bathroom to remove her tampon; (c) smoke some hash so she could be more relaxed; and (d) get a beer out of the refrigerator to further relax her. Actually she neither smoked hash nor drank beer (in reality she got a can of soda), but her use of physical force and her attempt to flee in addition to negotiations and delaying tactics led her to an opening where she was able to grab the knife. Then, threatening him with his own weapon,

she forced the half-undressed rapist to flee. He said: "And here I was, trying to be nice!"

Even under difficult circumstances some women were able to negotiate,
but they had to pretend to go along with the rapists' immediate goal (indeed
some of them *did* go along) and then watch for an opening. Most people,
including rapists, want to believe that they are nice people.

Storaska (1975), who provides much information about how to say no to
a rapist, says rapists need love (our major finding is that saying no or flattering the rapist is not enough). As long as the rapist's immediate goal is
reached, or he believes it will be reached, he might allow the woman some
leeway by behaving like a "nice guy."

CONCLUSION

This chapter dealt with women who avoided rape and how they did it
compared with women who were raped. In no way do we want to imply
that any woman can stop her rape (see Table 4.3). We *have* described
women who were overpowered; but even women who are not overpowered
or faced with an armed assailant are raped. Since some women are raped on
one occasion and avoid rape on another (see Chapter 4), we want to stress
that the women's "personality" does not cause rape. They are not "victimization prone." Women do not cause rape!!!

Although some women are naive, naiveté is not a crime. Middle-class
white women are not taught street smarts and are concerned about seeming
"paranoid" and hurting people's feelings, but the punishment for that
should not be to be raped.

Table 4.3. Strategies Summarized

Avoiders	Raped Women	No Difference
Physical strategies	Pleading	Talking, reasoning or using "feminine wiles"
Yelling/screaming	No strategies	(cognitive verbal strategies)
Fleeing or trying to flee	Depressed if raped and did not use physical	
Environmental intervention	strategies	
Multiple strategies (3 or more)	Depersonalization	
Primary fear of rape	Primary fear of death or mutilation	

Table 4.4. Consensual Sex and Rape Continuum

Consensual Sex	Altruistic Sex	Compliant Sex	Rape

Blaming a woman growing up in this culture for being raped is like blaming her for speaking English.

We live in a rape culture (Griffin, 1971) where many women cannot distinguish between consensual sex and aggression.[2] After working in this area for years, we are constantly aware that many sexual acts that we formerly defined as unpleasant and unwanted were actually rape, though they would not stand up in court. Bart has conceptualized a continuum of consent with rape at one end and consensual sex, equally desired by both partners, at the other (see Table 4.4). After consensual sex she has placed altruistic sex, and between altruistic sex and rape she has placed compliant sex. In the latter there is no overt threat of force, but the woman knows that if she does not comply, there will be unpleasant consequences. Few women have only engaged in consensual sex.

REFERENCES

Block, Richard, and Wesley C. Skogan. 1982. Resistance and outcome in robbery and rape: Nonfatal stranger to stranger violence. Unpublished paper, Center for Urban Affairs and Policy Research, Northwestern Univ.

Cohn, E., L. H. Kidder, and J. Harvey, 1978. Crime prevention vs. victimization prevention: The psychology of two different reactions. *Victimology: An International Journal* 3:285–296.

Fox, Greer Litton. 1977. Nice girl: Social control of women through a value

---

[2]After spending a day reading the cases of all the women who had been raped left me (Bart) feeling as if all my skin had been peeled off, and I stopped at a friend's house. She and a male guest were having tea, and he started to interrogate me about my work. At first I tried to avoid the interaction and said, "I don't talk to men about rape," but I couldn't stop him. He stated that it must be difficult to tell if a woman were raped. I said, "No, there was no problem at all." He then said, "I knew a girl that was raped once and she said it was the best thing that had ever happened to her." I became hysterical and left the room.

Shortly thereafter I was told that "girls say yes with their bodies and no with their mouths," i.e., that one did not have to take a woman's refusal seriously. This time I ended up tearing my hair out. Doing this kind of research decreases one's social skills and ability to carry on polite conversation.

construct. *Signs: Journal of Women in Culture and Society* 2(4): 805-817. Chicago: University of Chicago Press.

Kidder, Louise H., Joanne L. Boell, and Marilyn M. Moyer. 1983. Rights consciousness and victimization prevention: Personal defense and assertiveness. *Journal of Social Issues* 39(2):153-168.

McIntyre, Jennie J. 1980. Victim response to rape: Alternative outcomes. Final report of Grant MH 29045, National Institute of Mental Health.

Press, Aric and associates. May 20, 1985. Rape and the law. *Newsweek*: 60-64.

Queen's Bench Foundation. 1976. *Rape prevention and resistance*. San Francisco, California.

Sanders, William B. 1980. *Rape and woman's identity*. Beverly Hills: Sage Publications.

5 Socialization and Rape Avoidance: Guise and Dolls

Act like a lady. Be nice. Calm down. Don't raise your voice. (Assailant, case 94)

We do not believe that we are *simply* the products of childhood socialization. Nor do we believe, as classical Freudians do, that our character is formed by the time we are five. Yet childhood experiences affect behavior as adults. Significant life experiences, an indispensable part of "becoming" a person, do not end with childhood. As adults, we continue this process. No two people share *identical* life experiences. Nevertheless, there are common patterns in this process that are a part of the person's socialization. Since we all undergo childhood and adult socialization, what part of this process distinguishes raped women from women who avoided rape? What experiences in childhood or adulthood make a difference? Feminist analysts believe that learning to be "feminine," a theme of female socialization, results in our increased vulnerability to victimization.

CHILDHOOD

Parental Response to Childhood Aggression

Children commonly fight with their siblings and schoolmates. We found this was true both for women who avoided rape and for women who were raped. Furthermore, both groups were equally likely to use or not use force in these quarrels. Both groups were equally likely to win in these fights. However, parents of the two groups responded differently to the fighting. The parents of women who were raped were more likely to have intervened and punished their children for fighting. The parents of women who were raped were less likely to have advised their daughters to fight back when quarreling. For example, one woman who was raped (case 44) recalled that her parents "didn't want us to fight . . . they wanted us to walk away from it."

In contrast, a radio reporter who avoided being raped (case 24) noted

58

that after a childhood fight, when she went to her mother for protection, she was told: 'Go back downstairs' . . . she wasn't gonna let me in the house, I had to learn to take care of myself."

Childhood Play and Sports

Both groups of women were equally likely to play with dolls and read, behavior traditionally associated with growing up female. But sports is an area traditionally dominated by men. Girls are less likely to participate in sports than boys, and their participation is usually in noncontact sports such as baseball. Thus participation in noncontact sports was similar for both groups of women. However, women who avoided rape were more likely to have played football, a contact sport, than women who were raped. But it is not uncommon for tomboys to be discouraged from continuing their interest in sports generally and contact sports in particular.

> When I was in fourth grade I used to play tackle football with the boys. The teacher one day told me I had to stop playing with them because when I got to high school, the boys wouldn't date me and the girls wouldn't be my friend. I stopped. (Conversation with a raped woman)

Childhood Perception of What Life Would Be Like as an Adult

Raped women and women who avoided rape differed as children in their images of their futures. Women who were raped more often made statements such as: "I expected to get married and have children," or "I thought I was gonna be like Cinderella and I know that someday when I was 18 I wanted to get married. And I thought everything was gonna be rosy."

While 40 percent of the women who were raped envisioned a future of domesticity, one in which they would be married and have children, only 14 percent of the women who avoided rape mentioned this American Dream for females. They were more likely to speak of jobs or careers, making comments such as: "When I was growing up I thought I either was going to be a nurse or a physical therapist," or "I knew if I didn't stay in school and try to get my education that I would have no place in society."

ADULTHOOD

Adult Participation in Sports

Participation in sports on a regular basis has increasingly become a way of achieving improved mental and physical well-being. Women who avoided being raped were substantially more likely to engage in sports regularly: Almost half ($n = 21$) did so compared with approximately one fourth ($n = 10$) of the raped women.[1] What is the implication of this relationship? The causal links are difficult to establish. Whether avoidance is a by-product of a more "ready-for-action" physical condition, a more self-confident feeling of bodily capability, or some other factor (such as endurance) is unknown. However, a relationship exists. Women should know that regular participation in sports may provide them with skills that decrease their chances of being raped.

Adult Management of Stress/Emergencies

Extrapolating from research in other areas (i.e., disaster research), it seems reasonable to assume that experience in effectively managing stress and/or emergencies in one situation may carry over to other stressful/emergency situations. Obviously, being sexually assaulted is a stressful situation.

Women's reported response to common emergencies differentiated women who were raped from women who avoided being raped. For example, women who avoided rape were more likely than raped women to know how to extinguish a grease fire. In addition, almost three fourths ($n = 33$) of the women who avoided being raped also knew first aid procedures (excluding five for whom we had no information), while 56 percent ($n = 24$) of the raped women had these skills. A good example of the rhetoric of a woman without these skills is:

> I don't have too many emergencies in my life. I don't know how to react. [If I had to fix a flat tire] I wouldn't trust that the tire would stay on after I put it on. I would have to do it under somebody's supervision.

Many factors contribute to this concept of emergency readiness. One factor is knowledge of self-defense. As might be expected, knowledge of self-defense played an important role in differentiating raped women from women who avoided rape.

If a woman takes a course in self-defense, she is preparing to defend herself rather than to find some nice man to take care of her. She understands that the world is a dangerous place in which women must have basic mistrust. As one of the women (case 26) said, "We are engaged in guerrilla warfare." Such untraditional attitudes support the feminist analysis of the relationship between traditional socialization and victimization. Thus, it is not only the skills learned in self-defense courses that help women repel assaults, but the attitudes engendered and reinforced. These women are

---

[1]The relationship between regular participation in sports and outcome (rape or avoidance) is maintained when age is controlled.

not made of sugar and spice and everything nice. It is thus not surprising that avoiders were nearly twice as likely as raped women to have learned self-defense, although the number of cases is small (see Chapter 4 for elaboration).

Adult Role Models

Subjects were asked which women in public or private life they admired and why. Women who avoided being raped were more likely than raped women to mention a woman they knew personally (e.g., mother, friend) rather than one in public life. For both groups the overwhelming reason given for admiring these women, even if the women were in traditional roles, had to do with their strength.

> I admire my mother because she's taken her background and re-molded it . . . to what she needed and discarded the rest.

> [I admire] Margaret Mead . . . it's her outstanding, forging ahead type thing.

Sometimes women known personally and women in public life were combined: "I admire my mother, my grandmother and Barbara Jordan."

Only three women, all raped, gave a more traditional answer. They admired women who were able to successfully combine an occupation with their "role as a woman."

Feelings toward one's mother did not differentiate raped women from women who avoided being raped. The majority of women in both groups described their mothers in adjectives that would be classified as "strong." In addition, responses from both groups of women yielded fairly similar percentages of positive versus negative perceptions of their mothers.

The Women's Height and Weight

As one might expect, women who avoided being raped tended to be taller and heavier than women who were raped. Of the avoiders, 29 percent were 5'7" and over, while only 16 percent of the raped women were that tall. Of the women who were raped, 37 percent weighed 115 pounds or less, while only 18 percent of the women who avoided rape weighed that little. Thus it is no accident that the two women (cases 57 and 58) who were able to avoid being raped, despite the fact that they were attacked by armed assailants while they were asleep, were 5'7" or over.

The possible explanations for this difference are numerous. One plausible explanation is that the woman's size compared with the rapist's size makes a difference. But our data show that the rapist's build is not associated with the outcome, so we can eliminate this explanation.

SR-C*

Another possible explanation is cultural. Our society values tallness. Think of the phrases "She doesn't measure up to . . ." or "We need a man of stature," for examples of how this value is built into our language (Brodlie, 1981). The Yale psychologist Jerome Brodlie (1981) states that the over-emphasis on the value of tallness aggravates the sense of inadequacy felt by short children (see also Brooks, 1981 and Veevers and Adams, 1982). Such children are often dealt with in a condescending way by their parents and other adults, both in school and social settings.

Tall women are less likely to have the option of acting helpless. They, unlike short women, are less likely to have a trained incapacity to be competent and assertive. Therefore, they are less likely to have the option of assuming the traditional "feminine" role, which many rape analysts (e.g., Brownmiller, 1975; Griffin, 1971) suggest is conducive to being a rape victim.

Ordinal Position or Birth Order

The psychological literature is replete with examples of the effect of the order of birth (Brooks, 1984). Special characteristics have been attributed to oldest, youngest, and in certain instances middle children, as well as to only children. Parental expectations vary for children of different ages compared to their siblings. Parents usually expect more from the oldest child. What this usually means for oldest daughters is that they have greater responsibility for care of siblings as well as helping with housework.

Thus, it was not surprising that birth order was associated with rape avoidance. Oldest daughters (who were not only children) were more likely to avoid rape. Of oldest daughters (there were 57 oldest daughters) 68 percent avoided rape, compared with 46 percent of middle daughters (there were 28 middle daughters), and 43 percent of youngest daughters (there were 21 youngest daughters).

In addition, oldest daughters were somewhat more likely to have had major household responsibility such as full care of siblings and preparation of dinner than middle or youngest daughters. Of oldest daughters, 36 percent had such responsibility, compared with 25 percent of other daughters. These responsibilities require a relatively high level of competence and an ability to cope effectively with emergencies.

Further data analysis shows that both ordinal position and major household responsibility were independently associated with outcome.

Lesbians

Women, particularly lesbians, frequently ask whether lesbians were more likely to avoid rape. We did not ask the women if they were heterosexual. Nevertheless, six women said they were lesbian (all of these were lesbian before the current assault). Five of these six stopped their rapes. These self-identified lesbians differed in some important ways from the sample as a whole. Four of the six had studied self-defense, while only 18 of the remaining 88 women (about one fifth) had done so. All five who stopped their rapes used active, usually physical strategies, and three of the five stopped their rapes immediately. One fled as soon as she felt a sharp object in her back and the assailant ordered her to come with him. She said, "I took chances since I decided that I would run . . . I would rather be dead than have something like that happen to me" (case 3). Another immediately yelled the particular yell she had learned in judo (case 93). She also shouted "Get outta here!" and swung her bag full of women's movement papers at the man as he ran towards her. The third (case 73), attacked in her vestibule, said she

> pushed him away, kicked him and screamed at the top of my lungs all at the same time while he was . . . ripping my breast off and he left. Just kind of hobbled away . . . I think I kicked him in the balls. I know if I would have hit him on target as hard as I was kicking he would not have hobbled away, but I think I got him a little (case 73).

The two remaining women used delaying strategies rather than stopping their rapes immediately. One talked, pleaded (she was a virgin and said so), and kept pushing her assailant away until he finally realized that she was not playing games and really did not want to have sex. The fifth, a self-defense instructor, used the multiple strategies that are associated with avoidance.

Nothing explicitly sexual was done to three of the five lesbian women who avoided rape. The fourth was kissed and forcibly restrained, and the fifth had her breast grabbed and, as she put it, "he slid his hand on my ass." Four of the five women who avoided rape perceived that they were in danger immediately and took action rather than giving the man the benefit of the doubt, as other women sometimes did in ambiguous situations. These lesbians were not afraid to act on their feelings, to be "paranoid," or to hurt the man's "feelings."

The one lesbian who was raped was faced with a difficult situation. She was asleep in a hotel hallway in a strange city when she was grabbed by two strangers who said they had a knife and dragged her into a room. She waited for them to make a mistake so she could escape, but they did not slip up.

Some traditional advice, such as that given by Storaska (1975), has advised women to tell their assailants that they are lesbians. He further suggests that if two women are in danger of being sexually assaulted, e.g., being followed, that they should act like lovers. This ploy would so "turn off" and "disgust" their assailant that he would lose all interest in rape. Only one woman (case 74), a community organizer, lied and said that she was a lesbian. It didn't work. In fact, in two instances (cases 55 and 87) the assailant forced two women under attack to perform sexual acts with one another. So this advice is not supported. Indeed, the assailant might rape the woman precisely because he thought she was a lesbian, to "cure" her or punish her.

A rape victim advocate told the following incident. The woman for whom she advocated had met a man in a gay bar who said his sister was "gay." He felt that she needed help because she always stayed home and was embarrassed to go places where lesbians meet. The woman agreed to go to his sister's apartment with him to help her. When they got out of the car, presumably at his sister's apartment, he raped her in the gangway. He said: "This is what it's like to make love to a man" (Rondini, 1982).

It is reasonable to assume that women who volunteer the information that they are lesbian are less likely than are other women to be traditionally "feminine." So we can say, mindful of the small number of women, that the fact that only one out of six such lesbians was raped—and her situation was one in which no other woman was able to escape—gives further support for the feminist analysis: In order to avoid rape it is helpful to transcend traditional "feminine" socialization and style.

Women's Status/Class

Almost all the women were in the paid labor force when they were assaulted. Only two women were doing unpaid labor at home, and eight were unemployed.

Using education as an indicator of social class/status, the sample was heavily middle class or higher. A total of 89 percent ($n = 83$) had some college education: 19 percent ($n = 18$) had a four-year degree, and 26 percent ($n = 24$) had post-graduate education. Only 12 percent ($n = 11$) had a high school or less than high school education. We should realize that because our sample is young, the probability of having more education is increased. Education did not differentiate raped women from avoiders. The outcome of rape or avoidance was not associated with the woman's education, her occupation, or whether her occupation was traditional. When we examine parents' education and occupation, we find the following: Women who were raped were more likely to have had fathers with high school education or less, while women who avoided rape were more likely to have had mothers with college or post-graduate degrees. Because the numbers are small, we should hesitate to make inferences from these data.

Prior Sexual Abuse

The high level of sexual violence in women's lives emerged as the women started talking. We began by asking if the women had ever been attacked before the current assault. So much violence emerged that specific questions on male use of physical and sexual violence were added. This violence spanned both childhood and adulthood and included incest and other childhood molestation as well as adult rape/attempted rape, but did not differentiate raped women from avoiders. However, in some specific cases, it was apparent that the prior abuse was associated with the woman's response (see case 33 below).

Childhood Incest

Of the 94 women, 17 were incest survivors[2] or survivors of attempted incest (18 percent). Nine of these women were sexually abused by their father, stepfather, or foster father. One of the nine women (case 33) was not only raped by her father, but molested by her brother as well.

This woman's father began sexually abusing her when she was in the sixth grade. This abuse included "everything but [penile] penetration." She assumed that everything would cease when she began menstruating. When her menses began and he continued his molestation, she went to the authorities (police and a teacher). None of these persons, including her family, was supportive. She was given a physical exam and told: "Your story can't be true, because you're still a virgin." After this investigation, however, her father left her alone for three months. However, he began once again, and his resumption included sexual intercourse. This continued for three years until an older sister found them together. After this her father left the home, and a divorce followed. However, after her father left, a brother who was very close to her in age, "tried to pull the same shit." She threatened him, unlike in earlier episodes, with murder if he ever touched her. She recalled that her brothers had molested both her sister and herself when they were children.

The additional seven instances of incest involved other male relatives, primarily uncles.[3] Some of these experiences continued for an extended period of time, and others were isolated incidents.

Other Child Abuse

While incest was the most common type of childhood sexual abuse these women experienced, five women were molested by strangers, and nine were

---

[2]We use the term *survivor* on the advice of counselors who work with women who have been sexually abused by relatives. These counselors feel that the term *victim* can function as a self-fulfilling prophecy, while the term *survivor* emphasizes the woman's potential.

[3]The numbers total more than 17 because some women had more than one assailant.

abused by a nonrelative known to her when she was a child.[4] Thus a total of 25 of the 94 women were sexually victimized when they were growing up. This is similar to the Finkelhor (1979) finding of 20 percent[5] and Russell's finding that 15 percent of the wives she studied had experienced incest (1982).

Sexual Violence as Adults

Male violence against these women continued in their adult lives. Of the 94 women, 51 had been previously raped, attacked and avoided rape, or had multiple experiences in addition to the assault they came to talk about. A total of 24 women had been raped previously, and 32 had a previous rape attempt. Some women had experienced both rape and attempted rape in their pasts.

A prior history of sexual violence was as true for the women who were raped as for the women who avoided rape. (The terms *raped women* and *avoiders* refer to the incident that functions as the dependent variable in this study. This was the most recent sexually violent event the women reported.)

Those of us who have been in consciousness raising groups know that forced sex and attempts to force sex are common experiences that many women share. The results of this study are consistent with the feminist analysis of women's situation. *Violence is the bottom line of social control of women.*[6]

Dealing with Anger

As part of the attempt to learn whether women who avoided rape had deviated from traditional socialization, we asked them several questions about how they dealt with anger. Nice girls and ladies, after all, do not act

---

[4]The figures are more than 25 percent of the 94 women because they include women who had been subjected to attacks in more than one category of child abuse.

[5]Finkelhor (1979) found that 14 percent of the women in his sample and 8 percent of the men had sexual contact with a member of the nuclear family as children, but only 10 percent of these were cross-generational. Females were usually the victims of cross-generational incest. When sexual victimization was considered, he found that 19 percent of the women and 8.6 percent of the men had been sexually victimized as children.

[6]While this statement is not directly related to differentiating raped women from avoiders, we include it because it constitutes part of our analysis of why there is violence against women generally.

out their anger (Fox, 1977), so it is not surprising that one assailant said, "Act like a lady. Be nice. Calm down. Don't raise your voice" (case 94). We expected women who were raped to repress or at least not express their angry feelings and to feel guilty about them. Thus we asked them what they did if someone pushed ahead of them on a supermarket line and when was the last time they felt angry with someone. The results were not what was expected, although in retrospect they make sense.

An analysis of the responses of the women in this study by Kantor and Weinberger (1979) indicated that women were almost equally divided between those who felt rage at the rapist and those who directed their anger through other channels, such as self or society. Some saw the rapist as sick and in need of help. Both raped women and avoiders who directed their anger at the rapist had a greater proportion of positive feelings about anger. It frequently took time to become aware of anger toward the rapist. One raped woman said, "It took me a year and a half to even recognize that I was angry about it . . . now, I recognize the justification of my anger, instead of rationalizing it away." Some women who did not experience anger when they discussed the assault found this lack of anger difficult to deal with when speaking to other women.

When they were asked how they expressed their anger, there were marked differences between raped women and women who avoided rape. When asked if they ever got angry and yelled at their husband/friend/lover/children, more women who avoided rape said "never," or "it depends," than gave any other answer. Women who avoided rape appeared to be in control of their emotions, and their anger was dependent and selective according to situational determinants (Kantor and Weinberger, 1979). Women who were raped more frequently expressed anger and reacted to this expression either with guilt or with "good" feelings. The women who avoided rape behaved less like the female stereotype, since expressing emotion (especially being "hysterical") is traditionally viewed as a female characteristic. There were also differences in response to anger that were related to background factors. For example, women who were raped and who had a history of previous molestation were more likely to say they were never angry.

In trying to determine if women from different ethnic groups related to anger differently, we found that in no instance did a Black *raped* woman express her anger physically, while half of Black women *avoiders* were physically aggressive when they felt angry. Catholic women displayed the most negative reactions to expressions of anger (31 percent), compared with 18 percent of Protestants and 11 percent of the Jewish women. Protestant women were more likely to say they were never angry (30 percent) as well as to report turning their anger inward (21 percent). One Protestant subject stated that she never got angry and yelled, since "It's very un-Christian."

Table 5.1. Background Factors and Outcome

Associated with Avoidance	Associated with Rape	Associated with Neither
Childhood		
Lack of parental intervention in physical fights between subject and other children, including siblings	Parental intervention in physical fights with other children	Using force fighting with other children
Parental advice to fight back	Parents less likely to give advice on appropriate response to aggression	
Subject played football		Noncontact sports, e.g., softball
Subject more likely to have an image of her future that is untraditional, not the female "American dream"	Traditional expectations of future life, including domesticity, marriage, children. Less likely to mention job or career	Doll play

Reading

Sexually abused as a child or adolescent |
Adulthood		
Knowledge of first aid, how to control grease fire, and self-defense		
Engaged in sports regularly		
Role models they knew	Role models public figures not known personally	
5'7" or over	115 lbs or less	
Oldest sisters, especially with major household responsibility		
Mother having had college education, particularly postgraduate education	Fathers' education high school or less	Subject's education or occupation
Never expressed anger or expressed it situationally (depending on situation)	Expressions of anger resulting in guilt or "good" feelings (except if with a history of molestation)	
Lesbian [small number]		

Jewish women were the least physical in their manner of dealing with anger and the most verbal (65 percent).[7]

CONCLUSION

This chapter provided substantial but not complete support for the feminist analysis of the relationship between traditional feminine socialization and the risk of being raped when attacked. Table 5.1 summarizes the patterns we found.

REFERENCES

Bart, Pauline B. 1970. Portnoy's mother's complaint. *Trans-Action* 7(13):69–74.
Bart, Pauline, and Patricia O'Brien. 1980. How to say no to Storaska and survive. Paper presented at the annual meetings of the American Sociological Association.
Brodlie, Jerome. 1981. *New York Times*, November 30, p. 24.
Brooks, Andree. 1984. Helping the short child cope. *New York Times*, March 26, p. 16.
Brownmiller, Susan. 1975. *Against our will: Men, women and rape.* New York: Simon and Schuster.
Finkelhor, David, 1979. *Sexually victimized children.* New York: The Free Press.
Fox, Greer Litton. 1977. Nice girl: Social control of women through a value construct. *Signs: Journal of Women in Culture and Society* 2(4):805–817.
Griffin, Susan. 1971. Rape: The All-American crime. *Ramparts* 10:26–35.
Kantor, Glenda, and Gail Weinberger. 1979. Women and anger. Unpublished paper. University of Illinois at Chicago, Department of Sociology.
McIntyre, Jennie J. 1980. Victim response to rape: Alternative outcomes. Final report of Grant MH 29045, National Institute of Mental Health.
Queen's Bench Foundation. 1976. *Rape prevention and resistance.* San Francisco, California.
Rondini, Denise. 1982. Personal communication.
Russell, Diana H. 1982. *Rape in marriage.* New York: Macmillan, p. 179.
Sanders, William B. 1980. *Rape and woman's identity.* Beverly Hills: Sage Publications.
Storaska, Frederick. 1975. *How to say no to a rapist and survive,* New York: Random House.
Veevers, Jean E., and Susan M. Adams. 1982. Bringing bodies back in: The neglect of sex differences in size and strength. Paper presented to the Canadian Sociology and Anthropology Association, Ottawa.

---

[7]This finding is consistent with Bart's study (1971) of depression in middle-aged women or "Portnoy's Mother's Complaint."

6 Ethnicity and Rape Avoidance: Jews, White Catholics and Blacks*

> It was early in the morning and I cut through an alley on the way to Haganah (defense) training, which was illegal then because we were under the British mandate. Two British soldiers were there. One pulled me back and jumped on top of me. I tried to scream but couldn't. I kicked him in the balls, having learned judo in Haganah training. Then the scream came out and he left. He hit me hard in the face but I am not sure whether he did that before or after I kicked him and screamed.
>
> I felt pleased with myself, but lost a little of my faith in mankind. (Personal communication from an Israeli woman on learning of the rape avoidance study, December 1981)

When we first started interviewing, we noted with dismay that despite the fact that out of the first 18 women interviewed 11 avoided rape, the first 3 Jewish women interviewed were raped. It was not until the eighteenth woman was interviewed that we met the first Jewish avoider. Moreover, she had avoided rape by using verbal strategies, saying that she did not "want to" and asking her assailant not to "do anything" (case 18), a technique rarely effective for others in this study. The next Jewish woman interviewed avoided rape by kicking the gun out of the assailant's hand while she was seated on the washing machine where he had placed her. She had effectively used an active strategy in the assault situation, but when he had initially entered the laundry room, she had greeted him, saying, "Can I help you?" even though he was a stranger and she was alone in the room. Four of the next five Jewish women interviewed were raped.

When the study was completed we found that of all the ethnic groups

---

*This chapter is a revised version of a paper written by Pauline Bart, Patricia O'Brien and Jean Blanchard and presented at the World Congress on Women in Haifa, Israel, December 1981. We are very grateful to Jean Blanchard, who did all the computations and wrote the first draft. The section called "The Empty Cell" was originally written with the help of Brenda Eichelberger of the National Black Feminist Organization and was presented at the annual meetings of the National Women's Studies Association in Storrs, Connecticut, 1981.

(Blacks, white Catholics, and white Protestants[1]), Jews were the only group with more raped women than women who avoided rape. In the total sample, 46 percent (43) of the women were raped, and 54 percent (51) avoided being raped. There were 25 white Protestants. A total of 48 percent (12) were raped, while 52 percent (13) avoided rape. Of the Catholic women, 36 percent (9) were raped, while 64 percent (16) avoided being raped. The experiences of both Protestant and Catholic Black women were similar to those of Catholic women — 36 percent (5) were raped, and 64 percent (9) avoided rape. Jewish women were very different; 61 percent (11) were raped, while only 39 percent (7) avoided rape.

These findings surprised many people, who asked: "But aren't Jewish women aggressive?" One of us (Bart) was *not* surprised either by the responses of the Jewish women in the study or by the results, for although verbal skills are rewarded in traditional Jewish socialization, physical skills, particularly fighting, are considered un-Jewish (Bart, 1967). We believe that the statement about Jewish women's "aggressiveness" refers to their *verbal skills*, rather than to their physical prowess. It should be noted that Israeli culture which developed as a *reaction* against traditional *(shetl)* Jewish culture values physical skills.[2] In fact, only two Jewish women out of eighteen reported that their parents advised them to fight back when they were children. In contrast, the parents of 10 out of 14 Black women were reported to have advised their daughters to fight back, and 7 of these women were able to avoid being raped. Catholic women were less likely to have been given this advice: Only four subjects reported being told to fight back, but all four of these women avoided rape. For the sample as a whole, such advice was associated with rape avoidance.[3] Jews expressed their anger verbally much more frequently, while Protestants more often expressed theirs physically.

It was not simply childhood socialization factors that accounted for the high Jewish rape rate in this study. The situational factors that were associated with rape rather than rape avoidance marked the incidents that Jewish women experienced. Jewish women were more likely to be attacked inside their homes or in another indoor location by unknown armed assailants; these assailants generally committed another crime as well. Moreover, their attacks were likely to be sudden (called "blitz" in this study). The assailant was also more likely to be of a different race.

---

[1] There were too few Latinas (five) in this study to analyze separately.

[2] One of us (Bart) remembers that when a WASP friend of hers suggested she give her very agile daughter gymnastics lessons, she thought his suggestion absurd. Instead, she encouraged her daughter to take art and music lessons.

[3] We want to make it clear that we are not blaming parents. Since one of us is a Jewish mother (Bart — whose children were not told to fight back), we are hardly in a position to do so.

While the absence of these situational factors can partially account for the more successful avoidance by Catholics, it does not account for the high avoidance rates for Black women. While Blacks were less likely than were Jewish or Catholic women to be attacked by a man of a different race, they were more likely to be attacked by more than one assailant. Surprisingly, whether the assailant(s) were armed or not had no effect on the outcome for Black women. In fact, two of the three women who fought assailants with guns were young Black women.

Although 15 Jewish women were attacked inside buildings rather than outside, which made it more difficult to escape the rape, 5 of these women were either conned into letting the man in or went with the man into another inside location. Black women were far less naive. One Black woman let a man she knew from her church into her apartment; another was *forced* by two assailants to go to an apartment. Only one Black woman was duped into going inside with a man, and she was raped. Another Black woman (case 53) believed that men considered that crossing the threshold of her apartment implied consent for intercourse and that therefore she "had to give it to them." But since she was attacked at work, she fought back and stopped the rape.

JEWISH WOMEN

The first Jewish avoider (case 18), a law student, employed a strategy that rarely works. She simply asked the assailant not to assault her. At the time of the incident, she was living with her parents, and she stated that one of the problems they had as a family was her parents' insistence on treating her as if she were a child. She strongly felt that they were "stifling" her. This situation, coupled with the fact that her parents had always advised her to avoid fights, implies that in an assault situation she would be likely to be a victim. Fortunately, it did not turn out that way.

She was coming home from school, carrying a full backpack of books. She stopped to buy a bottle of wine. When she came out of the liquor store, paper bag in hand, she noticed a man on the street and, assuming that he was a neighbor, did not become unduly alarmed by his casual nod. When she walked into the vestibule of her apartment building, he followed her in: She still did not become alarmed. She related: "He came in and said, 'Hello, what's your name?' and I started to feel that it didn't seem right." At this point she decided against opening the door because she didn't want him to follow her upstairs. In spite of the awkwardness of the situation, he began telling her that he wanted to go up to her apartment and share her wine, because "people have to be friends." When this approach failed to work, he grabbed her around the neck. Although she claimed that he wasn't really hurting her, she was frightened and kept repeating, "Please let me go. Leave me alone." She did not scream because she thought it futile: There was "no one home to hear it." The man said that if she wouldn't let him kiss her, he was going to "take it all." Undaunted, she kept repeating her pleas and he finally left, saying, as he departed, that he "might see her again sometime."

The next Jewish woman (case 4) came from a "typical [Jewish] upbring- ing." She noted that despite what her friends were doing, she was a virgin when she married at 24 and had never slept with anyone except her hus- band. In her assault situation, however, she was not as fortunate as the other woman. She was also returning from school, but on a bike. It was raining hard. Although it was 10:30 A.M., she ran downstairs to the base- ment to put her bike away, because she didn't want to leave it outside. As she was coming back up the basement stairs, she saw an "enormous Black guy" standing in the doorway. Her initial reaction was that he was there for some legitimate reason, perhaps to "fix the washing machine." Within a very few moments he began to assault her, raising his arm in a fist, and her initial response was replaced by terror. She froze, unable to scream. She indicated that she

> was afraid to fight with anybody . . . I never did, [so it was not surpris- ing that I] was literally paralyzed and I was so terrified he was going to kill me. . . . [I did] not expect to be raped at 10 o'clock in the morning, [I did not] intrude on other people's property let alone their bodies and didn't expect that kind of thing to happen. . . . It was just self-preser- vation . . . that I would do whatever he wanted because nothing could be as bad as being killed.

The only thing she was able to do was shake and whimper. In retrospect, she said that she felt bad about the entire incident because she believes if she had resisted, "he would have just run." There is no way of knowing whether or not that's true; however, this added to her problems in dealing with the rape. In fact, after the rape, when she was in the hospital, she found herself defending the rapist to the police. He did not fit in with her stereotyped image of what a rapist would be like. He was not dirty and did not act in an uncontrolled fashion. He did not seem like a criminal.

Another Jewish woman (case 61) also described herself as coming from an overly protective environment: "I was never even kissed till I was 19 . . . most people consider me very sweet and sensitive, very feminine." She found herself in a situation much like that of the woman putting her bike away. Returning from a doctor's appointment where she had learned the sad news that she had a lump in her breast, she took a shortcut through an alley. She was preoccupied with the doctor's report and only vaguely aware of the presence of another person as she went through the backstairs entranceway to her apartment. As she started to put her key in the back door, he started up the stairs. She felt somewhat suspicious, but her suspicions were too late to help her. Although she unlocked and opened her door, he reached her before she was able to close it. Almost instinctively she screamed. He stopped her screaming by threatening to kill her with a hammer. She pleaded not to be killed, saying, "I'm the sole support of my son." Although she was terrified, she decided to "play it tough" in an effort to disguise her mounting fear. However, she said "I never tried to fight him off . . . I didn't know how at all." Initially, he made demands for her "diamonds" and any other valuables. She repeated over and over that she had nothing of value. He then began threatening to kill her son when he returned from school as added pressure to extricate her "valuables." When this also failed, he produced a tube of lubricating cream and raped her, noting that since she had nothing of value, he was "entitled to at least this." Upon completion, he gathered up some "worthless items" and left, leaving her tied up and lying on the bed. With a great deal of difficulty she managed to call the police before her son came home.

Not only did these Jewish women tend to come from overprotective homes, but they also tended to be inappropriately trusting and somewhat naive. One such woman (case 6) was attempting to find a new apartment. She made an appointment with the manager of a building in a somewhat safe neighborhood, but he failed to show up. While trying to decide what to do, she was approached by a man who had been standing with a woman and a child at a pay phone across the street. He asked her if she were looking for an apartment. When she said yes, he suggested she come with him to see some buildings that he knew of with vacancies. He claimed to work for the owner of these buildings. Initially she hesitated, hoping the building manager would arrive. However, the man said that one of the buildings was only two blocks away and that she could be back in no time. Finally, she agreed to go with him. As they headed for the building, the conversation was amiable, and she was unaware of the fact that he had taken her into an abandoned building. As soon as she entered the building, he closed the door, saying, "You shouldn't have come with me." She immediately offered him money, but he was not interested. He jabbed a rat tail comb with a long pointed metal edge at her stomach. She refused to remove her pants, so he slapped her. After this abuse, according to the woman, ". . . I thought, being the Jewish princess[4] that I am, that I had to take my pants off, cause I was scared to death." In disbelief she asked him how he could leave his wife and child and assault her: Her "whole assumption of trust was based on thinking here's this guy with his wife and kid." The assailant told her that he did not know those people and raped her. Afterwards, he took her money and threatened her with more bodily harm if she did not

---

[4] Jewish Princess or Jewish American Princess is an antisemitic label. Our inclusion of this term in the quote does not mean that we consider it acceptable.

write him a check, saying that she "came into the building of her own free will" and was "enjoying it." In the negotiation that followed, she not only convinced him that he would be unable to cash any check she wrote, but that she needed carfare money. He threatened to "hurt her badly" if she "moved before he returned." As he was leaving, he threw carfare money at her. Realizing that she was in great danger, she climbed out of a window and escaped, relieved that she was not wearing high heels so that such an escape was possible.

Another Jewish woman (case 68) found herself in an assault situation when she tried to help a stranger locate his friend, who was someone she vaguely knew. The stranger knocked on her door, and she let him in because, as she said, "I was in a stage of having to trust everybody. You know, like I never thought of not asking someone to come in and sit in the living room while I looked up the address the person needed." She knew that the man would never find his friend unassisted, as the area in which he lived was difficult to find. Despite the fact that she felt "bad vibes," she offered to give him a ride. In an effort to ascertain the man's trustworthiness, she made a brief stop first, leaving the keys and her purse in the car. She noted, "I couldn't admit to him that I didn't trust him . . . God forbid I should hurt someone's feelings." Returning to find everything intact, she proceeded to the desolate destination. When they arrived, she found out she had been wrong. He threatened her with a knife and, as she reported, "I couldn't conceive of being threatened with a knife or anything else." In an almost unreal series of events, she managed to escape from the car and run head on into a car of women who had inadvertently happened into the area. They rescued her from her knife-wielding pursuer. The assailant returned to the car, and a brief car chase ensued. After a time, he gave up.

Being a victim of basic trust rather than healthy mistrust was also a problem for some Jewish women with men they knew. In one instance, the woman (case 27) allowed her date into her apartment after a very pleasant evening, because he asked her for a cup of coffee. The evening had been nonthreatening, and he was "an educated man." It had been a long day for her, and she rested on the floor while he was drinking his coffee. Soon he began physically badgering her. When she showed signs of resistance, he twisted her arms behind her back. She protested further, telling him that he "was not going to enjoy it." He replied that she "had some problems . . . [she] was raping him." After the assault, as he was leaving, he told her that he would call the next evening. When he called, the police not only intercepted the call, but they arrested the assailant.

In another instance a woman (case 39) found herself in an assault situation as the result of her trust in "somebody that I did vaguely know, from my past . . ." Having encountered him on the street, she exchanged pleasantries, and they shared the details of their work situations—she was meeting success, and he was in a "financial crisis." Thus he asked her to lend him some money, and in exchange he would give her some record albums that he and his brother had made. As she had been involved in other barter situations, she agreed. She went to his apartment to collect the albums after he called and asked her why she had not come by earlier. She said, "It just never occurred to me to think that there was anything that was gonna be amiss." Moreover, she did not want to appear as though she were "acting racist," since he was Black. Upon entering the apartment he attempted to give her a hug, but she pushed him away, telling him, "You know, Joe, if you're into any funny stuff, forget it. I came up here for the albums. You borrowed money from me. I'm happily married." He replied, ". . . don't be worried. I haven't seen you for so long. . . . Don't worry. Just sit down. I want you to hear the albums . . ." After listening for nearly 20 minutes, she decided to leave. As she attempted to leave, he began his assault. According to the woman, "he knelt down, as if to get these albums . . . reached up and grabbed me, and tore off my underpants, in one stroke . . . slammed his fingers into my vagina and ass . . . so I was sort of being held from inside." She fought back fiercely, determined not to be raped. She bit his fingers until she "drew blood" and "gouged [her] fingernails into his balls." She also yelled so loudly that "people two apartment buildings away called the police. They heard me." She escaped from the room and avoided rape. She used all the strategies associated with avoidance and they worked.

BLACK WOMEN

The presence of a weapon did not stop Black women from trying to fight back, as it did for women of other ethnic backgrounds.[5] One Black woman (case 3), just discharged from the Army, was waiting for a bus when a man came up behind her and "put something in my back," some type of "pointed object." The assailant instructed her "not to move or fight," stating that if she followed his directives she would "be all right" and "wouldn't get hurt." Her first thoughts were to "take my chances and run," which she did. She could hear the sound of his running feet as he chased her, but she refused to stop. In her escape attempt, she fell down once, but she quickly recovered to continue her flight. After a four-block race, she was able to flag down a cab, return to her home, and call the police. According to this woman, she "would rather be dead than have something like that happen" to her. Her mother and sister had both been raped.

---

[5]The Black women in this study were not West Indian. Dr. Vickie Mays, a UCLA psychologist noted, when discussing this book, that West Indian Black women would not have reacted as aggressively (May, 1985).

Another Black woman (case 5) employed a similar strategy, despite the fact that the assailant openly displayed a gun. Early one morning as she was walking down the street, she noticed a man walking toward her. She thought him strange as he was wearing a heavy coat despite the 90 degree weather. When they reached each other, he refused to let her pass. He pointed a gun at her and told her to "turn around and walk." In an effort to figure out his motives, she offered him her purse. He refused and said that he wanted her to go with him to a nearby abandoned building. She felt strongly that he might kill her if she went with him to the building and that if she were going to die she "was gonna die out there [on the sidewalk] where somebody could find me rather than in an abandoned building." At that point she turned and ran until she was able to find help. She had been brutally raped three years earlier.

Discussion of rape appeared more common in Black families. One woman (case 20) reported that her mother had a great fear of getting raped and that she was warned incessantly to be careful. Despite a lifetime of warnings, she was an adult when she first faced an assault situation in New York City, soon after her arrival from Chicago. Leaving the terminal, she was approached by a man who saw that she needed a taxicab. He "grabbed [her] luggage really fast" and took it to a "non-traditional looking taxi . . . a jitney cab." He informed her that the "cab drivers were going out on strike" and that "they were already getting out the jitney cabs." Although she was a bit suspicious, she found his explanation plausible. Moreover, her father had been a jitney cab driver, and according to her "you think you're supporting the community when you take a jitney cab." As they began the ride she noticed that they "were going the wrong way." (She had some general sense of the location of things in New York having been there two or three times a year over a two-year period.) Thinking this was some oversight on his part, she informed him of his error in direction. About the same time, she also noticed that there were "regular cabs out" and began "feeling nervous." He turned off onto a side street, noting that he thought "something was wrong with the car." She got out with him; since nothing was wrong, they resumed the journey. At some point they had begun going in the right direction, but the driver still failed to act with "typical taxi driver behavior." He was asking her all "rapey type questions. Are you married?. . . . Are you going to meet a man? . . . meet a woman?" At one point in the trip a police car pulled up next to them as they were stopped for a light. The woman noted that "if I followed my gut instead of my head, I would have said something to them." When they were a block and a half from her destination, they encountered "road work type barricades." The driver told her that there had been a fire, and he'd be unable to get any closer. As she was reaching for her bag, he told her that he had a gun. Although she never saw any weapon (she was blind in one eye and the positioning of the two in the assault caused her "good eye" to be covered), she felt "something cold and metal." Initially he asked her for money. As she was only there for two days for a job interview, she'd "merely taken fifty dollars" with her. Discovering this, he demanded that she take her clothes off. She was attempting to comply ("Didn't want him to get nervous or upset"), but it was nearly impossible given the position he had her in on the backseat floor. What astounded her was the fact that "the car was double parked the whole time on a main thoroughfare under a street light . . . people [were] walking up and down the street the whole time," and yet no one came to her aid. She decided to use this to her advantage and told him that "someone might see them . . . move the car." Realizing his perilous position, he began to get out of the car, never ceasing his threats. When she "saw his shadow" outside the car, she "bolted out [of the car] screaming." However, the assailant chased her down the street. There were two men on the street, and the assailant told them to catch her. To her dismay, they attempted to do so, but she was able to "go under their arms." She told us, "those men all stick together . . ." She ran into a parking garage screaming at the top of her lungs, "wearing no bra, no blouse, a slip, no shoes . . ." begging the attendant to help her because a man tried to rape her. This benevolent soul gave her a quarter to call the police. Sometime after her entry into the garage the assailant drove away.

Despite the fact that they were assaulted by multiple assailants, several Black women were able to avoid rape. One woman, a nursing student (case 82), found herself seemingly surrounded by would-be assailants at a bus stop. Inadvertently she had taken the wrong bus to downstate Illinois, and this mistake meant she had to wait in East St. Louis for connecting transportation. She had been away from the area for a while and was not as aware as she might have been of the dangers involved in waiting alone for her ride. While she phoned to locate transportation, an adolescent male began bothering her. She effectively used physical strategies to handle the situation. As that episode was drawing to a close, she noticed a car behind her, containing two men. These "protectors" asked her if she wanted a ride to prevent further harassment, since the adolescent was "messing with her." Emphatically she declined. One of the duo got out of the car and blocked her exit from the pay phone. When she refused his offer of a ride, he became angry and grabbed her arm. Calmly she told him to release her. He grabbed her again. At this point her reaction was total anger, and she began to scream and curse. The first man was then joined by the other man, and they both attempted to force the woman into their car. By this time, she was not only screaming, but fighting and kicking as well. All this noise began to attract the attention of people in the bars near the scene. People began coming out, and their presence momentarily scared off the assailants, who got in their car and drove away. About the time the assailants left, another bus arrived dropping off "an elderly lady and a younger woman with a small girl." After the last struggle, the woman told us she was becoming frightened, so she decided to join the other women to wait. The assailants returned, obviously planning another attack. However, the additional women present kept them at bay. Fortunately, an ambulance happened by, and she knew the driver. This man called a cab and waited with the group until the cab arrived, and all the women were able to escape.

This woman noted in her interview that she trusts her "funny feelings," and in this situation she most definitely had "bad vibes. . . . I come from a ghetto . . . you have to take care of yourself or you won't survive . . ." She had heard her mother say that to avoid rape you have to "kick or pull . . . Kicking or just wring . . . just grab. You grab it, wring it and you just try to pull it off. . . . " She said that the assailants were shocked by her "gutter" language. But she was furious, stating, "He touched me, how dare . . . how dare you! How dare him! . . . I was just so angry. . . . How could you want to assault somebody else's body. . . . You just don't violate it. It's a sacred womb."

While several Black women reported direct advice on rape avoidance, other women in the sample did not report receiving such specific instructions when they were growing up. It is possible that, given the high rate of violence in Black women's lives, more so than in the other women's lives, advice on how to deal with violence was given in concrete terms, rather than the abstract fear of rape that other women learned.

Joyce Ladner (1971) reports a similar pattern of experience with violence and knowledge of how to cope with it in her study of a St. Louis public housing project, stating that "an eight year old girl has a good chance of being exposed to rape and violence." Although these children, like other children, are frightened by violence

> they have been educated by older children and adults as to the nature and possible consequences of aggressive activity. This enables them to . . . defend themselves against antisocial behavior more vigorously than would the child who has not had . . . experience with these overt acts. (pp. 62–63)

A student (case 8) faced multiple armed assailants in her assault. She usually went to school with a girlfriend every day, but when this friend failed to show up one morning, the woman went to school without her. However, while at home for lunch, she received an unusual phone call from her girlfriend, who was crying. When the woman asked her what was wrong, her friend dropped the phone. Concerned by this call, she and two other young women went to their friend's house. A man answered the door and, not knowing whether or not it was the friend's uncle, they entered the house. Once inside they were ordered to sit by two armed assailants, one of whom had a knife and the other a gun. Not long afterward, the woman they had come to check on staggered down the stairs. Despite the fact that she was seven and a half months pregnant, these men had raped her. The assailants, two Black and two white men, then began "talking vulgarly," asking the women questions about their bodies and sex lives. The men quickly tired of this interrogation and took one of the three women to the bedroom to be raped. The subject and another woman were taken to the kitchen at knife point. They were told to take off [their] blouses, take off [their] pants, and skirts and whatever [they] had on. The subject told the assailant that she "wasn't going to take [her] clothes off" and was threatened with death if she didn't comply. She indicated that at this point she became frightened, but she still refused to remove any clothing and noticed that one of the men in the kitchen seemed somewhat "afraid" and "insecure" about what was taking place. She also noted that he was the youngest of the group as well as being white. She decided to try and talk him out of it. She asked him why they were doing this and what they were getting out of it. The woman who was being raped in the upstairs bedroom had been screaming so loudly that neighbors finally called the police. Arriving at the home, the police came in both the front and back doors, ending the rape and preventing the woman we interviewed from being the next victim. Since she had been "making trouble," the assailants had decided to assault the other women first.

WHITE CATHOLIC WOMEN

White Catholic women were substantially more likely to use physical force than were Jewish women. One woman (case 62) had been having an extremely bad day on the date of her attack. She was in the process of ending a relationship and felt somewhat "paranoid" as well as hostile. She spent the early evening with friends but had to take public transportation home in the late evening. When she left the bus, she was convinced someone was following her. Looking over her shoulder she "saw this young Black guy about 18, 19, 20" following her. Initially she attempted to calm herself by assuming that she was being overly suspicious. However, earlier that week she had seen signs in the area warning of a rapist, which gave her a basis in reality for such feelings. The man continued following her into her apartment building courtyard, through an iron gate, and into the hallway. When she attempted to open the door, both her key and the door stuck. (There was a problem with the door, which the building tenants had repeatedly reported to the landlord without success.) At this point the assailant reached for her, and a struggle began. The struggle was "stalemated." She kept thinking, "Get out of this tiny foyer . . . back out to the courtyard." She was so intent on her goal that she put her elbow through the door, injuring it. However, the struggle was moved back to the courtyard, which was well lit and more populated. She began to scream, and the assailant became frightened and left. At this point, she was so angry that she chased him for two blocks. Realizing that to follow him further would trap her in a cul-de-sac and that she was covered with blood, she gave up her pursuit and returned home to call the police.

Situational factors also played a more important part in the assaults of Catholic white women than in those of Black or Jewish women. One Catholic woman (case 71) was on her way to an art exhibit when she was startled by a man who "cut in front of me . . . like he was gonna bump into me or he didn't see me." Her response at the time was to say "Hello," which was unusual for her because she "hardly ever look[ed] at or talk[ed] to any men on the street ever." Within seconds the man came up behind her and "grabbed [her] off the street." He dragged her down the street to a building near the alley and threatened her with his knife. He stated that "he hadn't decided yet [whether] he would kill me or he would rape me." Calculating her chances, the woman decided that since he "didn't kill me right away . . . maybe he'd talk." She kept up a steady barrage of questions and conversation. She suggested that they not have sex in the alley, but go to a bar around the corner first. "I told him I'd be happy to have sex with him. To be able to say that to this person was probably the hardest thing I've ever said to anyone." Right after she said that a siren went off, and he lessened his grip. Noting her chance for escape, she "kicked his leg or his knee or something" and managed her escape. She was able to stall with the various strategies she used until the siren went off (environmental intervention). She then used a physical strategy, kicking, and she was able to flee.

Another subject (case 92) indicated that as a child her parents had advised her to fight back in confrontation situations, to "put them in their places and stand up for [her] rights." Her assault situation was one of physical confrontation. She was on her way to celebrate a new job, when her car ran out of gas. She obtained the needed gas by hitchhiking to and from the gas station without problem. She was just finishing up "sprinkling some gasoline on the carburetor" when a car pulled up and a "savior" appeared. Over her objections he immediately took charge, stating, "Give me the keys, I'll start it." Without her consent he took the keys from her hand and started the car. After thanking him, she attempted to reenter the car only to find that he "blocked the door." After a few brief questions, he began kissing her. As the assault escalated, he "started pulling [her] off the road towards a grassy, bushy area." She kept struggling and attempting to flee while simultaneously pleading with him. Eventually, he produced a flashlight, which he threatened to use on her, saying, "If you don't take down your pants, I will hurt you." Realizing that struggling wasn't working, the woman began reiterating, in various versions, "Oh, we shouldn't do this,

this isn't the nicest place to do this sort of thing. We should go over to my place. I have a television, you can watch television. I have pumpkin bread, we can sit down, get to know one another." The struggle continued, and finally the assailant said, "Yes, we can go . . . let's go to your place." However, he wanted to take his car. When she protested, claiming that she had to care for her dog (who was in the back seat of her car), he once again dragged her into the bushes. The woman next suggested that they go up the road where she could buy him a milk shake, and they could "get to know one another." Initially this suggestion was greeted with more struggling and arguing over whether she could go in her car and he in his, but he gradually agreed to go in separate cars. As they approached the road, "he apologized" repeatedly to the woman. She was able to feign "forgiveness and understanding." When she reached the shop, she ran in to obtain help, and he left.

Two of the white Catholic women (cases 94 and 83) were different from most other women in that they verbally expressed a sense of entitlement. They both felt very strongly that their assailant had no right to invade their personal space, and both managed to mobilize this sense of outrage into effective strategies; they were concerned with not being raped rather than not being killed. Both women knew self-defense techniques, and both were feminists working or having worked in feminist alternative institutions such as rape crisis centers and women's health centers. The first two of these factors, concern with rape rather than with murder or mutilation and knowledge of self-defense, are associated with rape avoidance; the third factor, their feminist experience, reinforced their sense of the right to defend themselves (entitlement). The right of a woman to control her own body is a central part of feminist ideology.

The first woman (case 94) was working on a final exam when her door bell rang. She "answered the door, with the chain over it" as she usually did, to find what appeared to be yet another male campaign worker canvassing for one of the primary elections. When she undid the chain to accept the literature he was offering, "he pushed the door and entered the apartment." As soon as she had had a chance to scan the literature, she realized that "it wasn't campaign literature . . . something was amiss." When she indicated that the literature "didn't mean anything to" her, the assailant began to act confused, handed her his coat, and asked to use the phone. Instead of heading toward the phone, he pushed her "back against doorwell saying, 'I want to have a relationship with you.' " She countered with "There will be no relationship." He began making statements such as, "Don't get me angry. Act like a lady. Be nice. Calm down. Don't raise your voice." Although the woman said that her initial reaction was fear, she was able to engage in "verbally jockeying for position" with the assailant almost from the start of the assault. She did not limit herself to verbal warnings. She pushed her fist against his Adam's apple telling him, "I don't want your blood and guts on my floor. I don't want to hurt you, but I will kill a rapist." He seemed taken aback when she called him a rapist responding, "Oh, no, you're calling me a rapist, are you." When she repeated her statement, she added that he should "pick up his hat and coat and leave", he left. When this woman recounted her rage at the assailant, she noted that "I was a human being and he was infringing on my space . . . [I] let him know that very quickly. And I did say to him you have no right to be doing this. . . . I'm a human being. . . . And you have no right to touch me." The speed of her negative response was important, since rapidity of response is associated with rape avoidance. Her quick response is to be expected, since self-defense courses train women to be aware of and respond to danger early in a situation.

The second woman (case 83) was riding her bicycle along a canal when she noticed a man with a fishing pole. She stated, "Just something about him made me feel very suspicious." He was watching her approach so she "decided to move [her] bike over to the [bike] path" in order to minimize contact. As she passed him, he grabbed the handlebar causing her to fall off the bike. Instantly, he attacked her, but because she had some judo training, she was able to roll away before he made contact. She became "extremely angry, very violent, jumped up instantly and started yelling at him." She indicated that the assailant wasn't violent or mean. Nevertheless, he kept grabbing at her and attempting to pull her into the bushes, saying, "Come on Baby." Furthermore, he refused to release her bike, and they continued to fight over it. She'd been yelling throughout the assault, and at this point started shouting "FIRE." She screamed "fire" rather than "help" because of her knowledge of self-defense. Women are taught that the former is more likely to alert people to investigate, since the fire would also threaten them. Unfortunately, some people do not respond to cries for help because they do not want to become involved or put themselves in a dangerous situation.

The assailant finally ran off. Even though the woman avoided rape, she "really felt violated and disturbed and really put off by [his] knocking [her] off the bike . . . HE HAD NO RIGHT."

These cases illustrated not only individual variations, but variations differentiating ethnic groups. The following section will make these variations clearer by teasing out those characteristics, both background and situational, that predict rape or avoidance and how they vary among these ethnic groups. We have discussed the importance of these factors in previous chapters.

BACKGROUND DEMOGRAPHIC FACTORS

Catholic women in general were more often eldest daughters with major household responsibilities. Jewish women were less likely to be oldest and least likely to have had major household responsibility. Such training gives positive reinforcement, providing the woman training in competence and the ability to manage stress and emergencies. Jewish women were least likely to have younger brothers. We have noted in Chapter 5 that being an older sister and therefore having legitimate authority over younger brothers can lead not only to demystification of these males in particular, but to demystification of males generally. Such demystification is conducive to being able to manage a situation in which a male is threatening or using force. Some women who were teachers and taught boys or who worked with adolescent males said that training helped them avoid rape, since they knew what worked and what didn't and were not as afraid as women without such experience.

Catholic women were the most likely to be over 5'7", and Jewish women were least likely to be tall. Being tall is associated with rape avoidance. Additionally, having a mother who was a *competent* role model seems to be associated with rape avoidance. Black women were most likely to come from female-headed single parent households, where, by definition, the mother had to manage without a man. Of special interest is the fact that seven of the eight Black women who came from such households avoided rape. Only one woman from such a household was raped. This high ratio of rape avoidance did not occur in the cases of Black women who came from households with a father or stepfather present, although the number of cases is small. Such a finding is ironic because some behavioral scientists have considered women-headed households cradles of pathology, at least according to Senator Daniel Patrick Moynihan. Avoiding rape is not pathology. Additionally, *none* of the Jewish or Black women who were *raped* had mothers with a BA or graduate training, and *all* the Jewish women who avoided rape had such mothers. Daughters of mothers who were employed part-time rather than being full-time homemakers or employees were more likely to avoid rape, as we saw in Chapter 5. According to sociologist Myra M. Ferree (1976, 1981), who studied women with various employment patterns, mothers who managed to obtain such part-time jobs were very competent. They were able to juggle two ordinarily full-time responsibilities. Four of the five Catholics with mothers who held part-time employment when the subjects were growing up avoided rape, three of the four Jews with such mothers avoided rape, and the only Black woman with a mother who held part-time employment also avoided rape.

When we turn to the women themselves, we see that for Blacks, high educational attainment increases the likelihood that they will avoid rape. However, this finding is not true for Jews or Catholics.

What these data show is that we are not simply dealing with social class variables — working and lower class women avoiding rape and middle class women being raped. It is the middle-class Blacks, those with at least a bachelor's degree, and the Jews and Blacks with educated mothers who are more likely to avoid rape. Perhaps, for Blacks, it is the combination of formal education and street smarts that gives them the advantages — and disadvantages — of both worlds.

CHILDHOOD SOCIALIZATION

Jewish women were least likely to be advised by their parents to fight back in a confrontation situation, but the majority of Black women received this advice. Black women were also more likely to hold nontraditional views of the future when they were children. When asked what they had thought their future lives would be like as children, they were less likely to mention marriage and children and more likely to mention employment. Jewish women were least likely to have had such an image of their future.

ADULT SOCIALIZATION

We attempted to ascertain each woman's competence in crisis situations by noting her response to questions regarding the administering of first aid, the handling of a grease fire, and so on. Catholic women were more competent than Jewish or Black women in these two areas. No Catholic who knew self-defense (six) was raped. This finding was not true for Blacks or Jews.

SITUATIONAL FACTORS

When the assault occurred outside, all the Catholic women and 81 percent of the Black women avoided rape. However, none of the Jewish women who were assaulted outside avoided. It is also noteworthy that no Jewish women experienced environmental intervention such as an animal or another person happening to come along or a siren going off. But some Catholics and Blacks did have environmental intervention in their assault situations.

The presence of a weapon was associated with being raped for white women. However, Catholic women were least likely to be in an assault situation where a weapon was present. Jewish women, who had the highest rape rate, were likely to be attacked by an armed assailant. Black women seemed less intimidated by weapons than white women. We found no difference between the Black women who were raped and those who avoided as far as the presence of a weapon. Thus in examining situational factors, Jewish women were less likely than white Catholic or Black women to be in a situation that favored rape avoidance.

SR–D

STRATEGIES OF SELF-DEFENSE

In an assault situation, Jewish women were most likely to yell and least likely to run away. Almost half of the Catholic women used physical force against the assailant. Black women, on the other hand, used more kinds of strategies than did white women, and the strategies they used were more likely to be associated with avoidance. Unlike the other women, Black women always did something; at least one protective strategy was tried.

The Empty Cell — The Rape of Black Women by Black Men

A number of studies indicate that the rate of rape of Black women is higher than that of white women — for example, three times as high in one study (McIntyre, 1980). Moreover, the data also indicate that this finding is a result of Black women being assaulted by Black men. For example, there were fourteen Black women, in our study, and of these, thirteen were assaulted by Black men, and only one was assaulted by a white man (who was part of a gang of two Black and two white men).

The Chicago Defender, a Black newspaper in Chicago, on a front-page story appearing December 15, 1979, reported the increasing incidence of Black on Black rape, notably in the housing projects. Moreover, according to one researcher (LaFree, 1980), Black men who rape Black women are treated more leniently by the criminal justice system than when they rape white women. Despite the mounting evidence, this issue has been systematically ignored. We believe that the erasure of this aspect of the contemporary Black females' experience results from racism. This erasure is why this section is entitled "The Empty Cell."

The political Right does not address the issue because the most important factor in "founding a rape" (i.e., the police recording the event as rape) is the respectability of the victim (Clarke and Lewis, 1977). Black women, being, by definition, "unrespectable," are less likely to be considered rapeable. The male dominated Left also does not deal with the issue because no class analysis of the fact that Black men rape Black women is possible. Besides, it's embarrassing because the proletariat (those without power) are not supposed to be the oppressors[6] (Dixon, 1983, is an exception). The white women's movement does not deal with it because they are afraid of being called racists. However, to ignore the experiences of Black women is racist and not feminist. The only people willing to address this issue system-

---

[6] Angela Davis (1983) in her recent book, *Women, Race and Class*, only speaks of the rape of Black women by white men. Ann Jones, in her review (*New York Times Book Review*, Jan. 17, 1982) notes that most contemporary rapes of Black women are by Black men.

atically are Black feminists. *The Color Purple* by Black "womanist" (her term) Alice Walker (1982) and *The Women of Brewster Place* by Gloria Naylor (1983) dramatically address issues of the rape of Black women by Black men. But Black feminists are put down by some Black men and anti-feminist Black women for being feminists. They are told that the women's movement is a tool of white men used to get Black and white women together to attack Black men (Eichelberger, 1981). In fact, in the major theoretical piece on Black women in *Sturdy Black Bridges* (Carruthers, 1979), it is suggested that the women's movement is a plot by Jewish feminists to destroy the Black family.

Some of the most distressing cases in this study were those of Black women. Moreover, the attacks on Black women were more brutal. Four of the five Black raped women were forced to engage in multiple phallic acts (genital, anal, or oral penetration by a penis). Three of these four were subjected to multiple acts of traditional sexual intercourse, while the fourth was additionally subjected to fellatio. Only 13 of the 38 non-Black women were subjected to multiple phallic acts. It will also be recalled that Black women were more likely than the sample as a whole to be attacked by armed assailants. In spite of the greater brutality and seriousness of their assaults, they were treated worse than were the white women by the criminal "justice" system. In addition, eight of the fourteen Black women were attacked with weapons, and five were attacked by multiple assailants. This proportion was higher than that for non-Black women.

Not only were the assaults on these women more violent, but the women had more violence in their lives before this particular assault. Of the 14 Black women, 10 had been previously raped or attacked, and 8 Black women had been molested or attacked and had avoided molestation as children. In eight cases, the assault was incestuous. To erase the suffering of these women, to pretend it never happened, is unconscionable.

Some white feminists believe that women should not tell the police if their assailants are Black men because of the obvious racism of the police and the courts. From the women in this study we discovered that this view is not shared by women of color who have been sexually assaulted. No woman of color indicated that she would not turn her assailant in to the police because of the racism of the system. When asked this question by the researchers in this study, some of the responses of those women were as follows:

"I think they should be turned in. I don't care what color the person is. . . . If someone tries to hurt you, you know you're supposed to do something about it" (case 31). Some time after this woman had been assaulted she heard that one of her assailants was in jail, and she said she "was glad."

Another woman (case 24) noted that "even though most jails do more

Table 6.1. Ethnicity and Rape Avoidance

Avoiders	Raped Women	No Difference
Ethnicity	*Ethnicity*	*Ethnicity*
White Catholics, Blacks	Jews	White Protestants
Mother's education for Blacks and Jews		
Female-headed households for Blacks		
Demographics	*Demographics*	
Catholics 5'7" or over	Lack of younger brothers	
Major household responsibility		
Oldest daughter		
	Presence of a weapon	
	For white women	

harm than good" she wanted her assailants to be put behind bars. She added that "I believe he's done it before and like I said, if he did it to me and he had done it to the other woman on the platform, he would do it to my grandmother and my little cousin, my little seven year old cousin. It really made me mad." A third woman said, "They can hang him from the nearest lamp post for all I care" (case 13). One woman, in recounting the horrors of her rape three years prior to the avoidance she came in to talk about (case 5) testified at that assailant's trial. When she saw him on the street after his release, she felt compelled to move away. She said there should be legalized castration for rapists.

Another Black woman, when asked about the ethics of turning Black men in to a racist system, said: "Oh, because you're gonna get hassled by the police, you have a right to go out and rape people? So we're gonna become oppressed just to alleviate their oppression?" (case 54).[7]

---

[7]The following is a note from Black female psychiatrist Linda Freeman whom I (PB) asked to review the chapter to see if it were racist.

> Thank you for letting me read this. My comments also are that it is excellent. I am especially pleased that you did report the findings that Black women are raped more brutally, often, multiply, etc. I had not been aware that it was a liberal and/or radical ideology not to report rapes by men of color — but I agree with your interviewee *it's unfair to us* and dangerous not to. To suggest this occurs because of primitive, animalistic "instincts" peculiar to Blacks would be racist — but reporting is necessary and some exploration into the possible social historical causes for this would make the reporting responsible. I am very pleased that you began to do this.

CONCLUSION

The much-quoted psychologist Erik Erikson (1953)[8] divided the human experience into stages, each of which must be successfully resolved for the next level of development to occur and to ultimately achieve a successful maturity. He claimed that the successful resolution of the first stage is for the infant to develop basic trust rather than mistrust. What we have learned from reading the stories of Black, Jewish, and Catholic women is that his findings do not apply to women. For a woman to survive unraped, particularly in an urban setting, she must learn *basic mistrust*.

Because this study is exploratory, in the context of discovery rather than in the context of verification, as philosophers of science would say, we could follow up unexpected findings in the data analysis that might illuminate factors leading to rape and rape avoidance. One such clue was learning that Black women and white Catholic women were the ethnic groups most likely to avoid rape, while Jewish women were the ethnic group most likely to be raped. Catholic women were characterized by both background and situational variables associated with rape avoidance. They were most likely to be tall, to have been the oldest daughter, and to have had major household responsibilities. They were also most likely to have been attacked outside by an unarmed assailant, and they were less likely than Black or Jewish women to have had blitz attacks. Almost none of their assailants committed a crime or tried to commit a crime in addition to the sexual assaults.

In contrast, Black and Jewish women were confronted with similar situational factors, factors associated with rape rather than avoidance for the sample as a whole. They were likely to be attacked suddenly (blitz) by armed assailants. When we examined Black and Jewish women's accounts we learned that Jewish women were not socialized to prepare them to live unprotected in a situation somewhat akin to guerilla warfare. They referred to their overprotection, while Black women were advised by their parents to fight back when attacked. Black women were more likely to have street smarts and could perceive that a situation was potentially dangerous, while Jewish women reported that they trusted people. Black women, unlike the sample as a whole, were as likely to escape an armed as an unarmed assailant. The rape escapes by Black women are even more dramatic when we realize that they were more likely than the sample as a whole to be

---

[8]The lack of relevance of his theory to women does not surprise us. Since the women's movement and the burgeoning field of the psychology of women, we have learned that most of psychology, whether it be Freud's phallocentrism or academic psychology based on responses of male undergraduates, leaves women out, or when women are included the information is wrong.

attacked by more than one assailant, and when they were raped the rapes were more brutal than the rapes of the other women.

Jewish and Catholic women had similar educational attainments. Mother's education was associated with rape avoidance for Blacks and Jews. Coming from a mother-headed household was associated with rape avoidance for Black women. Thus the differences we are finding do not simply reflect class differences.

It is intellectually and politically dishonest to write about rape without discussing the racism in which the history of rape is embedded. Historically, charges of rape and the threat of such charges were used by the white community to control the Black community, since Black men were lynched because of such accusations. Thus the discussion of racism and rape has always focused on the accusations against Black men. Wolfgang and Reidel (1977) in their study of the death penalty for rape in the South from 1945 through 1965 found that Black men were executed for raping white women, although white men were not. Discussions of the rape of Black women usually deal with their rape by white men notably under slavery and in the South. In this chapter, however, we discussed the cases of Black men raping Black women and suggested why this problem has been ignored (even *Ebony's* special issue of June 1976 on Black on Black crime did not deal with rape). The erasure of Black on Black rape demonstrates the intersection of racism and sexism. The women of color in this study were willing and eager to turn their assailants in to the police, even though the system is racist. They recognized that the assailant would be a threat to other women they knew and cared about. Apparently the liberal and radical ideology which states that women should not report rapes by men of color is not shared by women of color in this study. (See Footnote 1, Chapter 3 for a further discussion of rape and race.)

It is fitting, we believe, to end this section with a portion of Ntozake Shange's *For Colored Girls Who Have Considered Suicide for Whom the Rainbow is not Enuf.* It was sent to one of us by a friend of a woman who had been interviewed by us. When *For Colored Girls* was presented on television, this part was omitted.

> lady in red
> but if you've been seen in public wit him
> danced one dance
> kissed him good-bye lightly
>> lady in purple
> wit closed mouth
>> lady in blue
> pressin charges will be as hard
> as keeping yr legs closed
> while five fools try to run a train on you
>> lady in red
> these men friends of ours

who smile nice
　　lady in purple
we must have known
　　lady in red
women relinquish all personal rights
in the presence of a man
who apparently cd be considered a rapist
　　lady in purple
especially if he has been considered a friend
　　lady in blue
& is no less worthy of bein beat within an inch of his life
bein publicly ridiculed
having two fists shoved up his ass
　　lady in red
than the stranger
we always thot it wd be

REFERENCES

Bart, Pauline. 1967. Depression in middle-aged women: Some socio-cultural factors. Doctoral Dissertation, University of California at Los Angeles. Dissertation abstracts 28:475–18 (University Microfilms No. 08-7452).

——. 1971. Depression in middle-aged women. 84–117. *Women in sexist society*, edited by Vivian Gornick and Barbara K. Moran. New York: Basic Books.

Carruthers, Iva E. 1979. War on African familyhood. In *Sturdy black bridges*, edited by Roseann P. Bell, Bettye J. Parker, and Beverly Guy-Sheftall. 8–17. Garden City, NY: Anchor Press.

Clark, Lorenne, and Debra Lewis. 1977. *Rape: The price of coercive sexuality.* Toronto, Canada: The Women's Press.

Davis, Angela. 1983. *Women, race and class.* New York: Random House.

Dixon, Marlene. 1983. *The future of women.* San Francisco: Synthesis Publications.

Eichelberger, Brenda. 1981. Personal communication.

Erikson, Erik H. 1953. *Childhood and society.* New York: Norton.

Ferree, Myra Marx. 1976. Working-class jobs: Housework and paid work as sources of satisfaction. *Social Problems* 23 (4):431–441.

——. 1981. Personal communication.

Freeman, Linda. 1982. Personal communication.

Ladner, Joyce A. 1971. *Tomorrow's tomorrow: The black woman.* Garden City, NY: Doubleday, 62–63.

LaFree, Gary. 1980. Assessing official reactions to rape: A multivariate analysis of the police response. Paper presented at the American Sociological Association.

May, Vickie. 1985. Personal communication.

McIntyre, Jennie. 1980. Victim response to rape: Alternative outcomes. Final report to Grant #MH29311 NIMH.

Naylor, Gloria. 1983. *The women of Brewster Place.* New York: Viking.

Shange, Ntozake. 1977. *For colored girls who have considered suicide and for whom the rainbow is not enuf.* New York: Macmillan.

Walker, Alice. 1982. *The color purple.* New York: Harcourt Brace Jovanovich.

Wolfgang, Marvin E., and Mark Reidel. 1977. Patterns of criminal homicide. In *Forcible rape*, edited by Duncan Chappell, Robley Geis, and Gilbert Geis. 115–128. New York: Columbia University Press.

7 Why Men Rape

Rapists Need Love Too
(printed on a t-shirt given at a meeting of Oregon attorneys to the lawyer who defended John Rideout, who raped his wife)

The offender needs an outlet for his sexual aggression and finds a submissive partner who unconsciously invites sexual abuse and whose masochistic needs are being fulfilled. . . . There can be no doubt that the sexual frustration which the wife caused is one of the factors motivating the rape which might be tentatively described as a displaced attempt to force a seductive but rejecting mother into submission. The sex offender was not only exposed to his wife's masculine and competitive inclinations, but also, in a certain sense, was somehow 'seduced' into committing the crime. (Abrahamsen, 1960, Psychoanalyst).

You'll feel better when I'm inside you. (Naprapath to patient on the examining table; case 19)

My feeling is that [rape] occurs because of the sexist orientation of our society . . . the majority of men tend to see women as sex objects, as created specifically and entirely for their pleasure . . . therefore, they have a right to this sex object that was created for them. (Avoider)

We address the issue of why men rape for two reasons. First, an understanding of the male world view can throw light on why some strategies are more effective than others. For example, as is shown in this chapter, many men attribute sexual meanings to behaviors that females consider neutral or friendly. These men think they have a right to force the woman to have sex because she has led them on. Thus it makes sense that active resistance, particularly physical resistance, is necessary to convince these men that the woman is not just playing hard to get. For example, we learned that when a hitchhiker (case 67) fought back long enough, her assailant realized she "really did not want it" and profusely apologized. He assumed that because she was hitchhiking and was willing to come to his apartment this behavior implied consent.

Second, we believe that one reason for scholarship on issues of concern to women is to answer questions they raise. Women frequently ask us and other sexual assault researchers why men rape.

Some people say that rapists are "wimps" (e.g., Geis in Sanders, 1980) or are badly socialized because they should have learned when they were growing up not to hit girls. They should have been taught proper ways of behaving with women. They should have been told not to be violent against women. Sure!!! Like they were taught the meek shall inherit the earth. When corporations provide courses in unassertiveness training for men we'll believe the latter, and when woman battery and rape are only done by men reared by wolves (psychologists call these "feral children") or in isolation tanks will we believe that rape results from inadequate male socialization. And then if men don't learn the lesson it is because of some woman's failure.

Indeed Steven Goldberg, in his epilogue to *The Inevitability of Patriarchy* (1974) maintains that even though men are aware that there are few women who can outfight or outargue them

> when a woman uses feminine means she can command a loyalty that no amount of aggression ever could. The experience of women is that the violence men often seek out is terrifying and overpowering, but that by using the feminine means that nature gave her woman can deal with the most powerful man as an equal. (p. 328)

WHAT THE WOMEN SAID ABOUT WHY MEN RAPE

What did the women tell us when they were asked why rape occurs, whose fault it was, and whether their feelings had changed since the assault? When we asked them, about half the women, mainly the women who were raped, gave psychological explanations (what sociologists call psychiatric vocabularies of motive). For example, one woman (case 7) said " 'cause definitely the men are sick [because as] many prostitutes that are on the street and as many ladies that are willing . . . to have sexual relationships with just about any man that comes, there's no reason for it." When the interviewer pointed out that men wouldn't want to pay for sex if they were raping to demonstrate power, she said "That's what I mean. They have to be sick." After their assault 13 women said that it became clear to them that rape was a sexist act or an act of power (sexist acts can be acts of power).

A nurse (case 34) said her feelings changed since her assault. Now she believes the reason men rape is "anger towards women." She was being threatened with death if she didn't drop the charges. Since she considers her assailant's behavior rational she no longer thinks he is "sick" but considers him insidious. She added that men are angry with women because they feel threatened by changing sex roles. Yet this could not be the sole explanation, she added, because there was rape before there was a women's movement. She then said that men might rape women to express their rage at other men. If women are viewed as property, then raping another man's "property" would be a way of expressing this anger. She talked about her boyfriend, who had insisted that she report the rape attempt although she did not want to. He was a student in a prominent medical school at which they would have stag parties where " . . . they would hire hookers. . . . This used to flip me out . . ."

No one blamed rape on women, although three women gave as their first answer that it was mainly men's and *partly* women's fault. Most women thought rape occurred because of society, because the rapist was "sick," or a combination of both these reasons. Sometimes the women spoke of the emphasis in the culture on sex and pornography. Nine women thought rape reflected male chauvinism and was a way to keep women in their place. When they were asked a more specific question on why rape occurs, 24 said to terrorize or control women—a power trip—and 7 said it was because women were viewed as sex objects. Another seven women said rape occurred because men could get away with it; it was men's "natures."

The first woman interviewed (case 1) stopped her rape by a man with a knife. She thought that he was a man who had either been hurt or felt he was being cheated. Such a man would want to impose his will and think "By God you were going to get your share of it no matter what." Another woman thought that assailants did not really see women as human beings and that they learned this dehumanization of women from society.

One woman, attacked while she was asleep (case 37), thought rape occurred because "people nowadays can do just what the hell they please," since they don't have to worry about being punished, particularly not for rape. A woman raped by a stranger (case 61) gave a combination of explanations. First she said men rape

> to humiliate and terrify . . . if painting a red stripe on someone's nose would be considered humiliating, in this society, that's what they would do. . . . [Rape was] a hostile act and men know they can get away with it, in our society so far . . . once women start doing things to defend themselves, and there's community awareness, I don't think it will happen as often. [She had taken a women's self-defense course since her rape.]

While most women used a combination of psychiatric and sociocultural reasons to explain rape, three women used biological vocabularies. Seven, all of whom were raped, gave both psychiatric and biological reasons for rape. One such woman (case 40) said "you could be a little bit into some sort of Freudian type thing or you could go into, you know, maybe it's the double Y chromosome."

Another woman said that she felt:

> Firstly sorry for the other women, and secondly sorry for him. I don't know why men do it. I guess 'cause they can. And I don't say that

means, you know, that I have something against them, because they
can do it. But because they can do it, they're the ones who do it.

CHANGES IN WOMEN'S IDEAS ABOUT RAPE

Some women changed their ideas about rape and about men after their
assaults. One (case 9) said:

> I hear that our sick society with the way men are, you know, they just,
> the aggression [sic] against women. . . . I just don't understand how
> anyone can like men. And I, I feel like I should start working on liking
> them again, but I don't . . . I really find it hard to see how any woman
> can like men at all.

Another woman (case 22) reported:

> . . . before [the assault] they were sick and needed help and now I feel
> they're sick and there *is* no help. They should just be taken away.

A third woman (case 46) who was raped by a professor at her college said:

> I feel like rape happens a million times more than I ever knew it
> did . . . that rape is a very common thing. [Eighteen other women gave
> similar responses.]

Not only did she now feel as if rape were more common than she had
thought before, but she no longer believed that it was necessarily physically
violent and gruesome or that the assailant was necessarily armed.

THE USE OF PSYCHIATRIC EXPLANATIONS

Psychiatric and psychological explanations for people's behavior are
common in our society. These explanations, or "vocabularies," are particularly common for crimes such as rape, incest, and woman abuse. However,
they function to maintain the status quo: male dominance and sense of
entitlement and female subordination and lack of a sense of entitlement.
Because these factors underlie rape, psychiatric explanations in fact reinforce the very behavior they are trying to explain.

If the guilty individual is "sick," then the solution is individual rather
than societal. Moreover, because he is sick, his responsibility is diminished.
The rapist should be treated by a mental health professional, such as a psychiatrist, psychologist, or social worker. Such professionals, however, even
if there were enough of them to treat all the men who are violent toward
women and children, do not have a good track record in "curing" or even
detecting rapists. Scully and Marolla interviewed a rapist who was seeing a
psychiatrist twice a week during the time he was raping and murdering
young women. The psychiatrist not only did not know during the time the
man was in "treatment" that his patient was raping and killing, but in

reviewing his notes, he said there was no hint that this behavior was going on (Scully, 1981).

Another disadvantage of a psychiatric vocabulary is that it is usually the mother who is blamed for causing the assailant's behavior. Indeed, when we review the psychiatric literature (Albin, 1977; Marolla and Scully, 1979), we find that rape is caused by *women*: the rapist's cold or close-binding mother, his "frigid" [sic] wife, and the "provocative" victim. Only the rapist has no free will. The Abrahamsen quotation at the beginning of this chapter is an example of such thinking.

Psychiatric vocabularies can also be used to prevent the rapist's conviction. Marolla and Scully (1979) note that traditional psychiatric explanations of why men rape ascribe rape to four causes: (a) uncontrollable impulse; (b) mental illness; (c) alcoholism; and (d) victim precipitation. These explanations ignore the sociocultural context that supports sexual aggression against women. It is interesting, if not suspicious, that each of these supposed psychiatric causes is put in the kind of legal language that can be used in court to defend the assailant so that he may be found not guilty (MacKinnon, 1981).

An alternative sociological explanation is that a substantial proportion of men believe forcing women to have sex is acceptable under many conditions. In the next section we will talk about "normal men" and rape.

"NORMAL MEN"

In order to find out why men rape it is useful to look at the behavior of normal men. Psychologists at UCLA (Giarusso, Johnson, Goodchilds, and Zellman, 1979) surveyed 432 high school students and found that by the time males and females reached high school, they constructed their sexual worlds differently. Males were more likely to attribute sexual meanings to events than females were (e.g., if the woman wore tight clothes, phoned him, went to his apartment, or to a wild party). Moreover, these researchers documented that under a number of conditions which the male interpreted as being "led on," he felt entitled to force the woman to have sex. Between 36 percent and 45 percent of the men thought it was "OK to force sex" if the man spent a lot of money on a woman; if the male was so "turned on he can't stop"; if he knew she had sexual intercourse with other "guys"; if the woman were drunk or stoned; if she let him touch her above the waist; and if they had been dating a long time. Women were substantially less likely to agree in each situation. Moreover, 54 percent of the men thought it was acceptable to force sex if the woman changed her mind about having sex and/or if she had "led him on." *Fifty-one percent* of the men believed forced sex was acceptable if the woman was "getting a man sexually excited." Here, too, the women were substantially less likely to agree. Thus, more than half of the men felt it was acceptable to force the woman to have sex (i.e., rape her) under certain conditions.

These differences are not unique to an adolescent population. Some of the women we interviewed found themselves in a sexual assault situation because the man involved felt entitled to sex. He misinterpreted some aspects of the woman's behavior. At no time did these women think that they were indicating a desire for sex. These scenarios used to be called "victim precipitated," but in fact they described situations that men (but not women) interpreted as sexual signaling (e.g., meeting a woman in a bar). Since the male perspective has been institutionalized, the courts frequently find the assailant not guilty in a rape case if the woman has "assumed a risk" (e.g., put herself in a situation that had the potential for assault). Underlying these assumptions is the image of male (but not female) sexuality as accelerating and uncontrollable once aroused, like a locomotive going downhill with the throttle open. Adolescent females are often taught to believe that arousing a man and not seeing that he has relief is a sin, somewhat less serious than genocide but more serious than manslaughter. "Cockteaser" was the worst epithet we could be called. If our date became aroused it was our responsibility to "do something" about it, or he would be afflicted with the dreaded blueballs. Rape therefore is a form of disease prevention.

Recently psychologist Neil Malamuth (1981) wrote "Rape Proclivity Among Males," in which he integrated the findings of a series of studies which demonstrated that many men in the general population possess a tendency to rape. About 35 percent of all men interviewed said that they might or would rape if they were sure that they wouldn't be caught. These men were similar to convicted rapists in their belief in various rape myths and in the degree to which they became sexually aroused to simulated rape scenes.

Finally, three southern sociologists (Wilson, Faison, and Britton, 1980) found that sexual aggression in dating situations was common. *Eighty-three percent* of college women surveyed had at least one

> forceful and offensive attempt by a male to achieve some type of sexual goal. *Twenty percent* had experiences which could legally be defined as rape. These behaviors were not a result of a failure to communicate since about one-quarter of the college men persisted in their behavior even though they knew it was disagreeable to the female involved.

The Malamuth summary of studies indicates that a substantial proportion of "normal" men say they would force a woman to have sex, particularly if they wouldn't be caught. The Wilson, Faison, and Britton research shows that male sexual aggression is common. These articles show that many "normal" men think that it is all right to be sexually aggressive, to force women to have sex against their will. Therefore to label rapists "sick" is inaccurate, unless you are willing to say that a large part of the male population is "sick."

UNDETECTED RAPISTS

How else can we answer the question "Why do men rape?" One traditional way is to look at rapists in prison. However, most rapists are not caught and convicted, much less sent to prison. Those in prison are primarily men who have raped strangers, who have a prior record of serious crime, and/or have used "excessive" violence in their assault.

Fortunately Smithyman's thesis, "The Undetected Rapist" (1978), is different. He interviewed adult males who had raped women and had not been caught. These men, who were mainly white, answered his ad and agreed to participate in an anonymous telephone interview. They said they raped because they wanted to have sex with a particular woman and/or they wanted to dominate and control their victims. Most of the rapes were planned rather than spontaneous. For the most part, the men felt that raping women had no negative effect on their lives or their self-image. "Indeed 16% felt that having raped had enhanced their self-image and had a positive effect on their lives." Their decision to rape was based on the potential reward (e.g., ego enhancement) and on the low probability of serious negative consequences such as bodily injury or imprisonment (see also Scully and Marolla, 1985).

Thus, one 22-year-old man, whose answer supports MacKinnon's thesis (1981) that rape is about "fucking," noted after having raped four women, that he raped because he liked "the idea that I can do whatever I want to a sex object. . . . you look at a girl and she looks like something out of *Playboy* and you have her there and you can do whatever you want."

Another, a 28-year-old high school custodian who had participated in from ten to fifteen rapes, said men raped because

> it is an easy way of doing it. You know you see a good looking woman walking down the street, sure everybody wants to fuck her. They can't touch her, but a lot of those rich bastards, just because they're rich, they got all the women in Beverly Hills. . . . But here we got 'em without worrying about all that stuff . . .

It becomes clear that women's bodies are the battlefield on which men engage in class war. Men who feel powerless in other areas fight this battle in the street against middle- and upper-class women rather than behind the barricades against the Fortune 500.

Not only do rapes reflect men's power, sexual motives, anger, and camaraderie motives, but also the desire to heal the hidden injuries of class (see Sennett and Cobb, 1972). Thus, former revolutionary, currently born-again Christian, Eldridge Cleaver raped Black women to practice raping white women in order to get at white men by despoiling their property (Cleaver, 1968). Cleaver said that rape was "an insurrectionary act. It delighted me that I was defying and trampling upon the white man's law, upon his system of values and that I was defiling his women . . . I felt I was getting revenge." (p. 28)

RAPISTS IN PRISON:
CONVICTED RAPISTS' ATTITUDES AND MOTIVES

What about imprisoned rapists? Groth (1979), whose work on rapists is widely quoted, classifies rapes in three ways: first, and most common, the power rape, in which sex is an expression of conquest (55 percent); second, the anger rape, in which sex is a hostile act (40 percent); third, the sadistic rape (5 percent), in which anger and power become eroticized. These motives can be combined.

Scully and Marolla (1981) studied 98 convicted rapists and a control group of 75 offenders convicted of other crimes (excluded sex offenses). While there was no difference between rapists and the control group on scales measuring attitudes toward women (both groups had relatively non-traditional views of women's roles), there was an important difference on the occupational and domestic spheres of women's roles. The convicted rapists were more likely to have a double standard of morality, expecting "an amount of virtue from women that was not expected from men." Moreover, they expected "unrealistic standards of moral behavior from their wives and/or girlfriends . . . and they had experienced a severe disappointment with respect to these expectations." (See other Scully and Marolla references for further data from this important study.)

WHY RAPE?

We live in a rape culture. Susan Griffin's words written in 1971 are equally applicable today.

> Far from the social controls of rape being learned, comparisons with other cultures lead one to suspect that, in our society, it is rape itself that is learned. (The fact that rape is against the law should not be considered proof that rape is not in fact encouraged as part of our culture.)

> . . . in the spectrum of male behavior, rape, the perfect combination of sex and violence, is the penultimate act. Erotic pleasure cannot be separated from culture, and in our culture male eroticism is wedded to power. Not only should a man be taller and stronger than a female in the perfect love-match, but he must also demonstrate his superior strength in gestures of dominance which are perceived as amorous. (p. 27, 29)

It is one of the myths about rape (as about men who batter) that men rape and otherwise abuse women because they are drunk or on drugs. Yet the women in our study reported that only 20 of the assailants had been drinking, and 12 had used drugs. Alcohol and drugs do not cause rape or battery, but they give the assailant an excuse, a vocabulary ("I wasn't myself") to rationalize his crime.

ENTITLEMENT

A woman (case 61) returning home from a worrisome medical appointment was too distracted as she approached her apartment to notice that she was being followed. When the man forced her to let him into her apartment he demanded her jewels. When she finally convinced him she didn't have any he said, "Well then at least I'm entitled to this" and raped her.

A 27-year-old man came home to find his mother drinking in her bed with her boyfriend. He threatened them both with a shotgun and raped his mother when the boyfriend left. After that incident he "initiated the sex relations when he was mad at the mother for allegedly neglecting his needs and therefore wanted to obtain revenge." This case is from the psychoanalytic literature and is called, "A Case of Consummated Mother-Son Incest," not rape (Margolis, 1977). This account not only demonstrates, although in exaggerated form, what men feel entitled to, but also shows that violence is the bottom line in the social control of women.

That men, as a class, feel entitled to goods and services from women as a class is clear in books on incest (e.g., Herman and Herschman, 1981; Rush, 1980), on woman abuse (e.g., Dobash and Dobash, 1979), on sexual harassment (e.g., MacKinnon, 1979), and in these interviews. One husband, raping his wife said, "You're my wife and you belong to me" (case 80). Many men deny that what they are doing is rape. "I'm not raping you, you're raping me," said an assailant at the end of a date (case 27). "You entered this place of your own free will," said another assailant (case 6), who had used a weapon. He had conned the woman into the building allegedly to show her an apartment for rent and then raped her. Several assailants said, "There's no such thing as rape." They were, therefore, entitled to have sex with the woman without having to consider it a criminal act.

The most seminal expression of the view that men as a class are entitled to goods and services from women as a class was stated by an imprisoned rapist in an interview with Scully (1985):

> Rape is a man's right. If a woman doesn't want to give it, the man should take it. Women have no right to say no. Women are made to have sex. It's all they are good for. Some women would rather take a beating but they always give in, it's what they are for.

Most women have no sense of entitlement. Thus a college student (case 40) raped by a professor said that she would have been able to stop it if she were in touch with her anger.

> I would have just . . . hit him and say "Get out of here, you measly lit-
> tle puny person." . . . if I had been in touch with any kind of sense of
> self-awareness or confidence of knowing that this should never happen
> to anyone . . . a real firm knowledge of that . . . it was a lack of a
> sense of power.

When we talk about our work and introduce the word *entitlement*, women in the audience nod their heads in agreement. The concept clarifies a great deal of male-female interaction by giving it a name.

NEUTRALIZATION

Sociologists use the term *neutralization* to explain the kinds of excuses the men were making. (Sykes and Matza, 1957). While the term was first applied to juvenile delinquents and the excuses they gave to justify their behavior, it is often applicable to rapists and can help us understand some of the strong things they say and do (Scully and Marolla, 1984). The relevant techniques of neutralization are as follows:

1. Denial of responsibility. The criminal sees himself as helplessly propelled into the rape situation. One rapist (case 77) said his behavior was caused by "the pollutants."
2. Denial of injury. This was the most common rationale men used. Who can forget the juror in the first trial of Inez Garcia, who shot one of her assailants after being raped. This juror found Inez Garcia guilty of murder, since "he [the assailant] was only trying to show her a good time." One of our friends was raped and forced to "have an orgasm" with the gun to her head. The assailant then demanded that she have another one but was "nice enough" to change his mind, since she "was probably too tired."

The women told us that rapists and would-be rapists made the following statements:

- "You're going to enjoy this" (as a man raped a woman at knifepoint; case 17).
- I know you won't mind what I do to you" (as a rapist was displaying a gun; case 35).
- "I don't want to rape you, I just want to screw" (as a rapist locked a woman in his room and penetrated her anus and vagina with his fingers, while she fought back vigorously and screamed, "You're not going to rape me!!"; case 39).

- "Well you know there is no such thing as rape. A man is doing a woman a favor" and later "It won't hurt. I'm small." (after a rapist conned a woman into his apartment, sodomized her, and forced her to have oral sex and masturbate him; case 51).
- "You're gonna feel good" and "I got a big one for you" (as a jitney cab driver viciously tried to rape his passenger; case 20).
- A naked man holding a knife mounted a sleeping woman and said he "wanted to make love" but if she did not cooperate he would kill her. (case 58 — the Champion Negotiator who was able to avoid). He left saying, "Here I was . . . trying to be nice." He also said that he was shy and it was too bad they had to meet that way.
- A napropath assured his patient whom he was treating for back problems, said "You'll feel better when I'm inside you" (case 19).

Several assailants denied that they were victimizing the woman and attempted to turn the encounter into a normal date. The landlord who tried unsuccessfully to rape his tenant assured her as she was fleeing that he'd call her. They'd have to have dinner (case 34). The man who conned his way into a karate expert's apartment by pretending to be a political campaign worker said, "I want to have a relationship with you" (case 94). And several assailants ended the interaction by kissing the woman, asking for her phone number, and complimenting her (e.g., "You're an all right chick.")

Perhaps attempting to turn a sexual assault into a date is not so strange if we remember the discussion of the amount of sexual aggression in dates. After all, it was a judge in Colorado who found a man innocent who had entered a woman's trailer, tore her clothes off, and tried unsuccessfully to rape her, because he said it was "normal courting behavior" as he recalled it. And it was a psychiatric resident at a seminar on rape who told one of us (Bart) that he could not understand what was wrong with forcing a woman on a date. He said, "That's the way it's done." As we said in Chapter 1, perhaps these assailants attempt to turn their rapes into dates because so many men turn their dates into rapes.

The question we should ask then, is not why men rape, but why don't *all* men rape.

CONCLUSION

In this chapter we have discussed what the women in our study said about why men rape, changes in women's ideas about rape resulting from the assaults, the use of psychiatric explanations to maintain the status quo, "normal" men and rape, the undetected rapist, the attitudes and motives of rapists in prison, and why the United States has been called a "rape culture." We also discussed entitlement (the feeling that many men have that leads them to believe they are entitled to goods and services, including sex, from women as a class) and neutralization.

We have seen the following:

1. Men and women view behavior differently. Men think that women are signaling sexual availability when women think their behavior is simply friendly or even neutral.
2. Many men believe that if a woman behaves as if she is sexually available they have a right to force her to have sex.
3. This reasoning is due in part to the current image of male sexuality, which is that it is like a locomotive going downhill. Once started it cannot be stopped.
4. About a third of male college students who were studied said they would rape a woman if they thought they could get away with it. The statistics on rape convictions show they generally can get away with it.
5. Psychological explanations (what sociologists call psychiatric vocabularies of motive) for rape diminish the rapists' responsibility for their behavior and increase the woman's responsibility.
6. Traditional white female socialization does not provide women with either the psychological or physical skills necessary to fend off attack.

REFERENCES

Abrahamsen, David. 1960. *Psychology of crime*. New York: Columbia University Press.

Albin, R. 1977. Psychological studies of rape. *Signs* 3:423–435.

Bart, Pauline B. 1968. Social structure and vocabularies of discomfort: What happened to female hysteria. *Journal of Health and Social Behavior* 9:188–193.

———. 1975. Rape doesn't end with a kiss. *Viva* 2(9):39–41; 100–101.

———. 1981. A study of women who were both raped and avoided rape. *Journal of Social Issues* 37(4):132–137.

Bart, Pauline B., and Patricia O'Brien. 1984. Stopping rape: Effective avoidance strategies. *Signs* 10(1):83–101.

Bart, Pauline B., and Kim Lane Scheppele. 1980. There ought to be a law: Self definitions and legal definitions of sexual assault. Presented at the annual meeting of the American Sociological Association, August.

Brownmiller, Susan. 1975. *Against our will*. New York: Simon and Schuster.

Cleaver, Eldridge. 1968. *Soul on ice*. New York: McGraw-Hill.

Dobash, R. Emerson, and Russell Dobash. 1979. Violence against wives: A case against the patriarchy. New York: The Free Press.

Frieze, Irene Hanson. 1983. Investigating the causes and consequences of marital rape. *Signs* 8(3):532–553.

Giarusso, R., P. Johnson, J. Goodchilds, and G. Zellman. 1979. Adolescents' cues and signals: Sex and assault. Paper presented at the Annual Meeting of the Western Psychological Association, San Diego, California.

Goldberg, Steven. 1974. *The inevitability of patriarchy*. New York: William Morrow and Co.

Griffin, Susan. 1971. Rape: The all-American crime. *Ramparts* 10:26–35.

Groth, A. Nicholas. 1979. *Men who rape: The psychology of the offender*. New York: Plenum Press.

Herman, Judith L. with Lisa Herschman. 1981. *Father-daughter incest*. Cambridge: Harvard University Press.

MacKinnon, Catharine A. 1979. *Sexual harassment and working women*. New Haven: Yale University Press.

———. 1981. Personal communication.

———. 1983. Feminism Marxism, method and the state: Toward feminist jurisprudence. *Signs* 8(4):635–658.

Malamuth, Neil M. 1981. Rape proclivity among males. *The Journal of Social Issues* 37(4):138–157.

Margolis, Marvin O. 1977. Mother-son incest. *Annual Review of Psychoanalysis*, 267–293.

Marolla, J., and D. Scully. 1979. Rape and psychiatric vocabularies of motive. In *Gender and disordered behavior: Sex differences in psychopathology*, edited by E. Gomberg and V. Franks. New York: Brunner/Mazel.

Riger, Stephanie, and Margaret T. Gordon. 1981. The fear of rape: A study in social control. *Journal of Social Issues* 34(4):71–92.

Rush, Florence. 1980. *The best kept secret: Sexual abuse of children*. Englewood Cliffs, NJ: Prentice-Hall.

Sanders, William B. 1980. Rape and woman's identity. Beverly Hills: California: Sage Publications. Introduction by Gilbert Geis.

Scheppele, Kim L., and Pauline B. Bart. 1983. Through women's eyes: Defining danger in the wake of sexual assault. *Journal of Social Issues* 39(2):63–80.

Scully, Diana H. 1981. Personal communication.

Scully, Diana, and Joseph Marolla. 1981. Convicted rapists' attitudes toward women and rape. Paper presented at the First International, Interdisciplinary Congress on Women, University of Haifa, Israel, 12/28/81–1/1/82.

———. 1984. Convicted rapists' vocabulary of motive: Excuses and justifications. *Social Problems* 31(4).

———. "Riding the bull at Gilly's": Convicted rapists describe the rewards of rape. *Social Problems*, 42 February 1985.

Sennett, Richard, and Jonathan Cobb. 1972. *The hidden injuries of class*. New York: Vantage Books.

Smithyman, Samuel David. 1978. The undetected rapist. Unpublished dissertation, Claremont Graduate School, Claremont, California.

Skyes, Gresham M., and David Matza. 1957. Techniques of neutralization: A theory of delinquency. *American Sociological Review* 22:664–69.

Wilson, K., Rebecca Fisson, and G. M. Britton. 1980. Cultural aspects of male sex aggression. Paper presented at annual meeting of American Sociological Association, New York.

8 Summary and Conclusion: What We Learned and What It Means

> Four months ago I was raped. . . . Following conventional wisdom, I reacted to the attack calmly, nonviolently, and tried to talk my assailant out of it. To this day I feel worse about having cried and pleaded than I do about the sexual act.
>
> I hope that you will do a follow-up study on women who have been attacked. I suspect you will find that even those who were ultimately raped have better feelings about themselves and are more easily readjusting to life. I am very grateful to be alive, and sometimes it seems foolish to even think this, but if there is a next time, they'll have to kill me. (From a letter sent to Bart, 1981)

All feminist rape analysts agree that traditional female socialization sets up a woman to be raped rather than to avoid rape when attacked. Deference to male authority is presented as the only appropriate behavior if a woman is to acquire a husband. Even though the idea that women are taught to win by losing is plausible, it had not been tested prior to our interviews. Therefore, about half of the interview schedule addressed issues of child and adult socialization into traditional female roles and the relationship of such behavior to rape or avoidance.

Examination of background factors (both socioeconomic and demographic factors and childhood and adult socialization variables) provided partial support for the feminist analysis of rape. When we looked at socioeconomic and demographic factors to see if they resulted in rape or rape avoidance, rape avoiders were more likely to be taller and heavier than raped women. Two thirds of the women who avoided rape had never been married, while women who had been married more than once or who were divorced were least likely to avoid rape. Oldest (but not only children) daughters were more likely to avoid rape, particularly if they had a major responsibility for housework and care of siblings; 69 percent of oldest daughters avoided rape when attacked. Although mothers of women who avoided rape had more college and post-graduate education than women who were raped, the occupation of mothers was not associated with avoidance, nor was the subject's holding a nontraditional job (e.g., electrician).

There are three childhood socialization variables that were associated with stopping sexual assaults: parental response to childhood aggression, childhood idea of what she thought her life would be like when she grew up, and childhood sports. Although it made no difference for rape avoidance whether the subjects fought physically with other children, or even if they won or lost those childhood battles, the parents of women who were raped were more likely to both have intervened in such fights and to have punished the use of violence. Moreover, the parents of women who were raped were less likely to have counseled their daughters to fight back in quarrels with their peers. It follows that women whose parents knew about the fights but did not intervene learned that they had to take care of themselves and had experience in doing so.

Women who avoided rape were more likely to have played football, a contact sport, than raped women. Football teaches women that physical contact — being knocked down, even hurt — is not the end of the world, something that most boys but few girls learn. It seems logical that such experience is helpful when a woman is attacked in less benign contexts.

Not only were the rape avoiders more likely to engage in contact sports and have had parents who allowed them to fight their own battles, but they were less likely to have mentioned marriage and children and more likely to mention paid employment when asked what they thought their lives would be like when they grew up.

So, these four factors — mothers' education, parental intervention in childhood aggression, football playing, and growing up with a nontraditional image of one's future — support the feminist theory about rape. Surprisingly, avoiders were not less likely to say that when they were growing up they believed a man would take care of them when they were adults.

When the women's adult socialization experiences were analyzed, the women who avoided rape were more competent in managing stress and/or emergencies and possessed skills enabling them to be independent.

As Henley (1977) pointed out:

> An attitude study in 1959 documented the psychological connection between chivalry and misogyny: attitudes favoring chivalry went hand-in-hand with those favoring the open subordination of women — and both were positively correlated with antidemocratic attitudes. (p. 65)

The practice of keeping women passive, doing things for them in the physical world such as opening doors and moving heavy furniture, not only gives women a feeling of inability to cope, but it alienates them from the physical world. A famous psychological experiment some years ago used a contraption called the "kitten carousel." Newborn kittens were strapped into it, one walking and the other riding around the track in a gondola. Both received the same visual experience of the environment, but the walking kitten had additional active physical experience, so that it could coordinate sight and movement. This experience gave normal development of motor abilities to the walking cat, but left the passive one, with the "soft life," deficient in such development. In an analogous way, passive women are taken for a ride — chivalrous treatment puts women into that crippling gondola. This point is well illustrated in this account by Jan Morris (1974) in response to the treatment she received from others after her change from male to female:

> The more I was treated as a woman, the more woman I became. I adapted willy nilly. If I was assumed to be incompetent at reversing cars or opening bottles, oddly incompetent I found myself becoming. If a case was thought too heavy for me, inexplicably I found it so myself.

This quote exemplifies the equation of trained incapacity with femininity.

Additionally, women who avoided being raped were more likely than raped women to mention a woman they knew personally rather than a woman in public life when asked which woman in public or private life they admired and why. Raped women were more likely to mention role models in public life. While the number of cases were small, it was only raped women who said that they admired women who were successfully able to combine an occupation with their *role as a woman*. Mothers of raped women were more likely to want their daughters to combine marriage with a traditional occupation, while mothers of women who avoided rape wanted them to have marriage and a career, although the career was not specified. Both groups of women described their mothers as strong, and they were similar in the ratio of positive-to-negative adjectives they applied to their mothers.

Men in prison are faced with the same threat of rape that women in society face on the streets and alleys of our cities. Thus, Marian Henriques Neudel (1980), an attorney, sent us the chapter on rape avoidance from a book of advice to male radicals who were going to be imprisoned, stating:

> Note especially the material I've marked, e.g., the references to physical modesty, not making eye contact, not accepting favors, not being too candid or friendly. All things, in short, that girls learn at their mother's knee by 11 or so (at least I did). From this it is not unreasonable to conclude that being a woman is the equivalent of a life sentence.

SITUATIONAL VARIABLES

> I was raped in my apartment . . . it was close to about four in the morning (case 65).

At the start of the interviews, we thought that the effect of situational variables, especially the presence of a weapon, would be extremely powerful, canceling out the effect of other factors. But we learned that while there are a number of situational variables associated with victimization, women have been able to avoid rape under the most threatening conditions. Situational variables by themselves do not account for the outcome. For example, there is no relationship between the woman's perception of the assailant's build and whether or not the woman is raped—women are not more likely to be raped by men they described as having heavy builds than by other less sturdy men. But it will be recalled that the woman's size correlated with the outcome, although this relationship was the result of women over 5'7" avoiding rape. Thus it is the background or socialization factors that are important. As predicted in the conceptual scheme (see Appendix B), both background and situational factors are associated with the outcome.

The following situational factors were positively associated with being raped:

1. The time of the attack was between midnight and 6:00 A.M. (the highest ratio of avoidance to victimization was during the day).
2. Another crime in addition to the sexual assault was committed or attempted (e.g., robbery).
3. The rape attack was a sudden, intense "blitz" rather than part of a more elaborate "con," and the rapist used force (including a weapon) to obtain compliance.
4. The rapist choked the victim (this was coded separately from the degree of force or beating).
5. No observer was present.
6. The woman lived alone.
7. The woman lived on the first floor.
8. The assault took place inside rather than outside.

The picture that emerges is that of an armed criminal who both robs and rapes, attacking a sleeping woman who is likely to be divorced and living on the ground floor. People are most vulnerable when they are asleep. (It is no accident that secret police also arrive between midnight and 6:00 A.M.) He takes her by surprise (blitz). She awakened to find his hands on her throat. She, quite understandably, fears for her life and, therefore, complies with his demand.

THE INTERACTION

I always heard that if you struggle it just excited them so I tried to use psychology, but it didn't work. (case 43)

Five active resistance strategies were examined: fleeing or trying to flee; screaming; physical resistance or force; cognitive verbal techniques—including reasoning with the attacker, trying to con him, insisting that she wasn't interested, flattering and/or attempting to make him see her as a human being (e.g., "My name is Mary, I live with my mother and teach in an elementary school—what's your name?"), and pleading. The effect of environmental intervention (e.g., a police car or passerby happening along) and no strategies was also analyzed.

Talking (but not pleading) was the strategy most frequently resorted to and was not notably effective. Of the 67 women who tried it, 36 avoided rape. Physical resistance was the second most frequently used strategy. Of the 44 women who tried it, 30 avoided rape. Third most frequent was screaming or yelling, resorted to by 40 women. This, too, was more effective than not: 25 of these women managed to avoid rape.

Fourth in frequency was pleading, which proved relatively ineffective. Of the 25 women who pleaded not to be raped, 11 ended up as rape avoiders. These results may be considered in the context of the feminist interpretation of rape as a male power trip: According to this view, pleading with the assailant is giving him what he wants—a victim who acknowledges his ability to dominate. Why should he quit while he's ahead?

In sum, of the five strategies, pleading was the only one disproportionately associated with being raped.

Bart suddenly realized the parallel between the accommodating strategies European Jews traditionally used in order to survive in a hostile environment and the strategies traditionally socialized women used in order to try to avoid rape, or if raped, to avoid death or mutilation. Jewish leaders thought that they could negotiate with the Nazis just as Jews with some exceptions (e.g., Spain) had successfully negotiated with heads of state and heads of communities since the Diaspora. But since the Nazi ideology demanded the *extermination* of the Jews, traditional strategies did not work. It was hard for Jews to grasp the enormity of The Final Solution, that genocide was occurring.

Similarly women have been taught (and perhaps have successfully used) "feminine wiles" to survive other difficult situations, from faking orgasms to crying and pleading. Kanter (1977) reports that crying is an effective strategy when used by secretaries. Bart wrote asking her why it was effective for secretaries but not for women trying to dissuade a potential rapist. Kanter (1978) replied:

> The use of crying or pleading is effective as a weapon when the powerful person needs the powerless person to do something, as with a boss and a secretary. However, it would clearly not work where the dominant person is simply getting pleasure out of asserting dominance, as I think is the case with rape; in that case, one could hypothesize that the more pleading and crying, the better for the rapist. With the boss, just the opposite is true.

These unassertive strategies depending on mutual self-interest and goodwill work neither with Nazis[1] nor rapists. (We do not intend to imply that these categories are mutually exclusive.) In analyzing the situation of Jews during the Holocaust and women during sexual assault, the use of traditional strategies is understandable.

Interestingly, the least frequently used of the five active strategies, fleeing or trying to flee, showed the most dramatic relationship with rape avoidance. Of the 21 women who fled or tried to flee, 17 avoided rape. Only environmental intervention proved more likely than flight/attempted flight to be associated with rape avoidance. Although outside intervention occurred in only 12 of the 94 cases, in 10 of these (83 percent), the effect was to thwart the rape attempt. Actually, environmental intervention covers several possible scenarios.

One such scenario is when the woman manages to stay calm enough to take advantage of events in the environment. For example, one woman (case 71) was struggling with her assailant in an alley, having already failed in her attempt to con him into going to a neighborhood bar with her. At the sound of a fire engine siren he loosened his grip, enabling her to break away and flee.

We have discussed the strategies as though they occurred in isolation, as if a woman chooses one strategy only. Clearly that was not the case. In fact, the most often used strategy for avoiders appears to have been a combination of screaming and use of physical resistance. Moreover, avoiders were more likely to use multiple strategies. The most frequent number of strategies used was three for avoiders *versus* only one for raped women. The five women who made absolutely no attempt to resist were all raped.

In addition to the strategies that were associated with rape or rape avoidance, another factor emerged in the interviews — the woman's primary concern when she was attacked. Some were most concerned with death and/or mutilation, and others had a gut reaction of rage that someone would dare try to rape them, to intrude on their space, along with a determination not to let that occur. It is not that the first group of women did not care whether they were raped, but rather they thought that by allowing the assailants to rape them they would not be injured or killed. However, since rapists are not characterized by the spirit of fair play, the women were sometimes injured anyhow. Statistically, 51 percent of the avoiders named fear of rape and/or determination not to be raped as their main thought.

---

[1]We do not wish to perpetuate the myth that Jews did not resist. There were many group uprisings (e.g., in the Warsaw Ghetto) and individual acts of sabotage committed by Jewish slave laborers. Jews who were political, whether Zionist or non-Zionist Left, understood the imminent danger and the need for action. We are referring to the majority of well-meaning leaders who did not understand the markedly different nature of fascism.

Only 7 percent of the raped women had these as their main concerns. Conversely, 65 percent of the raped women were primarily concerned with fears of death/mutilation *versus* 37 percent of the avoiders. The distinction remained when we controlled for presence of a weapon.

The following case is an example of this distinction between primary fear of death and primary rage at the prospect of being raped. A young Black woman (not in this study), shortly after leaving a convent, was asked out by a friend of her family. When they were together in his car, he said he was going to do her a favor because she had been innocent too long. Her reaction was: "How dare you! Someone I trusted and my family knew. If you do this you better kill me afterwards because if you don't kill me I'm gonna go and get me a gun and kill you." He responded by saying, "There's something the matter with you." She said, "There's something *deadly* the matter with you. Drive me home." And he did.

This woman did not originally label the event rape avoidance because she knew the assailant. And she had not thought of the event for years. But after hearing one of the authors (Bart) speak, it all came back to her.

Another woman, an engineer for a radio program that was taped in an effort to obtain subjects, shared an experience that happened to her too long ago to be used for this study. A man approached her with a razor, insisting that she allow him to rape her. She replied, "You want pussy. You're gonna get dead pussy. Get out of here." He fled.

Although talking, whether reasoning with the rapist or trying to con him, was by itself only rarely effective in dissuading him from forced intercourse, and pleading was counterproductive, 25 women were able to negotiate with their assailants. Some negotiated out of having to perform fellatio or sodomy. Some negotiated as to the length of the encounter. Some negotiated to protect the women they were with. Apparently, once the assailant believed he could rape the woman, he was willing to compromise on other issues.

Probably no aspect of rape research is as fraught with dilemmas of policy and practical application as whether women have more to gain or lose by physically resisting a would-be rapist. Two dimensions are involved. First, does a woman enhance or diminish her chances of avoiding rape by resisting physically? Second, regardless of whether a woman is raped or avoids rape, does physical resistance increase her chances of severe injury? One continued to get the impression from much of the media coverage on rape that this is precisely the situation (Heath et al., 1979).

It is striking how relatively few of the women in our study were severely hurt. Out of 94 cases, 5 women were brutally beaten (in 3 of these cases a weapon was also brandished). Physical resistance much more frequently resulted in rape avoidance than a beating. To cast further light on this matter, we compared two extreme groups: the five women who were severely beaten, and another five women who had used no resistance strategies whatsoever (all other women in our sample had tried *something*).

Of the five brutally beaten women, it seems that at least two of them did suffer additional physical damage because of their attempts to fight back. A third case is somewhat ambiguous. However, two of these three cases involved two assailants, and two of these cases also involved use of a weapon by the assailant. Two of the women who used no strategies were seriously injured and required medical treatment.

Each woman has to make her own decision about what risk she is willing to take. We will close this section with a quote from the mother of an avoider: "He broke her arm, but she won."

MYTHS ABOUT HOW TO AVOID RAPE: A MEANS OF SOCIAL CONTROL

> We recommend passive resistance, like getting a person's confidence by talking and doing what you were taught to do as girls growing up, to help resist attack. (Officer Hankins of Washington, D.C. Police, quoted in Dejanikus, 1981)

> Treat the rapist as a human being . . . gain his confidence . . . reassure him so that he knows you represent neither a mental or a physical threat to him . . . go along until you can safely react. (Storaska, 1975)

We have all heard myths about rape. We have heard that you can't rape a woman against her will because a woman can run faster with her skirt up than a man with his pants down, and, besides, you can't thread a moving needle; that legalizing prostitution would end rape; that nice girls don't get raped; that women enjoy rape (see Schwendinger and Schwendinger, 1974, for a debunking of these myths).

But many women also live with the fear of rape (see Griffin, 1971, for a discussion of how that fear enters our lives as girls and continues in adulthood). Riger and Gordon (1981) and Clarke and Lewis (1978) have shown that fear of rape causes women to restrict their lives. Women know that if they are raped after having been out, unaccompanied, in a place deemed unrespectable (e.g., a bar) at a time deemed indiscreet (night), they will have little recourse. Clarke and Lewis (1978) have shown that women who are not considered respectable are not classified as rapeable (their cases are not "founded") by the police. Fear of rape makes it difficult for women to exist independently of men, because women believe they need men to protect them from other men. But we realized after the press release on our work and McIntyre's work (1980) was widely disseminated that this new research was heretical. For two weeks the phone did not stop ringing with reporters wanting more color for their stories and talk show producers anxious to fill in empty hours. Reporters said that the findings that women who fight back are more likely to avoid rape, that talking by itself is relatively useless, and that pleading is associated with being raped challenged the conventional wisdom. Didn't we know that fighting back or even screaming would only excite the assailant and most probably result in the woman's serious injury? Women were thus advised to try to dissuade the rapist by guile; e.g., telling him she was menstruating, feigning insanity, telling him she had VD or cancer. Women were advised to humanize the situation, disclosing information about themselves so that they would be seen by their assailants as human beings and then, presumably, not be raped. We already knew that myths about rape acted to keep women in their place, beneath men. What we learned was that the traditional *advice* given to women, *avoidance myths*, were also mechanisms of social control, keeping women down and dependent. In no case in our study did the rapist become bored with lack of resistance and leave to look for another subject who knew karate so that he could become aroused.

Encouraging women to learn dirty street fighting, to kick and yell and gouge, to be rude to men on the street and refuse requests for help is, in fact, encouraging them not to act as women are expected to act. It is this traditional ideology that led a woman involved in the Human Service department of the city of Chicago to tell Bart that the department could not institute self-defense classes in the housing projects, even though rape is endemic there, because the men would consider it hostile. She said she could, however, set up counseling services for women *after* they were raped.

Advising women to try to humanize the encounter makes sense because objectification and dehumanization of women generally, and of the victim in particular, makes rape and other brutalizations possible (that is why many feminists believe all pornography, since it objectifies women, leads to rape; see the section on rape and pornography later in this chapter). Such strategies facilitate negotiations but *do not prevent rape*. For example, one woman who told her assailant about herself, presented herself as a good girl living with her mother, and expressed fear of becoming pregnant, was raped nonetheless. But the assailant withdrew before he ejaculated, assuring her that she would not become pregnant.

A women who tried to humanize the situation (case 29) was forced to perform fellatio, was sodomized, and was raped twice genitally. These sections from her interview can shed light on this process:

> I tried to talk as much as I could. I asked him a lot of questions. I don't even remember what he said, but I just wanted to be a person to him, not a thing. I didn't want him to just take out aggression on me, so I kept asking, I asked him what his name was. He told me his name was George. It probably wasn't but I called him George throughout the whole thing. And I asked him what kind of family he came from, how many sisters and brothers he came from, where he worked and all sort of things . . . so then we did the act and . . . after that he told me to

turn over and, I hate that. So then he did it from the rear and everything, and he didn't come at all. Then when I started to put my clothes
on, I think I had my clothes on, he said, "Should we fuck again?" or
something like that and I said, "George . . . ('cause in the process I
said, "Promise me after this we can go."). So then after that he said,
"Should we do it again." I said, "You promised me that we would go
after this." So then I got my clothes on and he put my head back into
his lap. And then he said, "Where should I drop you off at? . . . "
    BART: So it seems to me that you had all kinds of plans. You were
trying to make him think of you as a human being.
    S: 'Um-hmm. I didn't want to be a thing. I told him, "I'm getting
married. I have a boyfriend. I go to school." I told him all about
myself. You know, I tried to sound pleasant [laughs] which was really
hard at the time. This was all while I was down on his lap, en route to
where we were going.

Some advice given to women is not only incorrect and ideologically
regressive, but it is also dangerous. Storaska (1975), for example, states
that women should go along with the assailant at first, flattering him, and
even expressing sexual interest in him. Then, when the opportunity arises,
the woman should resist. But McIntyre and this investigation found that
women should react as soon as possible. One characteristic of the interaction between the assailant and the avoider compared with the interaction
between the assailant and the raped woman is that the avoiders first knew
they were in danger because of general behavioral indicators, while the
raped women did not know they were in danger until the assailant showed
them a weapon. *It is possible that it is this ability to perceive danger early
in the scenario from more ambiguous clues that enabled them to avoid the
attack.*

Researchers (Kidder et al., 1983; Cohn, Kidder, and Harvey, 1981) have
shown that one result of a woman's taking self-defense courses is that she
increases her ability to sense danger earlier by being aware of when her
space is being intruded. For example, in self-defense courses women are
taught to be suspicious if a man sits next to them in an almost empty bus.

The myths about rape and rape avoidance would have us believe that
women will not be raped if we restrict our behavior sufficiently, if we are
unwilling, if we reason, nurture or use guile. Thus it is no wonder that until
recently women jurors were considered unsympathetic to rape victims. All
the information they had been given implied that they and women like
them, "good" women, could not be raped. If a woman were raped, either
she wanted it, or she deserved it, or she was stupid and naive; and in the
case of rape, stupidity and naiveté apparently are crimes justifying rape.

The gang rape of a woman on a pool table in Big Dan's bar in New Bed-
ford, Massachusetts in 1983 exemplifies the persistence of rape myths as
well as their function in maintaining social control of women. Not only was
the woman publicly raped by several men (six were accused, four found

guilty), but none of the bystanders intervened or called the police, remaining unmoved by the woman's screams and cries for help. Since the trial was shown on cable television, and portions were broadcast on radio, the defense strategy was public. That strategy was based on discrediting the woman, i.e., showing that she was not rapeable, since, as we have stated in Chapter 1, only respectable women are "rapeable." The defense tried to show that she was not only on welfare but was a "welfare cheat," as well as a flirt and a liar. In short, their defense of the accused rapists was that the woman had "asked for it" — had indeed consented. Moreover, a large segment of the Portuguese community marched to protest the guilty verdict; factories were closed to facilitate a successful march. The marchers carried candles and wore tags saying "justice crucified." The march had a religious aura with the convicted rapists assuming the role of Christian martyrs.

That the gang rape of a poor woman was national news, and the assailants found guilty and sentenced to prison, shows progress. But that so many members of the community supported the assailants, and that the woman was in fact put on trial, shows how far we still have to go.

SELF-DEFINITIONS, ACTS, AND LEGAL DEFINITIONS OF RAPE AND ATTEMPTED RAPE

Attempted rape and rape can be thought of as a continuum extending from the first unwanted attention, to the rapist's penile penetration, to orgasm. When the woman's self-definition as having been raped or avoiding rape was compared with the acts that occurred, it became apparent that the important distinction was between phallic and nonphallic acts. Rape was what was done with a penis (genital intercourse, sodomy, fellatio), not what was done to a vagina (digital penetration, fondling and touching, cunnilingus).

Under the Illinois law that existed until July 1984, a woman who managed to stop a rape attempt short of genital penetration had not been raped. In order for the assailant to be charged with attempted rape he would have had to take a "substantial step" toward genital penetration, and this requirement has been interpreted very strictly by the courts (e.g., he has to have his pants off). When the legal definition was applied to the acts that occurred and compared with the woman's self-definition, it was found that there was little discrepancy between those women who said they were raped and those who met the legal requirements for such a charge. But there was a wide difference between those 51 women who considered themselves to have fended off a rape attack and those who met the legal requirements for a charge of attempted rape. Only 15 of these women could have charged attempted rape, 2 of them rape, and 3 of them deviate sexual assault. None of the five women who had no legal claim (e.g., their husbands raped them) reported their assaults to the police. Therefore the low rate of police recording ("founding") rape cases, of bringing rapists to trial, and of finding them guilty is not a result of women bringing "frivolous charges" (see Table 8.1 and Appendix C for an elaboration of these findings, as well as Bart and Scheppelle, 1980).

WHAT IS TO BE DONE

In this section, the women's ideas of effective and ineffective ways of avoiding rape will first be given. Next, their ideas on what other women could do to protect themselves from rape and how they would advise them are presented. The responses fell into 37 categories (including "Other"). The most frequent response, given somewhat more often by avoiders than by raped women, was "learn self-defense" ($n = 25$). Having a weapon or a lit cigarette available was stated by 12 women. As can be seen, a substantial group of women endorsed assertive strategies. The next largest category of responses had to do with the woman having heightened awareness and alertness to possible danger. There was no difference between raped women and avoiders in this category. The third largest category had to do with restricting one's behavior: A total of 16 women gave that advice and an additional 3 warned women not to dress or act provocatively. It should be pointed out that there was no increase in assaults in the warm months, and Chicago women dress in the winter as if they were about to scale Mount Everest. Only 2 women of the 94 women interviewed were attacked in clothes that some might consider provocative — one was walking from the beach wearing shorts and another was wearing a dress with spaghetti straps. When the women were asked what *precautions* they thought other women should take, 15 advised behavioral restrictions, such as not talking to strangers, not letting men in their apartments, with an additional 13 responses suggesting that the woman should restrict night-time behavior. Here again, 15 suggested learning self-defense, some advising that young girls be taught such skills. Nine women believed that carrying or having access to a weapon would be effective. When the women were asked what they thought would be an effective means of avoiding rape once accosted by a man, there was little consensus. The most common belief was using multiple strategies; the second most common was that it depends on the rapist, and the third was to keep calm. The avoiders were most likely to give the first and third responses and the raped women the second response. When they were asked what strategies would be *ineffective* in avoiding a rape once accosted, the largest group said being passive or submitting, the second largest group said pleading, and the third said using physical means. It was only the first strategy that differentiated the avoiders from the raped women, with more avoiders giving that response. A total of 28 women spontaneously mentioned what they would do if they were assaulted again:

Table 8.1. Relation Between Legal Definitions and Women's Definition of Incidents to Police

	Legal Definition						
	Rape[a] % (n)	Deviate Sexual Assault % (n)	Attempted Rape or Attempted Deviate Sexual Assault % (n)	Other Class X Felony[b] % (n)	Other Felony[c] % (n)	Other Misdemeanor[d] % (n)	Nothing Illegal % (n)
Reported to Police	80 (32)	40 (2)	67 (10)	100 (2)	77 (10)	79 (11)	— —
Not Reported to Police	20 (8)	60 (3)	33 (6)	0 (0)	23 (3)	11 (3)	100 (5)
Total n	(40)	(5)	(16)	(2)	(13)	(14)	(5)
Women's Definition							
Raped	80 (37)	5 (2)	2 (1)	0 (0)	0 (0)	2 (1)	5 (1)
Avoided	4 (2)	6 (3)	29 (15)	4 (2)	26 (13)	26 (13)	6 (3)

[a]Includes 15 cases of rape combined with deviate sexual assault.
[b]Includes 1 home invasion and 1 armed robbery.
[c]Includes 1 burglary, 1 robbery, 4 aggravated batteries, 4 unlawful restraints, 2 attempted kidnaps, 1 pandering.
[d]Includes 11 batteries, 2 aggravated assaults, 1 assault.

16 of them said they would fight back strongly (mainly avoiders), and 5 said they would kill the assailant (4 were raped women).

Spreading Information on Avoidance Strategies

The fact that it is possible to avoid rape when attacked should be widely disseminated, particularly in the mass media. News magazines and television should report in detail instances of rape avoidance so women can learn what works. The findings reported in this book as well as those in other studies in which rape avoidance has been analyzed should also be publicized. Women should be told about how to maximize the probability of avoiding rape when attacked and about the effectiveness of multiple strategies. Women should also learn self-defense, especially courses that are designed to teach women how to use "dirty" street fighting techniques and that include role playing in dealing with hassling as well as rape. Additionally women should be taught about the possibility of negotiating with their assailant(s).

Legal Changes

Those states that have not changed their sexual assault laws so that gender is unspecified (men can be raped, but almost always it is executed by other men) should do so. Those states in which it is not a felony to rape women with fingers or objects (rather than with a penis) should change their laws. In addition, the encounter with the judicial system should be made less traumatic for the victim. Several subjects said that the judicial process was worse than the rape. Vertical prosecution (the same attorney for the entire process) should be instituted, and the number of continuances should be limited. Furthermore, consent should be an affirmative defense. This means that the legal definition of rape would not include the phrase "against her will." It is assumed that if there were force or threat of force she had not consented. The burden of proving that the raped woman consented falls on the lawyer for the defense. The new Illinois sexual assault statute embodies the approach in a modified form. Consent may be a defense to the charge of rape, but it must be proven, not inferred.

> 'Consent' means a freely given agreement to the act of sexual penetration or sexual conduct in question. Lack of verbal or physical resistance or submission by the victim resulting from the use of force or threat of force by the accused shall not constitute consent. (Illinois Revised Statute 1983, Sections 12-17, p. 132)

In the absence of this definition, women who did not resist "enough," even when force or threat of force was used, were assumed to have consented.

Medical Changes

None of the subjects who went to hospitals for post-assault care were given "informed consent" when they were administered DES (the morning after pill). Several women said that had they known the possible side effects they would have risked becoming pregnant and had an early abortion. Such information should be provided, ideally by a rape victim advocate. Most women were pleased with the advocates provided by a women's group, but some complained about the clergy counseling service that was present in one Chicago hospital. We recommend that advocates be present in hospitals but that they should be female, since most raped women do not want to deal with men immediately after the assault.

We also advocate that all emergency room personnel be given appropriate skills for dealing with victims of sexual assault. In fact, physician and nursing education should include knowledge of how to appropriately treat women and children who are victims of male violence — incest survivors and other sexually assaulted children, battered women, and women (as well as men) who have been sexually assaulted. Items testing this knowledge should be included in licensing exams.

What About Men?

We can see from this study as well as others that men and women view sexual events differently. What is mere friendly behavior to a female is a sexual overture to a man, particularly crossing the threshold of his or her apartment. In one instance (case 93), the woman was picked up hitchhiking by a man, went skinny-dipping with him, but was unwilling to have sex. He threatened to break her arm, and she complied with the rapist's demand for sex (after which she learned judo and avoided the next incident). Incidents such as these were not uncommon. The men thought the women were willing to have sex. The women thought that they were merely being friendly.

Traditionally, the male definition of the situation has been institutionalized among the police and in the judicial system. It is important that these different meanings attached to the same act be openly discussed so that incidents of rape and attempted rape stemming from misunderstanding can be reduced.

There is a series of films funded by the government on acquaintance rape that addresses this issue. While the films are aimed at a teenage audience, they are useful for any age, since they show the disparity between female and male thinking and interpretation. The plot illustrates how normal interaction can escalate into a sexual assault scenario because of this disparity. (These films are available from Association Films, Inc., 1111 North 19 St., Suite 404, Arlington, VA 22209.)

Policy Implications

It is a useful exercise to ask women to imagine what it would be like to live in a rape-free society where there is no forced sex (Star, 1978). Margaret Mead claims that the "gentle" Arapesh are such a society, but most examples of societies where rape does not exist are found in the pages of the writers of feminist utopias and science fiction. Some, like first-wave feminist Charlotte Perkins Gilman (*Herland*; 1979), achieve this goal by having only women in the setting, although three men later arrive, which furnishes the plot. Some, like Sally Gearheart (*Wanderground*; 1979), restrict men, except for the "gentles." Men are unable to have erections outside the city walls, where the women live, and women "speak bitterness" about the old days when rape existed so it will not be forgotten. Some writers like Ursula Le Guin (*The Left Hand of Darkness*; 1980) and Marge Piercy (*Woman on the Edge of Time*; 1976) write about cultures peopled by gentle androgynous people. Clearly these "solutions" to the rape problem are not viable; at least there are no clear policy implementations that can be directly derived. In another constructed society, men rape and are violent against "their" women, but the group of women called "free amazons" are trained in self-defense and using weapons (Bradley, 1976).[2] They protect each other and cannot be raped. But we have been unable to find a society in fiction or in fact where it was considered manly to be aggressive, feminine to be gentle, and where economic success required competitiveness and aggressiveness (forcefulness, single-mindedness, and ambition if you prefer those terms) in which rape did not exist.

Eliminating rape would mean changing the structure of our society so as to bring about the elimination of gender inequality and its cause—male dominance. While it is apparent that such a complete transformation is one of our goals (and we prefer men becoming more like women to women becoming more like men), we do not know how to bring such a revolution about. Thus the suggestions we will present have a more modest goal—the reduction of rape by giving women the attitudes and behavior that seem to be most effective in rape avoidance both through institutional and personal changes. Even though men must also change, that is not the focus of this chapter, but a task for male sexual assault researchers. (See Pleck, 1981 for a critique of current theories of male psychology.)

The policy recommendations in this section flow from the data—from the variables that were associated with the avoidance of sexual assault, and the accounts of horror and triumph that were disclosed by women when they learned we were researching sexual assault accounts of rape cases and battery.

---

[2] The authors would like to thank Barbara Emrys for information on fantasy and science fiction.

The recommendations were based on general analysis of the endemic violence and misogyny in society (see Bart 1979a, 1979b for a more detailed exposition of this point) as well as the more commonly addressed issue of gender inequality, which we believe is maintained in part by the undercurrent of force and threat of force. [Komarovsky (1962) made this point years ago in her book on working class wives.]

Sports

Women who played football, a contact sport, when they were growing up and who engaged in sports regularly as adults were more likely to avoid rape. Therefore daughters as well as sons should be encouraged to be active in sports. The Title IX section of the Education Amendments Act that prohibits discrimination on the basis of sex in federally assisted intercollegiate and scholastic sports should be implemented. In our utopia no one would engage in competitive contact sports because of the ever-present danger of serious injury. But since such participation gives males skills that females need and do not possess, if such sports continue to exist, opportunities should be equal. Some female coaches are reported to have said that at adolescence females inhibit their ability when competing with males (Lichtenstein, 1981). This behavior should be discussed, if it occurs. If it cannot be changed, then females should have opportunities to compete in all female groups.

Childhood and Adolescent Socialization

Because competence and ability to manage the world (e.g., having major household responsibility when growing up) are associated with rape avoidance, parents should be advised to expect their daughters to be competent and reward them for these skills. Since parents of avoiders were less likely to intervene in childhood aggressive incidents, daughters should not be protected on the assumption that there will always be someone who will take care of them. Neither parents nor other adults in positions of authority should attempt to fit females into the "nice girl" role. [See the work of Greer Litton Fox (1977) for a discussion of this construct as a Procrustean bed that few would fit in if not squeezed or stretched.]

Because feelings about the integrity of one's body (about who has what rights over it, about who is responsible for sexual behavior) start early, children should be taught that they own their bodies. Children should be taught that no one has the right to touch them without their consent, whether that person be a member of their family or a stranger offering candy (our data as well as other statistics show the molester is usually someone the child knows). Since so many cases do not come to light because the child is afraid to disclose the incidents or is not believed when she does, parents and teachers should discuss the fact that such events occur so that children and adolescents know that they are not unique to them; moreover they should be believed until proven otherwise.

One woman in this study (case 33) reported her father's molestation to the police. Since she still had an intact hymen she was not believed. Her mother was told and threatened her with institutionalization if she ever said anything like that again. When subsequently her father started penetrating her, her sister found them and threatened to kill her. Unfortunately her experience is all too common, and such events set the stage for later assaults. Terry Schwartz, a child therapist who works with incest victims, notes that these children have the same feelings of guilt and responsibility that characterize adult raped women. These responses result from early learning that it is the female who is responsible for whatever happens sexually, that the demands of male sexuality are so imperative that men cannot control themselves and must have a release, and that it is the fault of "provocative" women that they are in this state.

As was previously mentioned, the UCLA study of adolescent attitudes toward sexual assault supports these assertions (Giarrusso et al., 1979). They found that adolescent males believe that females who wear tight jeans or no bra are giving a sexual "come on" and that any assertive behavior by a female, even a friendly phone call, is a cue for sexuality. These attitudes are particularly dangerous because male teenagers state they are willing to use force to have sex if they attribute their sexual arousal to the female's behavior, in which case they do not have to take responsibility for their sexual behavior. Moreover, many males also believe that they can use force to have sex if they have dated a long time or if the woman changes her mind from yes to no. Some, but not as many, female adolescents agree with these statements. (In Illinois consumers have several days during which they can revoke a contract to purchase major household items, but apparently women are not to be afforded that privilege when it comes to our bodies.) It is no accident that these attitudes are reflected in the enforcement and lack of enforcement of sexual assault laws. Date and boyfriend rapes are generally considered unprosecutable, and the woman's respectability, which can be discredited by her wearing clothes considered provocative, is an important factor in the outcome of the case.

It will be recalled that one of the factors that is associated with rape avoidance is a feeling of anger by the woman that anyone would try to rape her, to intrude on her space and person. Thus anything that enhances a woman's self-esteem so that she believes she is worth defending and that no one has the right to attack her should be associated with rape avoidance.

Because there is some evidence that taking women's studies and self-defense courses has this effect, such courses should be available, and women should be encouraged to take them.

Since there was moderate support in this study for the feminist analysis that rape is caused by traditional gender role socialization, the reexamination of such practices by parents and schools and an attempt to remove or at least mitigate sexism in textbooks and in classroom interaction must not be allowed to falter because of the new conservatism and "pro-family" atmosphere that permeates the current scene.

We have all heard horror stories about men who asked raped women whether they enjoyed it or if they had orgasms. This rarely occurred in this sample. One woman reported that a police officer told her and her raped roommate rape jokes and that the magazine *Hustler* was being passed around the police station when they were being questioned, which she found insensitive. Another said that her boyfriend "like all men, asked, 'was it good?'" But the kind of male behavior women have described in the study and in conversation is the male attempt to take control of the situation. Since the essence of the rape experience is the feeling of powerlessness, what helps the woman is to be empowered. What is *not* helpful is pressuring her to report the rape or trying to find the rapist and punish him. The former frequently results in additional trauma for the woman and the latter in her additional concern over what might happen to the man. This behavior should be stopped. Women should be validated for surviving, and their world view and construction of the event (unless they manifest guilt feelings about their character) should be supported (Janoff-Bulman, 1979).

Pornography as Pro-Rape Propaganda

Violence in pornography is increasing both in hard and soft core media (Malamuth, 1981). An emerging group of social psychological experiments grounded in learning theory (rather than in the Freudian catharsis model) is showing a relationship between being exposed to violence in pornography and pro-rape attitudes as well as in a willingness to engage in aggression toward a female experimenter (see Bart and Jozsa, 1980 and Russell, 1980).

The catharsis model states that pornography drains off sexual/aggressive feelings so that they do not have to be expressed. If the catharsis model were correct, then, since the amount, visibility, and legitimacy of pornography has been increasing, rape and other sexual violence against women should be withering away, like the state after the revolution. This does not appear to be the case.

The psychological experiments of Malamuth and Donnerstein (1984) show the links between viewing pornography and violence in an erotic context. Donnerstein and Linz (1984) demonstrate a causal relationship between viewing "R"-rated films that depict violence in an erotic context (e.g., "The Tool Box Murders," "Halloween") and male subjects' desensitization to rape. As men view more of these films, they laugh more at the violence, see less violence, and identify more with the assailant. When these subjects assumed the role of jurors in a simulated rape case, they judged less harm done to the raped woman. This finding is particularly disturbing in light of studies showing that about one third of men would rape if they were sure they would not be caught (Malamuth, 1981).

Additionally, Zillman and Bryant (1982) found that viewing sexually explicit but not "violent" pornography showing sexual activity between consenting adults results in college students becoming less sensitive to the harm of rape and more hostile to the women's movement. A "massive" exposure meant that the student subjects saw a *total* of 4 hours and 48 minutes of "erotic" films over a 6-week period. Those with medium exposure saw 2 hours and 24 minutes of erotic films and a similar quantity of nonerotic films. A third group saw only nonerotic films, and a fourth group no films at all. What is most striking about this research is that these films were about sexual acts between consenting adults without any overt violence. But the women in these films played one of the standard female roles in pornography—they were sexually insatiable and more eager for various acts than the men.

Zillman and Bryant measured disposition toward rape by the length of incarceration the students recommended for a man guilty of rape. Students who were "massively" exposed to pornography recommended "significantly shorter terms of imprisonment. . . . Such exposure, it seems, made rape appear a trivial offense." (p. 16)

This newer research demonstrates that pornography desensitizes men to violence against women and in fact can be considered pro-rape propaganda. The merger of sex and violence is exemplified by the fact that men who are "successful" with women are called "lady-killers."

An examination of the "neutralizing" excuse and explanations the rapists gave in the previous chapter shows the parallel between the rapists' vocabulary and the view of rape presented in pornography. Pornography presents a male ideology of sexuality that depicts women behaving in ways that are most pleasing to men. When men rape in pornography there is no injury, and indeed the woman enjoys the sexual experience as she never has before. The portrayal of rape in pornography is consistent with and reinforces a pro-rape atmosphere, especially since the woman is usually portrayed as enjoying the assault (Smith, 1976).

An original, and we think fruitful, way to remedy this pro-rape propaganda was conceptualized by Catharine A. MacKinnon and Andrea Dworkin who were teaching at the University of Minnesota Law School when the issue of zoning of pornography stores came up before the City Council.

The MacKinnon-Dworkin statute, first introduced in Minneapolis and passed in Indianapolis, conceptualizes pornography as a violation of women's civil rights, as well as those of men, transsexuals, and children "in the place of women."

Because pornography is a systematic practice of exploitation that sexually subordinates women, it violates the Fourteenth Amendment, which guarantees civil equality to all citizens. Under the Fourteenth Amendment, human rights are violated when people are abused, exploited, or held in an inferior status because of a condition of birth. Although some say such a restriction violates the First Amendment, Lawrence Tribe, Professor of Constitutional Law at Harvard Law School, wrote in January 1984 to Councilwoman Charlee Hoyt, one of the two council members who introduced the bill, that "the ordinance, as drafted . . . rests on a rationale that closely parallels many previously accepted exceptions to justly stringent First Amendment guarantees."

The implications of current research and analyses such as this one are that pornography is not a victimless crime. It ought not to be viewed as a set of isolated magazine purchases by men or a developmental stage through which individual adolescent males pass. Pornography is a social phenomenon in which men are socialized into an insensitivity to female needs and are reinforced in their inaccurate fantasies about women. Myra Marx Ferree (1983), when trying to eliminate the showing of pornographic films in the dormitories at the University of Connecticut, was told by the upperclassmen that it was necessary for the new male students to see the films so they would know how to act on dates. When women outside of pornography are expected to behave as women in pornography do— particularly those women in pornography who "enjoy" pain and brutalization, or are sexually "insatiable"—the stage is set for physical and mental abuse of women. The advent of pornographic home video, both on television and privately purchased, exacerbates this problem. The issue is not primarily the effect of a single film or magazine, but the cumulative effect on women and men of life in a society pervaded by pornography.

Since rape and the response to rape is a paradigm of sexism in society (Bart, 1979a), a reduction of sexism should be reflected in a reduction in rape and attempted rape. In a scholarly book such as this, it is difficult and perhaps inappropriate to express one's feelings after conducting all these interviews. But we cannot simply present a traditional, "professional" data analysis after living with these experiences for over seven years. So, we will end with two poems, because it is the poets who get at the essence of human experience. The first is from a long poem written by a raped woman, describing what is called in other contexts the "rape trauma syndrome" (Burgess and Holmstrum, 1974).

SR-E*

The Rape Journal
by Dell Fitzgerald-Richards (1974)

. . . i did not bring this man upon my self
he came in the night
with knife and mask
I did not invite him into my home or bed

and i have to live with it
to deal with it (oh and i do mean that literally
oh so literally)
deal with it
every day at least once. . . .

i hope that it warns you my luckier sisters
that you will be careful
both night and both day
and be alert
because we are at war even though
we are not ready and
we have not chosen this
not yet at any rate
and i hope that helps you
my other sisters
who have shared my experience . . .
that it will fire your anger
make you learn to fight back and kick and claw
hate even when necessary
more so to know
and be ready for that necessity
perhaps even learn to use knives and guns
but at least your own body
to protect yourself
for i love you my sisters
and we have been playthings too long

The second poem was written anonymously and is about the death of Virginia Woolf. It appeared in the feminist newspaper, *off our backs*, Feb. 2, 1977.

I am thinking of a woman who walked into the waters
    of a river with stones in her pockets
I am thinking of the waters of the rivers of my life
I am thinking of the stones in my pockets
All women are born with stones in their pockets
Empty them. Empty them. Empty them. Swim!

Rape and fear of rape are stones in our pockets. We hope, through this research, to empty them so we can swim.

REFERENCES

Bart, Pauline. 1979a. Rape as a paradigm of sexism in society. *Women's Studies International Quarterly* II (3):347–357.

——. 1979b. Victimization and its discontents. Paper presented at a meeting of the American Psychiatric Association.

Bart, Pauline B., Linda Freeman, and Peter Kimball. 1984. The different worlds of women and men: Attitudes toward pornography and responses to "Not a Love Story" — A film about pornography. Paper presented at the Second International Interdisciplinary Conference on Women, Groningen, The Netherlands. Forthcoming in a Special Issue of the *Women's Studies International Forum* 8(3) in 1985.

Bart, Pauline, and Margaret Josza. 1980. Dirty books, dirty films and dirty data. Observations on pornography research. In *Take Back the Night*, edited by Laura Lederer. 204–217. New York: Thomas Morrow.

Bart, Pauline, and Kim Lane Scheppele. 1983. Through women's eyes: Defining danger in the wake of sexual assault. *Journal of Social Issues* 2:63–81.

Bradley, Marion Z. 1976. *Shattered chain*. New York: DAW Books.

Burgess, Ann Wolbert, and Lynda L. Holmstrum. 1974. The rape trauma syndrome. *The American Journal of Psychiatry* 131:981–986.

Clarke, Lorenne, and Debra Lewis. 1977. *Rape: The price of coercive sexuality*. Toronto, Canada: The Women's Press.

Cohn, E., L. H. Kidder, and J. Harvey. 1981. Crime prevention vs. victimization prevention: The psychology of different reactions. *Victimology: An International Journal* 3:285–296.

Dejanikus, Tacie. 1981. New studies support active resistance to rape. *off our backs*. (February): 9–23.

Donnerstein, Edward, and Daniel Linz. 1984. Sexual violence in the media: A warning. *Psychology Today* 18 (January):14–15.

Ferree, Myra Marx. 1983. Personal communication.

Fitzgerald-Richards, Dell. 1974. *The rape journal*. Oakland, CA: Women's Press Collective.

Fox, Greer Litton. 1977. Nice girl: Social control of women through a value construct. *Signs: Journal of Woman in Culture and Society* 2(4):805–817.

Gearheart, Sally. 1979. *The wanderground — Stories of the hill women*. Watertown, MA: Persephone Press.

Giarrusso, R., P. Johnson, J. Goodchilds, and G. Zellman. 1979. Adolescents' cues and signals: Sex and assault. Paper presented at annual meeting of the Western Psychological Association, San Diego, California.

Griffin, Susan. 1971. Rape: The all-American crime. *Ramparts* 10:26–35.

Gilman, Charlotte Perkins. 1979. *Herland*. New York: Pantheon Press.

Heath, Linda, Margaret Gordon, Stephanie Riger, and Robert LeBailey. 1979. What newspapers tell us (and don't tell us) about rape. Presented at the American Psychological Association meetings, New York.

Henley, Nancy. 1977. *Body politics: Power, sex and non-verbal communications*. Englewood, NJ: Prentice Hall.

Janoff-Bulman, Ronnie. 1979. Characterological versus behavioral self-blame: Inquiries into depression and rape. *Journal of Personality and Social Psychology* 37:1798–1809.

Kanter, Rosabeth Moss. 1977. *Men and women of the corporation*. New York: Basic Books.

Kanter, Rosabeth Moss. 1978. Personal correspondence.

Kidder, Louise H., Joanne L. Boell, and Marilyn M. Moyer. 1983. Rights consciousness and victimization prevention: Personal defense and assertiveness training. *Journal of Social Issues* 39(2):155–70.

Komarovsky, Mirra. 1962. *Blue collar marriage.* New York: Random House.

Lederer, Laura. ed. 1980. *Take back the night: Women on pornography.* New York: Thomas Morrow.

Le Guin, Ursula. 1980. *The left hand of darkness.* New York: Harper & Row.

Lichtenstein, Grace. 1981. The wooing of women athletes. *New York Times Magazine* 130 (February 8):26.

Malamuth, Neil, M. 1981. Rape proclivity among males. *Journal of Social Issues* 37(4):138–157.

Malamuth, Neil, M., and Edward Donnerstein. 1984. *Pornography and sexual aggression.* New York: Academic Press.

McIntyre, Jennie J. 1980. Victim response to rape: Alternative outcomes. Final report to Grant #MH 29045 NIMH.

Morris, Jan. 1974. *Conundrum.* New York: Harcourt Brace Jovanovich.

Neudel, Marian Henriques. 1980. Personal correspondence.

Piercy, Marge. 1976. *Woman at the edge of time.* New York: Knopf.

Pleck, Joseph H. 1981. *The myth of masculinity.* Cambridge, MA: MIT Press.

Queens' Bench Foundation. 1976. *Rape prevention and resistance.* San Francisco, California.

Riger, S., and M. Gordon. 1981. The fear of rape: A study in social control. *Journal of Social Issues* 37(4):71–92.

Russell, Diana. 1980. Pornography and violence: What does the new research say? In *Take back the night: Women on pornography*, edited by Laura Lederer, 218–238. New York: Thomas Morrow.

Schwendinger, Herman, and Julia Schwendinger. 1974. Rape myths: In legal, theoretical and everyday practice. *Crime and Social Justice: A Journal of Radical Criminology* 1 (Spring-Summer):80.

Smith, Don. 1976. Sexual aggression in American pornography: The stereotype of rape. Presented at the annual meetings of the American Sociological Association, New York.

Star, Susan Leigh. 1978. The politics of wholeness, II. *Sinister Wisdom* (5) Winter: 82–105.

Storaska, Frederick. 1975. *How to say no to a rapist and survive.* New York: Random House.

Zillmann, Dolf, and Jennings Bryant. 1982. Pornography, sexual callousness, and the trivialization of rape. *Journal of Communication* 32(4):10–21.

Appendix A:
Getting Better Estimates on Rape

FBI statistics on rape and other crimes underestimate their incidence. This underestimation is particularly important when sexual assault is discussed, because a substantial number of rapes are "unfounded" by the police (not counted as rape). In Chicago this was true for about half of the rapes the women reported to the police. Moreover women are less likely to report acquaintance rapes than stranger rapes, so a bias is built in.

In an effort to get around the problems of the FBI's method of tabulating rape and other crimes, the Law Enforcement Assistance Administration (LEAA) began to collect its own information in 1972. Instead of relying on police reports, the LEAA's National Crime Surveys interview thousands of people each year, obtaining valuable information about the actual incidence of crime.

In 1974–1975, a special survey was done in 26 cities in the United States. About 10,000 households were contacted in each city, with about 22,000 interviews in each city. From this survey, a great deal was learned about rape (McDermott, 1979), since the group of women with sexual assault experiences was large enough to permit detailed analysis of rape by strangers.

These kinds of surveys are more accurate in detailing rapes because they include women who have not reported the rapes to the police. Women are often reluctant, however, to report their experiences to survey interviewers, particularly since many of these interviews are done with other family members present. Some of the same biases that exist with police records also exist with survey responses, because women are much less likely to report rapes by people they know than rapes by strangers; if the event is still very difficult for the woman to talk about, she won't report it to interviewers either. (See Russell and Howell, 1983 for a more detailed critique.)

Victimization surveys report crimes as they are perceived by the people who were subjected to them, not as they are perceived by the police. This is an important difference. If a woman interprets her experience as an attempted rape, then the survey interviewer will mark down "attempted rape" rather than "assault" (which the police might do). While this helps a bit, there is still a technical problem with the victimization survey we will be reviewing. Subjects were first asked if they had been attacked. If the answer was "yes," then the subject was asked how she was attacked and what injuries she suffered. If the subject did not answer "rape" to either of these two questions, then the event was not classified as a rape or attempted rape. No direct questions about rape were asked. We are aware there could still be substantial misclassification of attempted rapes and rapes as lesser crimes such as assault or battery. In addition many women who have had nonconsensual sex do not call it rape.

129

The survey reports the rape rates per 100,000 females 12 years of age or older in the covered area, not for each 100,000 women in the United States. Also provided is information the FBI figures do not give — information about the characteristics of the situation in which the attack occurred. From these figures, we can make better inferences about the risks of rape to different groups of women under a variety of circumstances.

There are two problems, however: The victimization survey only presents results for women attacked in the 26 cities, and rape rates in metropolitan areas are higher than those in nonmetropolitan areas. Because of severe underreporting problems in cases where the rapist was known to the woman, the analysis that we will review was limited to those rapes involving only men not known to the attacked woman. In what follows, then, the rates apply only to women living in metropolitan areas attacked by strangers.

Most of these exceptions work to bring the rate of rape and attempted rape down, even in the victimization surveys. Although reporting metropolitan rapes might inflate the figure a bit, the fact is that most women, about three quarters, live in urban areas in this country, according to the U.S. Census Bureau. In other words, these are probably quite conservative estimates.

Even so, the rape rate for women in this country stood at 255 rapes or attempted rapes per 100,000 women 12 or over in 1974–1975 when this victimization survey was done. We know that official rates have increased almost 50 percent since that time. Rape has reached epidemic proportions.

The most recent data on the prevalence of rape in the United States (Russell and Howell, 1983) is based on a randomly selected sample of 930 San Francisco women who were extensively interviewed. The authors conclude "that there is at least a 26 percent probability that a woman in that city will become the victim of completed rape at some time in her life, and a 46 percent probability that she will become the victim of rape or attempted rape" (p. 692). They conclude that since the rate of rape is larger for the younger cohort, the feminist analysis of rape, which states that sexual violence against women is endemic, is supported by research.

There are, however, some grounds for optimism in these alarming statistics. While the FBI figures indicate that fully 77 percent of rape attacks are "completed," the victimization survey finds just the reverse. Only 33 percent of rape attacks reported to interviewers were completed. That means two thirds of the women who were attacked avoided being raped. The radical difference between the FBI and victimization survey estimates probably results in part from avoiders being less likely to report their attack to the police than to interviewers. The main cause, however, can probably be found in recording more than in reporting. Even when avoiders report, their attacks are seldom recorded by the police as "attempted rape."

THE DISTRIBUTION OF RISK

Not all women are equally likely to be attacked. Although there are no groups of women who are free from sexual attack, some groups are more likely to be attacked than others. Based on evidence gleaned from the 26 cities victimization study (McDermott, 1979), we will quickly review who is at risk.

There is an inverse correlation (starting with mid-teens) between age and chances of being attacked. From mid-teens to the mid-twenties, women have the odds most heavily stacked against them. Women aged 16–19 had a rape rate of 671 per 100,000, of which 64 percent resulted in rape avoidances. Women aged 20–24 had a rate of 712 per 100,000, with a 69 percent avoidance rate. The chances of being attacked rapidly declined after the mid-twenties until age 65 and over, when the rape rate was 29 per 100,000 women. The avoidance rate for this group was only 48 percent, however, indicating that women who are attacked at this age are less likely to avoid being raped (McDermott, 1979).

Race is another significant factor in assessing risk of rape. Black and minority-race women had a much higher rate of attack than white women — 328 compared with 221 (McDermott, 1979).

Women who had never been married and women who were divorced or separated had higher rates of attacks (495 and 400, respectively) than women who were married or who had been widowed (with rates of 123 and 51) (McDermott, 1979). It is probably true that the high rate for single women and the low rate for widows is a function of their age. The difference in rates between married women on the one hand and divorced/separated women on the other is more complex. Since married women who are forced to have sex with their husbands are less likely to consider the forced sex rape, it is less likely to be included in the statistics. Indeed the wording of the victimization study refers to *crimes*, and marital rape has only recently been considered a crime and only in some states under some circumstances. If the difference in rate is "real," it probably reflects the fact that divorced women are more likely to live in areas where there are other women not living with men, and according to the Chicago police, rapists prey on women in those areas. These statistics also demonstrate the function of rape and fear of rape as a means of social control over women. If women learn that it is only by being married that they are afforded protection from rape (unless they are widowed), then this may motivate them to seek protection from men by men.

Women who were in school (467) or were looking for work (433) had higher rates of attack than women who were working for pay (286) or keeping house (194). In addition, the lower the family income of the woman, the higher her chances were of being attacked (McDermott, 1979). This relation between income and risk is partly a function of age (lower incomes are often associated with younger ages) and partly a function of race (black and minority-race women have lower family incomes on average than white women).

REFERENCES

McDermott, Joan. 1979. *Rape victimization in 26 American cities.* Washington, DC: U.S. Department of Justice.

Russell, Diana E. H., and Nancy Howell. 1983. The prevalence of rape in the United States Revisited. *Signs* 8(4):688–695.

Appendix B:
Strengths and Limitations of Our Sample

Our sample underrepresents Black women. While LEAA estimates that 31 percent of all sexually assaulted women are Black, in our study only 15 percent of the women interviewed were Black. Despite our efforts to locate more Black women willing to talk about their experiences, we were unable to increase our numbers. Still, the racial composition of the women in our study was closer to the victimization survey figures than most other similar samples.

In the distribution of women by marital status, our sample does quite well. Although we slightly undersample married women and oversample divorced and separated women, the overall distribution is quite close to the LEAA distribution and much closer than most of the other similar studies. Our sample has 58 percent single women, which is just about identical to national surveys of sexually assaulted women.

In work status, our sample has more employed women than a random national urban sample would have. We have very few women who are homemakers without jobs in the paid labor force. At the same time, we have a generally representative proportion of students and unemployed women, certainly a much more reasonable representation than any of the other studies examined. One of the biggest problems in studies of women who had been raped, from the point of view of sampling design, has been the oversampling of students. This oversampling is probably because many researchers work closely with student populations.

Our sample is somewhat older on average than other similar samples and the LEAA study. Part of the reason for this is that we limited interviews to women who were 18 years old and older. We did this because of problems of obtaining informed consent of women under 18 and still promise complete confidentiality. The rights of minors to confidentiality cannot be insured since parental consent to participate in the study may be needed. As a result, we don't have as many younger women as a random sample of sexual assaults would lead one to expect.

On education, our sample proves to have more years of schooling than one would expect from other samples, but in the absence of national data on educational distribution of assaulted women, it is very difficult to say how far off our sample is. Part of the problem in estimating the relationship between education and sexual assault is that many women are still students (and therefore have not completed their education) when attacked. It is clear, however, that any sample of assaulted women would be in general better educated than the general public, because younger, employed women have more education on average than older women or women who are not in the paid labor force.

On all of the factors associated with the rape event itself, our sample is remarkably close to the national averages. While 33 percent of rape attacks nationally are "completed," about 46 percent of ours were. While 40 percent of attacks nationally involve assailants with weapons, 46 percent of the attacks we are studying did. Virtually identical percentages of women were attacked by multiple assailants in the national and Chicago samples. Although the women in our sample were more likely to have reported their attacks to the police than any other sample we have seen (other than those drawn directly from police records), we are not that far off the national average as reported by LEAA. In our sample, 71 percent of the attacks involved strangers, compared to 82 percent of the national urban sample. Overall, this is quite a close correspondence in the distribution of situational factors.

The validity of our data is strengthened by the fact that we used neither a sample based on official records nor a snowball sample based on friendship chains. However, we must remember that the sample is not random and is vulnerable to the effect of using volunteers. The reality of time and cost constraints limits any study. Using a large random sample from which data are collected systematically is good for some purposes. Such studies are complemented by those using small samples that are studied intensively. Data collected in this manner allow a processual analysis. It was precisely because we had processual data that we could describe how accosted women prevented rape in Chapter 4. We were able to separate those women who talked first and then fought from those who fought first and then talked. Moreover, the nature of our subject matter made a face-to-face interview, with no time limitations, particularly appropriate.

In summary, we believe our sample is much better than might be expected from a convenience sample. The women we talked to were different from other samples of sexually assaulted women because they were disproportionately older, better-educated, working in the labor force, and white. Although our sample is much better than many of the other studies that have used similar methods, it is also important to be aware of the limitations of the sample group.

It is reasonable to assume that the relatively high rate of reporting, 66 percent, stems from the high proportion of rapes by strangers in this sample. Indeed, 75 percent ($n = 50$) of the women attacked by strangers reported their rape to the police, while 44 percent of women attacked by known assailants reported their attacks ($n = 12$).

Additionally when we examine reporting by outcome (rape or rape avoidance), we find that 70 percent ($n = 21$) of women who were raped by strangers reported to the police. Seventy-eight percent ($n = 29$) of women who avoided rape by strangers reported the attack to the police. We cannot attribute the high rate of reporting simply to an interaction among degree of acquaintance, outcome, and reporting. A substantial proportion of women attacked by men they knew in some way also reported the assault to the police. Indeed for avoiders, an equal number of women (seven) who were attacked by strangers and who were attacked by men they knew reported. The women who did not report to the police were asked why they did not. However, the numbers in the different categories are too small to analyze meaningfully. It may be of interest to some readers to know that five women, four avoiders and one raped woman, stated that they did not report the attack to the police because they heard of mistreatment by the police of such cases.

THE INTERVIEWS

When women learned of our study, they called and were asked if they were 18 or over and if they had been attacked within the past 2 years. Both of these questions served as "screeners." The women who answered "yes" to both were then asked whether they had been raped or whether they had avoided rape when attacked. Through answering this question, women defined their own situations as rapes or avoidances. This definition process is significant in itself, because it enabled us to learn what factors went into the self-definition as having been raped or having avoided rape.

At the time of the phone call, the women were told that they would be paid $25 if they completed the interview and that their expenses (carfare, childcare, etc.) would be covered. Confidentiality of individual responses was assured, and mutually convenient times for interviews were arranged.

When the women arrived for the interview, they were asked to fill out a questionnaire including such items as age, marital status, race, and other background questions. This was followed by an in-person interview with either Dr. Bart (80 percent of the interviews) or Dr. Grossman, a female psychologist (20 percent of the interviews). The semistructured interviews consisted of a series of questions that had been pretested with 30 other women.

Because of the exploratory nature of the study, questions were added as patterns began to emerge. Women were encouraged to talk as long as they wanted to, and interviews lasted anywhere from one and one-half to six hours. Women were asked fairly nondirective questions, such as, "Why don't you tell me in your own words what happened?" This enabled women to define the situation any way they wished and allowed them to focus on the aspects of the attack that were especially important to them. Only after a woman's story was complete did the interviewers ask more focused questions to ensure that the same information was available from each woman in the study. Women were not only asked about their attacks, but also about their childhood and adult experiences.

Because there was no time limit for the interviews and the questions covered so many different topics, many of the women were able to talk about very personal matters. It is possible in the interviews to see the intricacies and textures of the lives of these women. We think that the information in these interviews is of exceptionally high quality for these reasons. Women seemed to open up during these sessions, talking quite freely about topics they had often not been able to talk about before. The analysis of their stories and the patterns we observed led to our conclusions about rape and rape avoidance. After the interview the women were told that they could have one psychotherapy session at our expense with either Dr. Marlyn Grossman, one of the interviewers, or Dr. Anne Seiden, a psychiatrist with experience with female victims of male violence. We also offered them information on where they could find self-defense courses and legal assistance.

METHOD OF ANALYSIS

The interviews were taped and transcribed, and about 250 pieces of information were coded from these transcripts to facilitate computer analysis. As it turned out, however, the computer analysis was used only to help us locate possible patterns in the data. We then returned to the transcripts and reread them, looking for patterns the computer suggested we might find. We have only reported the results when the initial hint was confirmed by reading the cases. We present cases as well as tables to back up many of our results. This reflects the view that cases presented in their context are often more informative than descriptions of tables.

The fashion in social science circles these days is to report the results of quite elaborate statistical analyses. We decided against this "data crunching" approach. The following reasons help to explain our decision:

1. With 94 cases, tabular analysis is quickly limited to the scrutiny of very small numbers of variables. It became apparent to us that many of the most interesting patterns in the data involved clusters of variables that would have exhausted the capacity of tables to illuminate the interrelationships.

2. Correlation-based techniques (multiple regression and similar methods) become very difficult to interpret when the dependent variable is dichotomous. In our study, whether a woman avoided rape or was raped was the main thing we wanted to "explain." Under these circumstances, the standard errors of the regression coefficients would have been unreliable, making any evaluation of the significance or even of the size of the coefficients almost impossible.

3. The general solution in these sorts of cases is to use logit models, but the technique is not widely understood in the social sciences and would have greatly limited the audience to which we could speak.

Because of these statistical problems and because we wanted to communicate our findings not only to the academic community, but also to other women who might make use of our findings, we decided to present in this book a more qualitative analysis. It should be noted, however, that many of the patterns that we described in the data were first seen on the green and white computer paper generally associated with quantitative inquiry. The computer in this study was used primarily as a signaling device. We used it to locate the patterns, which we then went back to the cases and confirmed. What we have presented are the conclusions and the cases.

VARIABLES COLLECTED BUT NOT ANALYZED

An attempt was made to measure the extent to which the women in the study held values that were consistent with traditional or feminist sex role perspectives. The hypothesis, of course, was that women who held traditional values would be more likely to use more passive strategies when confronted with a rape scenario. Responses to the five items were collected as part of the interview (Miller, 1979). Subsequent analyses indicated that there was virtually no variance in the responses provided, because answers were almost uniformly nontraditional.

The variable of whether the woman grew up in a high crime or dangerous area had to be discarded because whether the neighborhood was considered dangerous varied systematically. Thus, while whites considered Hyde Park a dangerous neighborhood, Blacks considered it safe. What we are tapping is relative safety and danger—what Hyde Park is being compared to. Blacks differentiate between housing projects, which they call "the ghetto," and the southeast section of Chicago other than the projects. These neighborhoods are considered safe, compared with "the ghetto," although whites would consider them dangerous. Were we to redo the study we would ask more precise questions on their neighborhood experiences to ascertain whether or not they had "street smarts," a factor that presumably would be associated with rape avoidance.

The other following variables were rejected because of low intercoder reliability:

1. Strength of assailant.
2. What the woman thought being raped would be like (before the attack) and whether her ideas have changed.
3. What the woman believed she would do about a rape (before her attack).
4. How violent a woman thought a rape would be.
5. The woman's experience of the rape (pain, anger, hatred, impersonal).
6. Mechanical precautions the woman had taken in her house or apartment when she moved in.
7. Flashbacks to prior rape or attempted rape.

REFERENCE

Miller, P. Y. 1979. Female delinquency: Fact and fiction. In *Female adolescent development*, edited by Max Sugar. New York: Brunner/Mazel.

Appendix C:
The Women's "Legal Claim"

We are including this appendix, even though it does not bear directly on the factors that are associated with avoiding rape, for the following reasons.

First, many states are currently revising their sexual assault laws and knowing the relationship between the woman's self-perception and the legal definition of what occurred facilitates basing policy change on social science data. One purpose of this study is to provide a data base for social policy.

Second, one of the rape myths is that women frivolously bring charges against innocent men for vindictive purposes or in order to provide an acceptable excuse to significant others (e.g., parents of an unmarried woman living at home) for having intercourse. None of the women in this study brought charges when they had no legal claim. In fact, 23 of the women who had legal claims did not report these claims to the police, even though 11 of them were raped, sodomized, and/or forced to perform fellatio.

Process of Determining the Women's "Legal Claim" in the Sexual Assault

Since we have complete reports of the incidents from the woman's point of view (and since this is generally all police or lawyers have to go on when they categorize a case), we evaluated all the cases, indicating what charges could be brought against the attacker if the case came to court.

We assumed that all of the cases would be brought in Chicago under then existing Illinois criminal law. Since most interviews were conducted in Chicago, this was a reasonable assumption. But a number of the respondents were attacked in places other than Chicago, including several in foreign countries. Whether the woman would be able actually to bring a suit in the jurisdiction where the event occurred, we cannot say.

We assumed away some of the most difficult problems that confront lawyers in deciding which cases actually to bring to trial. We make no judgment about the sufficiency of the evidence, since our information on that aspect of the prosecution is incomplete. We have assumed that women's stories can be supported by admissible evidence in sufficient quantity to warrant a full prosecution. In addition, we have assumed a lack of consent, since all but two of the women in our study reported to us that they made some substantial effort to resist. In these two cases, however, it seemed clear to us that it would be extremely difficult to show that the woman failed to consent. In one case, a woman ran into her former boyfriend and spent the night with him. He raped her when she had fallen asleep, even though she had refused sex because she did not have her diaphragm with her. In the other case a woman was entertaining a friend's son with whom she had considered having intercourse. In both cases there was little resistance, although each woman indicated to us that she did not want intercourse at that time.

While in a real prosecution, multiple charges would be filed against the offender, in our study we have used only the most serious offense. Multiple codes would, in our view, add confusion rather than clarity. Thus a case that could be prosecuted as rape and robbery we have counted as rape, and a case that included both home invasion and attempted rape was counted as only home invasion. Seriousness, for the purpose of coding, was defined as the maximum length of sentence one could get for such a crime.

We have assumed that the women would be willing to report all of these incidents to the police. In fact, this did not occur. Twenty-nine percent of our respondents did not report to the police the attacks that they reported to us. In evaluating these cases, conservative criteria were used. Legal definitions of the crime codes were obtained from the Illinois criminal code.

Women Who Say They Were Raped

In each of these 38 cases, the victims were forced to have sexual intercourse against their will. A total of 15 of the 38 cases also could be prosecuted for deviate sexual assault, meaning that they also involved anal sex, and/or either type of oral sex. Two of the raped women experienced what the law considered deviate sexual assault without rape, and one raped woman, who was stripped, kissed, fondled and had a knife stuck between her legs, had a strong case for attempted rape. Finally, the two women who considered themselves raped, yet have no legal claim, were the two who did not forcefully resist the attack and who would not have objected to having a sexual relationship with the men in question at some other time.

Women Who Say They Avoided Rape

The avoiders have much more varied legal claims. Two women actually experienced penetration, but both were able to make the attacker stop. The three cases of deviate sexual assault involved one case of fellatio, one case where the attacker forced cunnilingus on the woman, and one case where a woman was forced at gunpoint to engage in cunnilingus with her roommate. Fourteen of the avoiders experienced what the law would be willing to call attempted rape. All of these cases involved the man either ripping the woman's clothes off or informing her he was going to rape her (in conjunction with a physical attack) or getting on top of the woman with both of their clothes removed. The one case of attempted deviate sexual assault involved a husband separated from his wife who attempted to sodomize her in front of their young son.

There was one case each of home invasion and armed robbery, and one case each of burglary and robbery. All four of these cases involved a specific sexual component. The home invasion case involved a man armed with a knife who climbed in the woman's window and got into bed with her. The armed robbery occurred only after one of the attackers digitally penetrated the woman's vagina at knife point. The burglary involved a man climbing in a second-floor window and kissing and fondling the woman before her screams scared him away. And the robbery occurred only after the woman was knocked to the ground, and the man ripped her coat open.

The aggravated battery and simple battery cases are similar. In almost all of the cases, there was an explicit sexual component, although not enough to be called an attempted rape. The main characteristics distinguishing the aggravated battery from the simple battery cases was the presence of a weapon during the attack. Typical battery cases in our study are those where a stranger attacked a woman on the street or in her apartment lobby, grabbing at her breasts or her crotch, or wrestling her to the ground while trying to stick his hand in her pants.

The assault cases involved a man threatening a woman. The two aggravated assaults included weapons as part of the threat. The one of simple assault involved a man running threateningly at a woman at night on an otherwise deserted street.

Unlawful restraint and attempted kidnapping are similar offenses, the former occurring when a man refuses to let a woman move from where he first confronts her and the latter occurring when a man attempts to force a woman to move somewhere else with the intention of concealing her. In one unlawful restraint case, a woman was held at gunpoint while the attacker's associates raped her friend. One of the attempted kidnapping cases was a man trying to drag a woman into a car.

In one case a male stranger who pulled up in his car next to a woman and offered her money if she would have sex with him was subject to a charge of pandering. A month later, he approached her on the street and began asking questions and following her. Given his previous behavior, this second otherwise unactionable encounter could be the occasion to arrest him for the first.

Finally, there are three cases among the avoiders in our study where the women had no legal claim. All three occurred in the course of an ongoing dating or friendship relation.

Appendix D:
The Conceptual Scheme

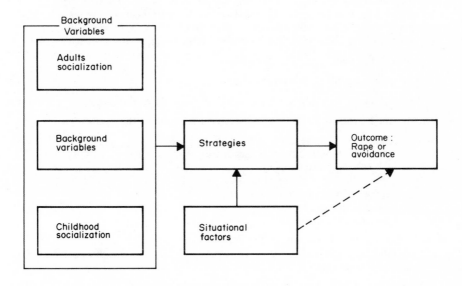

Dotted line: This is theoretically possible, but did not occur in our study.

Appendix E:
Self-Report Questionnaire

The purpose of this study is to obtain from women who were victims or potential victims of a sexual assault some information about themselves, their assailants and their experiences. Before discussing your experiences, we would like to have some general information about your background. Your replies to the questions below (and to the questions raised in the interview) will be confidential. Your identity will be protected in any use of the responses you provide. As you complete this questionnaire, if you have any questions feel free to ask about them. Please read the following statement which says that you, of your own free will, are willing to be interviewed. If you agree with the statement on the form, please sign your name.

1. How old are you? _____ years

2. Approximately how tall are you? _____

3. Approximately how much did you weigh at the time of the assault? _____

4. How much schooling had you completed at the time of the assault?

    a. less than 8th grade
    b. some high school but didn't graduate
    c. high school graduate or GED
    d. some college but didn't graduate
    e. degree from junior college
    f. degree from four year college
    g. post-graduate work

5. If you are currently employed, or have ever been employed, what kind of work do you usually do? _____ (such as secretarial, waitress, teacher, etc.)

6. What kind of work did you do at the time of the assault? _____

7. In what religion were you raised?

    a. Catholic
    b. Protestant
    c. Jewish
    d. Other (which)? _____
    e. no religion

8. In what country were you born?

    a. U.S.A.
    b. other (specify) _____

9. Who did you live with most of the time before your 14th birthday?

    a. mother and father
    b. mother and stepfather
    c. mother only
    d. father and stepmother
    e. father only
    f. other relations
    g. others, not related

10. What kind of work did your father (or stepfather) do (such as plumber, engineer, factory worker, teacher) most of the time when you were growing up?

_____

11. How much schooling did your father (or stepfather) complete?

    a. less than 8th grade
    b. some high school but didn't graduate
    c. high school graduate or GED
    d. some college but didn't graduate
    e. degree from junior college
    f. degree from four year college
    g. post graduate work
    h. don't know

12. Did your mother (or stepmother) have a job outside the home most of the time when you were growing up?

    a. yes, she had a full-time job
    b. yes, she had a part-time job
    c. no, she didn't work outside the home

13. If she was employed, what kind of work did she do (such as secretary, factory worker, teacher. etc.)? _____

14. How much schooling did your mother (or stepmother) complete?

    a. less than 8th grade
    b. some high school but didn't graduate
    c. high school graduate or GED
    d. some college but didn't graduate
    e. degree from junior college
    f. degree from four year college
    g. post graduate work
    h. don't know

15. How many older brothers or step-brothers do you have? _____

16. How many older sisters or step-sisters do you have? _____

17. How many younger brothers or step-brothers do you have? _____

18. How many younger sisters or step-sisters do you have? _____

19. What is your marital status?

    a. married, living with husband
    b. married, but not living with husband
    c. divorced

    d. widowed

    e. never married (If never married, skip to question 25).

20. How many times have you been married? _____

21. How many years living with (present) husband? _____

22. How old were you when you were married (the first time)? _____

23. What kind of work does your husband (or former husband) do? (Such as plumber, engineer, factory worker, teacher, etc.) _____
_____

24. How much schooling did your husband (or former husband) complete?

    a. less than 8th grade
    b. some high school but didn't graduate
    c. high school graduate or GED
    d. some college but didn't graduate
    e. degree from junior college
    f. degree from four year college
    g. post graduate
    h. don't know

25. Who do you live with?

    a. my husband
    b. my husband and my children
    c. my children
    d. my parents
    e. a man who is not my husband
    f. one or more women friends
    g. a group of men and women
    h. alone
    i. other (specify) _____

26. How many children have you had? _____

Appendix F:
Case Profiles

INTRODUCTION

We are presenting the data in this form because in the text we identified women by case number, giving little additional information about them. Therefore we are including this summary of cases by number so that the reader may learn more about the women being discussed. Additionally, reading through this abstract of the cases can familiarize the reader with the data, since it is only in this appendix that some relevant demographics, the strategies the woman used, and her self-definition are included. We are not presenting more information (e.g., exact age, occupation) so as to reduce the probability of the woman being identified. This omission fulfills our commitment to the NIMH and the women that the data would be confidential.

Information on each woman in our study will be presented as follows:

a. Age of the woman
b. Religion
c. Race
d. Birth order
e. Number of assailant(s)
f. Race of assailant(s)
g. Weapon
h. How well did the woman know the assailant(s)
i. Woman awake or asleep
j. Woman alone or in the company of another person
k. Strategies employed by the woman
l. What sexual acts took place
m. Woman's definition of herself as a raped woman or an avoider

CASE PROFILES

Case 1

a. Under 30 years of age
b. Greek Orthodox
c. White
d. Oldest
e. one assailant
f. Hispanic
g. saw a knife
h. stranger
i. woman was awake
j. woman was alone
k. scream, physical force, affective verbal strategies
l. no acts took place
m. Rape Avoider

Case 2

a. Over 30 years of age
b. Protestant
c. White
d. Oldest
e. one assailant
f. Black
g. took her cane and threatened her with it; said he had a gun
h. stranger
i. woman was awake
j. woman was alone
k. cognitive verbal strategy
l. tried to penetrate her but was physically impossible due to vaginal shrinkage caused by radiation therapy
m. Rape Avoider

Case 3

a. Under 30 years of age
b. Protestant
c. Black
d. Not oldest
e. one assailant
f. Black
g. did not see, but a "pointed object" was put to her back
h. stranger
i. woman was awake
j. woman was alone
k. fled
l. no acts took place
m. Rape Avoider

Case 4

a. Over 30 years of age
b. Jewish
c. White
d. Oldest
e. one assailant
f. Black
g. no weapon
h. stranger
i. woman was awake
j. woman was alone
k. affective verbal strategy
l. vaginal intercourse, sodomy, fellatio
m. Raped

Case 5

a. Under 30 years of age
b. Catholic by choice, although raised Protestant
c. Black
d. Youngest
e. one assailant
f. Black
g. saw a gun
h. stranger
i. woman was awake
j. woman was alone
k. cognitive, affective verbal, fleeing strategies
l. no acts took place
m. Rape Avoider

Case 6

a. Under 30 years of age
b. Jewish
c. White
d. Oldest daughter
e. one assailant
f. Black
g. long rat tail comb used as a weapon
h. stranger
i. cognitive verbal strategy
j. vaginal intercourse twice
k. Raped

Case 7

a. Under 30 years of age
b. Catholic

c. Hispanic
d. Not oldest
e. one assailant
f. Hispanic
g. saw a razor
h. worked in school she attended
i. woman was awake
j. woman was in the company of a female friend
k. cognitive verbal strategy
l. no acts took place
m. Rape Avoider

Case 8

a. Under 30 years of age
b. Protestant
c. Black
d. Oldest
e. four assailants
f. two Black, two White
g. saw both a gun and a knife
h. strangers
i. woman was awake
j. woman was in the company of two other women
k. cognitive verbal, environmental intervention strategies
l. no acts took place
m. Rape Avoider

Case 9

a. Under 30 years of age
b. No religion, although parents were non-practicing Catholics
c. White
d. Oldest daughter
e. one assailant
f. White
g. no weapon
h. stranger
i. woman was awake
j. woman was alone
k. screamed, physical force, cognitive verbal strategies
l. assailant put his hand down her pants
m. Rape Avoider

Case 10

a. Over 30 years of age
b. Catholic
c. White

d. Oldest
e. one assailant
f. White
g. no weapon
h. met him in a bar earlier that evening
i. woman was awake
j. woman was alone
k. physical force, cognitive verbal strategies
l. fondling and touching of sexual parts, kissing
m. Rape Avoider

Case 11

a. Over 30 years of age
b. Catholic
c. White
d. Oldest
e. one assailant
f. Black
g. saw a knife
h. woman was awake
i. woman was alone
j. stranger
k. cognitive and affective verbal strategies
l. vaginal intercourse, cunnilingus, fondling and touching of genitals
m. Raped

Case 12

a. Under 30 years of age
b. Catholic
c. White
d. Not oldest
e. one assailant
f. Black
g. no weapon
h. woman was awake
i. woman was alone
j. knew him by sight and by name; met him that day
k. screamed, physical force, fled, and cognitive verbal strategies
l. digital penetration of vagina; fondling of genitals
m. Rape Avoider

Case 13

a. Over 30 years of age
b. Protestant
c. Black

d. Oldest
e. one assailant
f. Black
g. used cord from phone to attempt strangulation
h. knew him from church; had been working with him
i. woman was awake
j. woman was alone
k. screamed, physical force, cognitive verbal strategies
l. slight vaginal penetration
m. Rape Avoider

Case 14

a. Under 30 years of age
b. Protestant
c. Black
d. Not oldest
e. two assailants
f. Black
g. saw both a knife and a gun
h. knew them by sight
i. woman was awake
j. woman was alone
k. fled, screamed, physical force strategies
l. numerous acts of vaginal intercourse; fellatio
m. Raped

Case 15

a. Under 30 years of age
b. Protestant
c. White
d. Oldest
e. one assailant
f. White
g. no weapon
h. stranger
i. woman was awake
j. woman was alone
k. fled, screamed, physical force, and cognitive verbal strategies
l. vaginal intercourse, kissing, touching of breasts
m. Raped

Case 16

a. Under 30 years of age
b. No religion
c. Oldest daughter

d. White
e. two assailants
f. White
g. no weapons
h. stranger, although picked her up while she was hitchhiking
i. woman was awake
j. woman was alone
k. cognitive verbal strategy
l. vaginal intercourse; kissing
m. Raped

Case 17

a. Under 30 years of age
b. Jewish
c. White
d. Youngest
e. one assailant
f. Black
g. saw a knife
h. stranger
i. woman was awake
j. woman was alone
k. screamed, used physical force
l. vaginal intercourse
m. Raped

Case 18

a. Under 30 years of age
b. Jewish
c. White
d. Only child
e. one assailant
f. Black
g. no weapon
h. had seen him on the street a few minutes before the assault
i. woman was awake
j. woman was alone
k. affective verbal strategy
l. kissing
m. Rape Avoider

Case 19

a. Over 30 years of age
b. Protestant
c. White
d. Oldest
e. one assailant
f. White
g. no weapon

h. used his professional services several times over a 5-year period
i. woman was awake
j. woman was alone
k. physical force, cognitive verbal strategies
l. partial penetration, manipulation of breasts
m. Rape Avoider

Case 20

a. Over 30 years of age
b. Protestant
c. Black
d. Not oldest
e. one assailant
f. Black
g. said he had a gun; felt something cold and metal
h. stranger
i. woman was awake
j. woman was alone
k. fled, screamed, cognitive verbal strategies
l. no acts
m. Rape Avoider

Case 21

a. Over 30 years of age
b. Protestant
c. White
d. Not oldest
e. two assailants
f. Black
g. saw a gun
h. strangers
i. woman was awake
j. woman was alone
k. cognitive verbal strategy
l. vaginal intercourse with both assailants
m. Raped

Case 22

a. Under 30 years of age
b. Jewish
c. White
d. Oldest daughter
e. one assailant
f. White
g. saw a gun
h. stranger
i. woman was awake

j. woman was alone
k. fled, physical force, cognitive verbal strategies
l. licked her crotch
m. Rape Avoider

Case 23

a. Under 30 years of age
b. Protestant
c. Black
d. Oldest
e. one assailant
f. Black
g. thought he might have a gun; something was covered with a cloth
h. stranger
i. woman was awake
j. woman was alone
k. screamed, cognitive and affective verbal strategies
l. vaginal intercourse, fellatio
m. Raped

Case 24

a. Under 30 years of age
b. Catholic
c. Black
d. Only child
e. two assailants
f. Black
g. no weapons
h. strangers
i. woman was awake
j. woman was in company of a female friend
k. physical force, environmental intervention and cognitive verbal strategies
l. fellatio
m. Rape Avoider

Case 25

a. Under 30 years of age
b. Protestant
c. White
d. Not oldest
e. one assailant
f. unsure of race, as did not see
g. no weapon per se, but smothered with blanket
h. assumes stranger

i.   woman was asleep
j.   woman was alone
k.   physical force and affective verbal strategies
l.   vaginal intercourse
m. Raped

Case 26

a.   Over 30 years of age
b.   Protestant
c.   White
d.   Oldest
e.   one assailant
f.   Black
g.   saw a knife
h.   face seemed familiar, but basically a stranger
i.   woman was awake
j.   woman was alone
k.   fled, screamed, environmental intervention and cognitive verbal strategies
l.   kissed and fondled her
m. Raped

Case 27

a.   Over 30 years of age
b.   Jewish
c.   White
d.   Not oldest
e.   one assailant
f.   White
g.   no weapon
h.   a date, although a casual date
i.   woman was awake
j.   woman was alone
k.   physical force, cognitive verbal strategies
l.   vaginal intercourse
m. Raped

Case 28

a.   Over 30 years of age
b.   Jewish
c.   White
d.   Oldest daughter
e.   one assailant
f.   Black
g.   saw and had used on her a knife
h.   stranger
i.   woman was awake
j.   woman was alone
k.   cognitive verbal strategy

l.   vaginal intercourse
m. Raped

Case 29

a.   Under 30 years of age
b.   Catholic
c.   White
d.   Youngest
e.   one assailant
f.   White
g.   saw a knife
h.   stranger
i.   woman was awake
j.   woman was alone
k.   cognitive verbal strategy
l.   vaginal intercourse, digital penetration, sodomy, fellatio
m. Raped

Case 30

a.   Under 30 years of age
b.   Protestant
c.   White
d.   Not oldest
e.   one assailant
f.   White
g.   no weapon
h.   sister's boyfriend
i.   woman was awake
j.   woman was alone
k.   physical force, affective and cognitive verbal strategies
l.   vaginal intercourse, fellatio
m. Raped

Case 31

a.   Under 30 years of age
b.   Catholic
c.   Black
d.   Oldest daughter
e.   one assailant (two instances)
f.   Black
g.   no weapon
h.   friend of a former boyfriend; boyfriend's cousin
i.   woman was awake
j.   woman was alone
k.   screamed, physical force, affective and cognitive verbal strategies
l.   vaginal intercourse both times
m. Raped

Case 32

a. Under 30 years of age
b. Protestant
c. White
d. Oldest
e. one assailant
f. White
g. no weapon
h. traveling companion of a man she knew
i. woman was asleep
j. woman was alone
k. screamed, cognitive verbal strategies
l. kissing
m. Rape Avoider

Case 33

a. Under 30 years of age
b. Protestant
c. White
d. Not oldest
e. two assailants
f. Black
g. said they had a knife, although not seen
h. strangers
i. had fallen asleep and at that time the assailants grabbed her
j. woman was alone
k. cognitive verbal strategy
l. vaginal intercourse
m. Raped

Case 34

a. Under 30 years of age
b. Protestant
c. White
d. Oldest daughter
e. one assailant
f. White
g. no weapon
h. landlord
i. woman was awake
j. woman was alone
k. screamed, physical force, and cognitive verbal strategies
l. fondling of breasts, kissing
m. Rape Avoider

Case 35

a. Over 30 years of age
b. Catholic
c. White

d. Oldest
e. one assailant
f. Black
g. saw a gun
h. stranger
i. woman was awake
j. woman was alone
k. environmental intervention, affective and cognitive verbal strategies
l. no acts
m. Rape Avoider

Case 36

a. Under 30 years of age
b. Protestant
c. White
d. Oldest
e. one assailant
f. Black
g. said he had a knife, but she never saw one
h. stranger
i. woman was awake
j. woman was alone
k. cognitive verbal strategy
l. no acts
m. Rape Avoider

Case 37

a. Over 30 years of age
b. Catholic
c. Hispanic
d. Not oldest
e. one assailant
f. Hispanic
g. used a belt to try and strangle her
h. may have met him earlier through her son; saw him afterward
i. woman was asleep
j. woman was alone
k. fled, cognitive verbal strategies
l. vaginal intercourse
m. Raped

Case 38

a. Under 30 years of age
b. Protestant
c. White
d. Youngest
e. one assailant
f. White

g. no weapon
h. stranger
i. woman was awake
j. woman was alone
k. fled, screamed, physical force, and cognitive verbal strategies
l. no acts took place
m. Rape Avoider

g. no weapon
h. had bothered her once before on the street
i. woman was awake
j. woman was in the company of a small child
k. fled, cognitive verbal strategies
l. no acts took place
m. Rape Avoider

Case 39

a. Under 30 years of age
b. Jewish
c. White
d. Not oldest
e. one assailant
f. Black
g. no weapon
h. knew vaguely from school and the neighborhood
i. woman was awake
j. woman was alone
k. fled, screamed, physical force, and cognitive verbal strategies
l. vaginal and anal digital penetration
m. Rape Avoider

Case 42

a. Under 30 years of age
b. No religion
c. White
d. Not oldest
e. one assailant
f. Hispanic
g. no weapon
h. lived in her building and she knew him
i. woman was awake
j. woman was alone
k. screamed, physical force, environmental intervention, cognitive verbal strategies
l. acts not disclosed
m. Rape Avoider

Case 40

a. Under 30 years of age
b. Catholic
c. White
d. Not oldest
e. one assailant
f. Black
g. saw a gun
h. stranger
i. woman was awake
j. woman was alone
k. cognitive and affective verbal strategies
l. vaginal intercourse, digital vaginal penetration, cunnilingus, fondling and touch of sexual parts, kissing
m. Raped

Case 43

a. Under 30 years of age
b. Protestant
c. White
d. Not oldest
e. one assailant
f. Black
g. saw a gun
h. stranger
i. woman was awake
j. woman was alone
k. no strategies
l. vaginal intercourse
m. Raped

Case 44

a. Under 30 years of age
b. Catholic
c. White
d. Oldest daughter
e. one assailant
f. White
g. saw a knife
h. stranger

Case 41

a. Over 30 years of age
b. Catholic
c. White
d. Oldest
e. one assailant
f. White

i. woman was awake
j. woman was alone
k. screamed, affective and cognitive verbal strategies
l. vaginal intercourse
m. Raped

Case 45

a. Under 30 years of age
b. Protestant
c. White
d. Oldest
e. one assailant
f. Black
g. no weapon
h. stranger
i. woman was awake
j. woman was alone
k. screamed, affective and cognitive verbal strategies
l. vaginal intercourse, kissing
m. Raped

Case 46

a. Under 30 years of age
b. Protestant
c. White
d. Not oldest
e. one assailant
f. Black
g. no weapon
h. she designated him as a friend
i. woman was awake
j. woman was alone
k. cognitive verbal strategy
l. vaginal intercourse
m. Raped

Case 47

a. Under 30 years of age
b. No religion
c. White
d. Oldest
e. two assailants
f. Black
g. saw a knife
h. strangers
i. woman was awake
j. woman was in the company of a female companion

k. fled, physical force, environmental intervention, cognitive verbal strategies
l. digital vaginal penetration, fondling and touching of sexual parts, kissing
m. Rape Avoider

Case 48

a. Over 30 years of age
b. Jewish
c. White
d. Oldest
e. two assailants
f. Black
g. saw a gun
h. strangers
i. woman was awake
j. woman was alone
k. screamed, cognitive and affective verbal strategies
l. vaginal intercourse, fellatio, fondling and touching of sexual parts, masturbation by one assailant between the woman's legs
m. Raped

Case 49

a. Over 30 years of age
b. Jewish
c. White
d. Not oldest
e. one assailant
f. Black
g. thought it was a knife, felt it against her neck, could have been a scissors
h. stranger
i. woman was awake
j. woman was alone
k. cognitive verbal strategy
l. vaginal intercourse, had to masturbate rapist
m. Raped

Case 50

a. Under 30 years of age
b. Catholic
c. White
d. Oldest daughter
e. one assailant
f. White
g. saw an ice pick

h. stranger
i. woman was awake
j. woman was alone
k. screamed, physical force, cognitive verbal strategies
l. fellatio, fondling and touching of sexual parts
m. Raped

Case 51

a. Under 30 years of age
b. Protestant
c. White
d. Not oldest
e. one assailant
f. Black
g. no weapon
h. stranger, although had briefly interacted with him on the street
i. woman was awake
j. woman was alone
k. physical force, cognitive verbal strategies
l. fellatio, kissing, had to masturbate the rapist
m. Raped

Case 52

a. Under 30 years of age
b. Jewish
c. White
d. Oldest daughter
e. one assailant
f. Black
g. no weapon
h. stranger
i. woman was asleep
j. woman was alone
k. screamed, physical force, cognitive verbal strategies
l. vaginal intercourse
m. Raped

Case 53

a. Under 30 years of age
b. Catholic
c. Black
d. Oldest
e. one assailant
f. Hispanic
g. no weapon
h. co-worker
i. woman was awake

j. woman was alone
k. fled, physical force, environmental intervention, cognitive verbal strategies
l. tried cunnilingus, fondling and touching of sexual parts, rubbed his body on her
m. Rape Avoider

Case 54

a. Under 30 years of age
b. Catholic
c. Hispanic
d. Oldest
e. one assailant
f. Hispanic
g. no actual weapon, used towel to smother her
h. stranger
i. woman was awake
j. woman was alone
k. affective verbal strategy
l. vaginal intercourse, digital vaginal penetration, sodomy, fondling and touching of sexual parts, had to masturbate rapist
m. Raped

Case 55

a. Under 30 years of age
b. Protestant
c. White
d. Not oldest
e. one assailant
f. Black
g. saw a butcher knife, said that he had a gun
h. stranger
i. woman was awake
j. woman was in the scenario with another woman and a man
k. vaginal intercourse, fellatio, rammed a wine bottle up her vagina, forced to perform cunnilingus on the other woman, rammed the handle of the knife up her vagina
l. environmental intervention, cognitive verbal strategies
m. Raped

Case 56

a. Under 30 years of age
b. Protestant
c. Black

d. Only child
e. five assailants
f. Black
g. saw a gun
h. knew them from the neighborhood; two had tried to date her
i. woman was awake
j. woman was alone
k. physical force, cognitive verbal strategies
l. vaginal intercourse, unclear if anything else
m. Raped

d. Only child
e. one assailant
f. White
g. no weapon
h. boarder in boarding house in which she was staying
i. woman was awake
j. woman was alone
k. cognitive verbal strategy
l. began vaginal intercourse but switched to anal intercourse; kissing
m. Raped

Case 57

a. Under 30 years of age
b. Protestant
c. White
d. Not oldest
e. one assailant
f. Black
g. saw a knife
h. was a resident in the residential center in which she worked
i. woman was asleep
j. woman was alone
k. screamed, physical force, environmental intervention strategies
l. no acts
m. Rape Avoider

Case 60

a. Under 30 years of age
b. Catholic
c. White
d. Oldest
e. one assailant
f. White
g. drugged the woman
h. was an acquaintance; worked with him
i. woman was drugged
j. woman was alone
k. affective verbal strategy
l. from the nature of her injuries, both vaginal and anal intercourse
m. Raped

Case 58

a. Under 30 years of age
b. Protestant
c. White
d. Oldest daughter
e. one assailant
f. White
g. saw a knife
h. stranger
i. woman was asleep
j. woman was alone
k. fled, screamed, physical force, cognitive verbal strategies
l. attempted digital vaginal penetration, fondling her breasts
m. Rape Avoider

Case 61

a. Under 30 years of age
b. Jewish
c. White
d. Oldest
e. one assailant
f. Black
g. saw a hammer
h. stranger
i. woman was awake
j. woman was alone
k. screamed, affective and cognitive verbal strategies
l. fondling breast, not sure if vaginal or anal intercourse
m. Raped

Case 59

a. Under 30 years of age
b. Greek Orthodox
c. White

Case 62

a. Over 30 years of age
b. Catholic
c. White

d. Oldest
e. one assailant
f. Black
g. no weapon that she saw
h. stranger
i. woman was awake
j. woman was alone
k. fled, screamed, physical force strategies
l. no acts took place
m. Rape Avoider

Case 63

a. Over 30 years of age
b. No religion
c. White
d. Only child
e. one assailant
f. Black
g. knife she saw
h. relative stranger; had interacted with him briefly prior to assault
i. woman was awake
j. woman was alone
k. screamed, cognitive verbal strategies
l. fellatio, cunnilingus, manipulation of breasts, digital vaginal penetration, vaginal intercourse
m. Raped

Case 64

a. Over 30 years of age
b. Catholic
c. White
d. Only child
e. one assailant
f. Black
g. saw a knife and had it used on her
h. stranger
i. woman was awake
j. woman was alone
k. no strategies
l. vaginal intercourse, fondling of breasts
m. Raped

Case 65

a. Under 30 years of age
b. Jewish
c. White
d. Not oldest
e. one assailant
f. Black

g. saw a knife
h. stranger
i. woman was asleep
j. woman was alone
k. no strategies
l. vaginal intercourse
m. Raped

Case 66

a. Over 30 years of age
b. Catholic
c. White
d. Not oldest
e. one assailant
f. White
g. no weapon
h. well known to the woman
i. woman was awake
j. woman was alone
k. no strategies
l. vaginal intercourse
m. Raped

Case 67

a. Under 30 years of age
b. Catholic
c. White
d. Not oldest
e. one assailant
f. White
g. no weapon
h. had hitched a ride with the man
i. woman was awake
j. woman was alone
k. fled, physical force, cognitive verbal strategies
l. kissing
m. Rape Avoider

Case 68

a. Under 30 years of age
b. Jewish
c. White
d. Oldest
e. one assailant
f. White
g. saw a knife
h. had stopped at her home for directions and interaction minimal
i. woman was awake

j. woman was alone
k. fled, cognitive verbal strategies
l. no acts took place
m. Rape Avoider

Case 69

a. Over 30 years of age
b. Protestant
c. White
d. Oldest
e. one assailant
f. Black
g. no weapon
h. stranger
i. woman was asleep
j. woman was alone
k. cognitive verbal strategy
l. kissed, fondled breast
m. Rape Avoider

Case 70

a. Under 30 years of age
b. Catholic
c. White
d. Oldest
e. six assailants (juveniles)
f. five Black, one White
g. no weapon
h. had seen them in the area
i. woman was awake
j. woman was alone
k. fled, physical force strategies
l. touched her in the "most intimate places"
m. Rape Avoider

Case 71

a. Under 30 years of age
b. Catholic
c. White
d. Oldest
e. one assailant
f. Hispanic
g. saw a knife
h. stranger
i. woman was awake
j. woman was alone
k. fled, environmental intervention, cognitive verbal strategies

l. rubbed up against her, touched her
m. Rape Avoider

Case 72

a. Over 30 years of age
b. Catholic
c. White
d. Oldest
e. one assailant
f. Black
g. saw a gun and a lead pipe
h. had briefly interacted with him earlier
i. woman was awake
j. woman was with her husband
k. cognitive and affective verbal strategies
l. no acts took place
m. Rape Avoider

Case 73

a. Under 30 years of age
b. Protestant
c. White
d. Oldest daughter
e. one assailant
f. White
g. no weapon
h. stranger
i. woman was awake
j. woman was alone
k. screamed, physical force strategies
l. grabbed her breast, fondled her buttocks
m. Rape Avoider

Case 74

a. Under 30 years of age
b. Protestant
c. White
d. Oldest
e. one assailant
f. Black
g. no weapon
h. relative stranger; had to come to his home for an interview
i. woman was awake
j. woman was alone
k. screamed, physical force, cognitive verbal strategies
l. digital vaginal penetration, fondling and touched sexual parts
m. Rape Avoider

Case 75

a. Over 30 years of age
b. Protestant
c. White
d. Not oldest
e. one assailant
f. White
g. no weapon
h. stranger
i. woman was awake
j. woman was alone
k. fled, screamed strategies
l. grabbed genitalia
m. Rape Avoider

Case 76

a. Over 30 years of age
b. Catholic
c. White
d. Oldest
e. one assailant
f. White
g. no weapon
h. stranger
i. woman was awake
j. woman was alone
k. affective verbal strategy
l. no acts took place
m. Rape Avoider

Case 77

a. Over 30 years of age
b. Protestant
c. White
d. Oldest
e. one assailant
f. Black
g. stranger
h. saw a knife
i. woman was awake
j. woman was alone
k. physical force, cognitive verbal strategies
l. vaginal intercourse, kissed
m. Raped

Case 78

a. Under 30 years of age
b. Protestant
c. White

d. Oldest
e. one assailant
f. Black
g. no weapon
h. estranged husband
i. woman was awake
j. woman's child was present
k. environmental intervention, physical force, affective and cognitive verbal strategies
l. rubbed himself between her buttocks but no penetration
m. Rape Avoider

Case 79

a. Under 30 years of age
b. Jewish
c. White
d. Not oldest
e. one assailant
f. Black
g. never saw or was threatened with a weapon
h. stranger
i. woman was awake
j. woman was alone
k. screamed, affective verbal strategies
l. no acts took place
m. Rape Avoider

Case 80

a. Over 30 years of age
b. Jewish
c. White
d. Not oldest
e. one assailant
f. White
g. no weapon
h. husband
i. woman was awake
j. woman was alone
k. physical force, cognitive verbal strategies
l. vaginal intercourse, fondling of breasts
m. Raped

Case 81

a. Under 30 years of age
b. Catholic
c. White
d. Youngest

e. one assailant
f. White
g. no weapon
h. date
i. woman was awake
j. woman was alone
k. cognitive verbal strategy
l. kissing
m. Rape Avoider

Case 82

a. Over 30 years of age
b. Protestant
c. White
d. Not oldest
e. two assailants
f. Black
g. no weapon
h. strangers
i. woman was awake
j. woman was alone
k. screamed, physical force, environmental intervention strategies
l. no acts took place
m. Rape Avoider

Case 83

a. Under 30 years of age
b. Catholic
c. White
d. Oldest daughter
e. one assailant
f. Black
g. no weapon
h. stranger
i. woman was awake
j. woman was alone
k. screamed, physical force strategies
l. no acts took place
m. Rape Avoider

Case 84

a. Over 30 years of age
b. Catholic
c. White
d. Only child
e. one assailant
f. White
g. no weapon

h. stranger
i. woman was awake
j. woman was alone
k. screamed, physical force strategies
l. no acts took place
m. Rape Avoider

Case 85

a. Under 30 years of age
b. Catholic
c. Hispanic
d. Not oldest
e. one assailant
f. Hispanic
g. no weapon
h. man she was dating
i. woman was awake
j. woman was alone
k. screamed
l. vaginal intercourse
m. Raped

Case 86

a. Under 30 years of age
b. No religion
c. White
d. Oldest
e. one assailant
f. said he had a weapon but not shown
g. Black
h. stranger
i. woman was awake
j. woman was alone
k. environmental intervention, cognitive verbal strategies
l. no acts took place
m. Rape Avoider

Case 87

a. Under 30 years of age
b. Jewish
c. White
d. Oldest
e. one assailant
f. Black
g. saw a gun
h. roommate had briefly interacted with him
i. woman was awake
j. woman was in the company of a female friend

k. fled, screamed, cognitive verbal strategies
l. perform cunnilingus on her roommate and allowed her roommate to perform cunnilingus on her
m. Rape Avoider

Case 88

a. Under 30 years of age
b. Jewish
c. White
d. Oldest daughter
e. one assailant
f. Black
g. no weapon
h. relative stranger, although appeared to be a friend of two women hitchhikers the woman had picked up earlier
i. woman was awake
j. woman was alone
k. screamed, physical force, cognitive and affective verbal strategies
l. no acts took place
m. Rape Avoider

Case 89

a. Under 30 years of age
b. Protestant
c. Black
d. Not oldest
e. one assailant
f. Black
g. no weapon
h. employer
i. woman was awake
j. woman was alone
k. fighting back, talking and yelling
l. genital intercourse
m. Raped

Case 90

a. Over 30 years of age
b. Catholic
c. White
d. Oldest
e. one assailant
f. White
g. no weapon
h. husband
i. woman was asleep
j. woman was alone

k. no strategies
l. anal intercourse
m. Raped

Case 91

a. Under 30 years of age
b. Catholic
c. White
d. not available
e. three assailants
f. Hispanic or Italian
g. no weapon seen, but hit with object
h. strangers
i. woman was awake
j. woman was alone
k. fought, screamed, said she had VD
l. was unconscious part of the time because of physical beatings, so she doesn't know exactly what happened
m. Rape Avoider

Case 92

a. Under 30 years of age
b. Catholic
c. White
d. Only child
e. one assailant
f. White
g. threatened with flashlight
h. stranger
i. woman was awake
j. woman was alone
k. physical strategies and cognitive verbal strategies
l. kissing, breast grabbed, hand put down her pants
m. Rape Avoider

Case 93

a. Under 30 years of age
b. Catholic
c. White
d. Not oldest
e. one assailant
f. Black
g. stranger
h. no weapon
i. woman was awake
j. woman was alone

k. yelled judo yell followed by "Get outta here" and swung her bag at him
l. no acts
m. Rape Avoider

Case 94

a. Under 30 years of age
b. Catholic
c. White

d. Not oldest
e. one assailant
f. Black
g. stranger
h. no weapon
i. woman was awake
j. woman was alone
k. threatened to kill him, put her fist in his throat, called him a rapist, pushed him
l. no acts
m. Rape Avoider

Appendix G:
Case Transcript

INTRODUCTION

We here present a transcript of one complete interview. Proper names and places have been edited to preserve confidentiality. This transcript will give the reader a better understanding of the interview procedure and the extent of the women's responses.

TRANSCRIPT

PB: Would you tell me in your own words what happened?

S: I was at my apartment. This was back in March. It was right around . . . I was taking a take-home final exam that I had been working on for many hours and I was not very much with it at that point. And it was right around primary election time and I had had several campaign workers at my door the previous week, and when this guy came, I answered the door with the chain over it as I usually did, and he asked me if I was registered to vote and he had some literature and stuff and that had set my mind at ease, "Oh, another campaign worker," you know. So I undid the chain on the door to take the literature out of his hand and he pushed the door and entered the apartment. And it took me, well, it seems, in retrospect, a surprisingly long time—you know, like a half a minute or so—to realize that something was amiss, you know . . . that this wasn't right and that . . . he was taking off his coat, you know, and . . .

PB: What was it that made you feel that something was amiss?

S: That . . . oh, I had taken the literature out of his hand and was reading over it and it didn't mean anything, it wasn't campaign literature, and I said, "This doesn't mean anything to me." And he started acting kind of confused and by that time he had taken his coat off and he was handing it to me to hang it up and something wasn't going right, but I still couldn't quite make sense out of the situation, and he started to say, "Well, can I use the phone?"—acting as though he inadvertently took a wrong turn somewhere, you know. And I said, "The phone is over there." But he didn't move toward the phone. He pushed back on me against the . . . we hadn't moved from the doorwell. It amazes me, I get so nervous every time I tell the story. And . . . pushes me back against the doorwell, and that was when it started falling in place that this guy was not working for someone running in the primary and that I was in trouble.

PB: It was when he pushed you against the doorwell, not when you didn't know . . . not when you saw that the literature didn't mean anything . . .

S: Right, that's . . . something seemed funny then, but it still wasn't _____ something was really amiss. And my first reaction was, "I'm taking a final exam. You can't be interrupting me!" — this kind of thing — "I don't want to have to deal with this. I've got to be able to think!" And, he . . . I pushed him back after he had pushed me initially. I pushed him back against the other side of the doorwell. And he said, "I want to have a relationship with you." And . . . I pushed him back. I said, "There will be no relationship." And . . . he . . . started . . . feeding me a lot of lines like, "Don't get me angry," "Act like a lady," "Be nice," "Calm down," you know, "Don't raise your voice." And he was getting kind of hyper. He didn't seem to be armed or anything, at least he didn't show any weapon. He had . . . I hadn't hung up his coat, so he dropped it on the floor or something . . . he had some comment, "This could take a while," you know. And . . . I said "There would be no relationship," and . . . he . . . We spent some amount of time more or less verbally jockeying for position. My . . . my initial reaction was fear — this stunned kind of thing, you know. And that, thankfully, left at some point. And I realized that I was supposed to know what to do in these kind of situations!

PB: Why did you think you were supposed to know?

S: I had spent so much time doing self-defense (clinics). I had worked on the work with rape counseling centers and in my angrier days, I was convinced I would wring the neck of any man who had approached me . . . I was suddenly feeling like an absolute marshmallow. And I remember saying to him, of all stupid things, "I don't want your blood and guts on my floor. I don't want to hurt you, but I will kill a rapist." And he was really . . . he stepped back and said, "Oh, now you're calling me a rapist, are you." I said, "You've pushed your way into my apartment and you have no right to be pushing yourself on me like this. Yes, I'm calling you a rapist." And I told him to pick up his hat and his coat and leave. And, he did. Now, that's the end of the story, he left, you know, and I was really relieved. The whole scene, though, went on about ten minutes and the inner — about the inner five, you know — was, as I say, kind of bantering for position, you know that . . . we must have pushed each other back and forth across that doorwell half a dozen times . . . and . . . we kept really steady eye contact and were just talking to each other . . .

PB: Is this something you learned . . . by keeping eye contact . . . is that something you learned in self-defense or . . .

S: One of the first things that came to me is that . . . was — how can I say it — that I was a human being and he was infringing on my, you know, my space and to let him know that very quickly. And I did say to him, you know, that you have no right to be doing this, you know, this is . . . I'm a human being! . . . you know, this kind of thing. "And you have no right to touch me." That didn't really seem to make an impression, but the eye contact was really important to me because I felt that . . . that . . . somehow we were communicating . . . that eventually he did back down and eventually I did get the upper hand and that when I told him to leave, he did. Also . . . I didn't . . . I remember pushing back against him and feeling his ribs right at my fingertips, you know, and feeling a real strength but just the complete impotence of his . . . of his . . . you know, all of his threats were just kind of dissipating, you know, because he seemed so absolutely . . . so completely uncapable of carrying them out, you know. He seemed really incompetent generally. And I think that's . . . certainly looking at his record and his performance in court and stuff like that, that was very much borne out . . . but, uh . . . it . . . it wasn't . . . you know, it wasn't like a really dangerous situation for me, you know, and I guess my reaction to it afterwards, I was really shaken, but . . . in retrospect, I mean, he doesn't strike me as a really dangerous kind of character. I can't really give myself much credit for being able to handle the situation.

PB: Oh, I don't know. I would not say that.

S: Well . . . he's . . .

PB: I'm not just saying it to support you, I mean, not that I wouldn't support you, but I would guess that many women would not have—I can't tell you how many, because I haven't done my analysis or anything—but like certainly a substantial proportion of women would have allowed him to rape them under those circumstances.

S: Well . . . something that had really crossed my mind and that I had never understood before and it really hit home was the idea that I want to get this thing over with, you know, I want to get him out of my apartment so, you know, I can return to normalcy, so to speak and . . .

PB: And take your take-home exam.

S: Right, you know, as quickly as possible. And I want this to be, you know, as neat a scene. And for the first time it really made sense to me where . . . you know, why women would give a little . . . they have maybe some inviolable line that they won't go beyond but up to that point . . . "Well, it's better than getting killed" kind of thing. That wasn't the alternative I was confronted with, but it really made sense to me then as it never had before the idea of just, you know, "Take what you want and get out of here!" kind of thing, you know, this . . . kind of a . . . "Let's get this over with!"—you know . . . and, uh . . . that's . . . . That was very surprising to me . . . it was really . . . .

PB: I want to clarify . . . did at any point you think that he might kill you?

S: No. First, he wasn't armed and it was . . . and . . . his initial presence was stunning and frightening, but subsequently, as I mentioned, he just struck me as being a weaker and weaker type person, you know, that . . . unable to even carry out his own threats, unable to really even take care of his own stance, much less be aggressive.

PB: Now, some women, in order to get the guy out real fast, would have just let him rape them and _____ leave real fast, but you didn't choose that alternative.

S: Right.

PB: I mean, well some women will tell me, "Well I just wanted to get it over with." You know, that kind of thing. But I thought you said something . . . that it crossed your mind that you could understand why women might . . .

S: Yeah . . . well, that . . . that I was really struck by . . . the . . . the . . . move not to make this messy, you know, not to make it too disruptive, we're going to have this very . . . you know . . . I didn't . . . I didn't at any point seriously think of striking him, you know, just punching him out or kneeing him in the groin, you know. I did crunch my fist and I put it, you know, to his throat and when I was saying that I would kill him . . . and I think . . . I mean, I know at that point that I really was just . . . just trembling with a kind of determination that I know at that point that I meant it . . . that I didn't use any violence on him at all, and . . . and . . . prior to that I had been talking and talking very calmly with him, and he said at some point, "I really like you. Do you like me?" You know? It was just this . . . it was really a piercing kind of thing . . . such an emotional (wrought) kind of situation, you know, it was . . . so much unlike I would have imagined any kind of (interview) with an assaulter.

PB: What was your idea of what rape would be like or an attempted rape would be like? Assault, or whatever?

S: Well . . . as a very impersonal kind of thing, I mean, I think . . . by . . . at least it strikes me it almost seems very . . . the meaning of rape . . . that the woman is not a human being . . . she's an instrument . . . some kind of political pawn, I don't know quite how to put it, but that the last thing that a rapist would want from a woman that he's going to rape would be her to like him, you know.

PB: Is this the rapist that tried and raped a whole bunch of women in Hyde Park and wrote this letter to one of them? Or was this a different rapist, because _____ was involved with that guy and I'm curious because I had one of his subjects, too . . . .

S: Well, I don't think that this man would write notes, so I think that's a different person. I say that because he doesn't strike . . . I mean, he didn't strike me as being educated enough to write notes. In fact in court he mentioned he had been through first grade . . . O.K.? But he had been . . . there were two other assaults right in the same time, but the women did not press charges . . . .

PB: O.K., I just wondered, because I'm always pretty _____ because who else gets caught.

S: Right! Exactly!

PB: While you were on the phone, you said that while you had been trained in self-defense you didn't use it. Now, it could be that my self-defense class, which is really dirty street fighting — it's _____ course, which I'm almost finished with — is different from your training, but my perception is you did stuff that one learns and I just wonder what you meant when you said you didn't use it . . . .

S: In my mind, I did use it — 100 percent — I mean, again, a thought that raced through my mind was my karate instructor's line that the best fight is the one that doesn't have to be fought.

PB: Yeah.

S: And that was something I really wanted to carry out right here on the spot, you know, I wanted to have enough mastery of the situation that I didn't have to fight.

PB: So you are saying that you did use . . . .

S: So . . . yes . . .

PB: O.K., fine, because I was . . . you know, I have a friend, too, who is a purple belt who said, "Well, I didn't use it," except she did, really, in a sense, you know, the assumption being that you _____ or something, I don't know. I mean, it seemed to me that you did. But I just wanted your perception of that.

S: In my mind, that . . . I really have no qualms about how I acted . . . I don't feel badly about it, but when I . . . when the police . . . I think why I say I didn't really use it is that I would never try to justify that, I mean like when the police came and they said, "You say you know karate. Why didn't you use it!?" — you know — or, "These women who think they can take care of themselves . . . " was a line I got . . .

PB: Oh, wonderful . . .

S: . . . that "I know there's one of our . . . one of our girls at the police station has been taking self-defense and one of these times I'm going to come up from behind her and startle her and I bet she'll scream" — you know, this kind of thing. Really digging kind of cuts at women . . . I mean, "I did not brutally attack him" was signed "I did not use karate," so that's the spirit in which I'm saying I didn't use it.

PB: I don't want to put words in your mouth, but I think you _____ what your karate instructor said.

S: Yeah.

PB: Now I'm going to ask you a whole bunch of questions. I will not ask you questions that you've already told me unless I want to get it worded precisely for coding purposes. You have the misfortune of being interviewed after I have started coding and I know all the ambiguities, which will make it much more useful an interview for me but may make it a little more boring for you.

O.K., what time of day was it?

S: About 3:10 . . . 3:10.

PB: In the afternoon?

S: Yes.

PB: And it was a weekday or weekend?

S: Weekday.

PB: O.K., weekday. And you said it was March, and that's of, let me see, '78. One assailant. Had you ever seen him before?

S: No.

PB: About how tall is he?

S: Five-nine, five-ten.

PB: And how's he built? Heavyset, average, light.

S: I would say light. As I said when I pushed back I felt his ribs right there. He was kind of a skinny guy.

PB: Was he white, black, Spanish (-speaking) . . .

S: He was black.

PB: About how old was he?

S: Late twenties.

PB: Do you know if he was married? Did that come out in the course of . . .

S: Not to my knowledge. I would think not, but I guess if you can get better records there, then I would go ahead . . .

PB: Do you know what kind of work he did? Roughly.

S: Well, he had been in and out of jail for ten years, and I don't think that he had a consistent job.

PB: He had sexually assaulted women before, you told me.

S: Yes.

PB: Did he _____ and everything?

S: Well, I . . . told me of the concurrent cases, but then, also in the . . . and she also was talking about his record . . . that he had been in jail for several years for attempted rape and previous assaults—I mean, I saw his record . . .

PB: . . . he seemed _____ for getting into jail for attempted rape. O.K., at the time you were a student, right?

S: Right.

PB: You were living in Chicago. How long had you lived in Chicago?

S: I had moved here last September.

PB: Now you said that you were so tired because you were taking your exam, but some people have told me that they just sort of had a feeling like that that wasn't their day and other people didn't have any kind of feeling like that. Did you have any kind of feeling like that?

S: No. The exam was even going well.

PB: Now . . . you first realized you might be in danger not when you saw the primary literature wasn't primary literature, but when—what was it, he gave you his coat, or he pushed you . . .

S: He pushed me back against the door.

PB: How would you say that he first communicated to you that he intended to sexually assault you rather than do something else to you.

S: When he said, "I want to have a relationship with you" and pushed me back against the door, I didn't think he meant an intellectual conversation.

PB: Or taking your money.

S: Right.

PB: O.K. You were in your house. _____ it's harder to get out of it if you're in your house.

S: I don't know, I felt safer in being in my own territory than I may have felt elsewhere . . . being in my own element.

PB: On-the-street contingency you might have . . . I mean, like you might scream and somebody might hear, or a police car might _____ while in your house _____.

S: That's true . . . that's true.

PB: The question is, how much time elapsed after he communicated his intent to assault and the assault, and it seems to me it was sort of simultaneous, if you consider his pushing you an assault.

S: Right.

PB: O.K., now, after he communicated his intent to assault, I have a lot of adjectives from another study, so that I can — which I didn't write — so I can use comparative data, so some of these sound silly. That's why I'm asking you these apparently silly adjectives, and it has to do with how you perceived his manner. Now did he seem charming?

S: No.

PB: Did he seem (helpful)?

S: No. This is right as he's pushing me back against the door, saying "I want to have a relationship with you"?

PB: Did he seem threatening?

S: Yes, initially.

PB: Did he seem contemptuous?

S: No . . . he seemed very angry.

PB: You hesitate a lot on "contemptuous" and that's why . . . .

S: Yeah, I . . . it's no . . . that . . . I was just thinking back to the overwhelming feeling that I got as I was looking at his eyes . . . not that he was a hateful person, but that he was full of hate, is what I was saying . . .

PB: Did he seem afraid?

S: Yeah.

PB: Did he seem calm and matter-of-fact?

S: No.

PB: Did he seem righteous?

S: No.

PB: Did he seem sexually aroused?

S: No.

PB: Are there any other adjectives about him that you would like to mention?

S: Angry. Driven . . . he seemed a little compulsive, a little agitated. Nervous, unsure of himself.

PB: What made you think that he seemed unsure of himself and nervous and agitated and driven and very angry?

S: Well, it seemed like . . . boy, I (do) don't want to play amateur psychologist, but I just got the impression that he was . . . that his anger was just like driving him to do something, you know, to go through this assault thing, but he was caught in his own incompetence, you know, so he seemed to be like waging his own war with this overpowering anger and his own fear, you know. Like when I told him . . . After I'd looked over the literature and said "This means nothing to me," he seemed like at a loss for, like, "What do I do next? Where's the cue card?" kind of thing, and he was just kind of staring at me blankly for a minute, you know, just . . . and then he said, "I want to have a relationship with you."

PB: Now when you said that you will kill a rapist and he said, "Oh, so you think I'm a rapist . . . " "Now you're calling me a rapist . . . " do you think that he didn't think he was a rapist?

S: Yeah . . . yeah . . . I think that it really didn't dawn on him that . . . what kind of violation he was after. I think, also, that maybe he just saw that as an "out," that, you know, that was time to leave, you know . . . .

PB: O.K., now, did you have a plan when you realized that something was going wrong?

S: No. I don't think I had any plan, but . . . if there was a plan, it had crossed my mind to . . . to . . . establish my own ground and defend it kind of thing, but let him know, let him see me as a person, and, if that counts as a plan, I don't know.

PB: It's . . . yeah . . . you behaved in a very direct and consistent way, and I don't know how much of that just happened automatically or how much of that was a conscious thing, but it was a very logical kind of thing that you did, so what I'm trying to figure out is how much that was something _____ because you wanted to establish your own ground, right, and defend yourself and have him see you as a person. Now, having him see you as a person, the eye contact was part of that. Establishing your own ground was pushing him?

S: Uhm . . . yeah . . . but I thought I meant that a bit more figuratively, too, just to defend some footing kind of thing, you know.

PB: Do you remember when you threatened him, you said you would kill a rapist, but was that like an unconscious thing or was that something that you thought about doing?

S: I did not think about doing it until it was done . . . I mean, the words to me seemed (distilled) I can't believe I said them, more or less, you know . . . but, you know, it was very spontaneous, but it . . . it went in line with a growing sense of . . . of control that I was feeling in the situation evidently.

PB: O.K., so, did the way he acted influence you know the kinds of things that you were doing?

S: Yeah, yeah . . . I think that there was definitely an exchange going on there.

PB: And they influenced your response . . . wait a second, I have two questions here and I want to see if we can differentiate them. One is, did the way the assailant acted influence your plan — let us assume that, you know, what you did was planned, it was sort of this, as you say, to establish your own personal ground and defend it — did the way he acted influence the plan or would that have happened regardless of how he had acted?

S: Well the plan was general enough that, yes, I would say that it would have happened anyway. I mean, it wasn't . . .

PB: In other words, you're saying that the plan was not affected by his behavior or was affected by his behavior.

S: My *actions* were affected by his behavior, I'll put it that way.

PB: O.K., fine, that's a distinction. Your actions . . . yes. And do you want to specify how your actions were affected by his behavior?

S: Uhm . . . well I didn't know what I was going to do, but it slowly . . . but, of

course, the action kind of unfolded with the exchange, you know . . . uhm
. . . and . . . I kept . . . I was getting progressively more assertive and com-
manding in what I was saying . . . uhm . . .

PB: Why were you doing that? I mean, you said you were in control, I mean, was
there something that he was doing or not doing in respect . . .

S: Yeah . . . it was definitely a point at which he back down. I told him to take
his hands off of me and he did and that was when it kind of clicked that
"We're getting somewhere" you know.

PB: At what point did you tell him to take his hands off you and he did?

S: Well, as I'd mentioned, we'd kind of pushed each other back across
the . . . and he had pushed me back and he had his hands on my . . . on the
top part of my arms, and we were . . . we were talking . . . and . . . I told
him — I don't remember what precipitated the comment — but I said, "Take
your hands off of me." And he dropped his hands.

PB: That was before you put your fist at his throat?

S: Oh yeah . . . yeah. Because that was the last thing I did.

PB: O.K. Did he try to steal anything?

S: No.

PB: Do you know if he was drinking?

S: Uhm . . . I didn't detect any alcohol on his breath, and we were rather close!

PB: Do you think he was on any drugs before the assault?

S: Uhm . . . he seemed very spacey, but I don't think he was on drugs, I think he
was just spacey.

PB: Had you been drinking prior to the assault?

S: No. Coffee.

PB: Had you used drugs, and this is like immediately prior to the assault?

S: No.

PB: O.K., I'm asking about clothes now, you know, not because I think that
women are provocative, but it has to do, particularly on street stuff, with getting away. That's why, you know, I guess, I always apologize for asking . . .
O.K., were you wearing a skirt or pants or other . . .

S: It was . . . like a . . . housedress, I don't know what to call it . . . like a . . .
kind of a robe sort of thing . . .

PB: Well, if I call it a bathrobe, would that be O.K., or . . . ? Or a caftan, or . . . ?

S: Yeah, a caftan. I don't know how that would code up in a book . . .

PB: What kind of shoes were you wearing?

S: None.

PB: Were your hands free?

S: Yeah.

PB: O.K . . . . now, help me try to get your compliance . . . what was the most
coercive thing that he did?

S: Uhm . . . the most force that he showed was in pushing me back against the
wall. His most demanding verbal _____ with the effect of "Act like a lady,
or I'll hit you," you know, this kind of thing . . .

PB: He did threaten to hit you a few times?

S: Yeah . . . yeah . . . "Act like a lady or I'll hit you. Don't raise your voice or
I'll hit you," you know, this kind of thing. And again, I have to hand it to the
karate, that you no longer get worried about pain . . .

PB: You no longer get worried about . . .

S: Being hit, I mean it doesn't strike you as being a threat anymore!

PB: That is very interesting . . . we'll have to go through that . . . O.K . . . . "Act
like a lady." That's such a wonderful line! I think I may call an article that:

"Act like a lady, or I'll (rape you)." That's a wonderful line! I mean it's so . . .

S: Oh, he'd be proud!

PB: Contradictory. Uhm . . . O.K., now, you resisted . . . uhm . . . both by talking and forcibly, by pushing him back . . . O.K., so let me see, you talked to him, you maintained your territory, you pushed him back and then at some point he dropped his hands and then you made the threat, you know, you said the thing about, you know, you would kill a rapist and you don't want his blood and guts on the floor . . .

S: Yeah, what had happened . . . I told him to drop his hands and he did . . . and there was a little bit more exchange of conversation, and then he pushed me back again . . .

PB: Do you remember what the exchange was?

S: Oh, boy . . . I jotted some things down after it had happened, but I . . . I'm not so hot on order at this point . . . The sense that I remember, though, is that "Oh, we're really getting nowhere," you know. That was what provoked me to putting my fist under his throat and pushing him back and telling him I would kill him.

PB: Yeah, because he tried . . . after he dropped his hands, then he started again . . . .

S: Yeah, then he started in again and it . . . you know . . . it seemed sick like and I thought, wait a minute, try a different tactic or something like this, you know, and . . . that was when I was more forceful, you know, and . . .

PB: So you just like put your fist at his throat; you didn't push his whatever . . . .

S: Yeah, I made contact, you know, but did not . . .

PB: You made contact with the . . .

S: The jugular . . .

PB: The thing you're supposed to push.

S: I made contact, but I wasn't hurting him at all.

PB: O.K., you answered this one before, that you were not concerned with being killed . . . you were . . . what would you say you were primarily concerned with?

S: I think the concern changed. At the outset, while I was feeling frightened and stunned, I was concerned with being raped. I mean, at the outset it seemed like a possibility . . .

PB: Being raped . . . .

S: Yeah, it seemed . . . or compromised in some self-respect kind of way, you know. Then I was . . . immediately it was the concern that I'm not going to be able to think, you know, I've lost my concentration for the day kind of thing . . . scrap this day, this is not going to be a pleasant scene. Then I was concerned with getting it over with as quickly as possible and getting him out of my apartment. Then . . . after that concern kind of faded and I just . . . there was none that . . . came in its place.

PB: There is something that emerged from the study that I didn't expect at all, but I'll tell you after the interview . . . . At what point do you think that he decided not to rape you?

S: I think right at the end.

PB: You mean when you put your . . . .

S: I got the impression that he abruptly decided, "This is it. I'm leaving" kind of thing, then . . . if he had changed his mind earlier about assaulting me, then it really didn't come across.

PB: And what do you think made him decide that?

S: Uhm . . . because I think . . . maybe two things: he wasn't getting anywhere and I think he realized that and also the overwhelming anger that I detected at the first wasn't there at the end. It seemed to be a lot more of a confusion and nervousness, and, offering him a way out, he wanted to take it kind of thing.

PB: Do you think there was anything you could have done that would have made it turn out differently?

S: . . . . Well, yeah . . . sure . . . I mean . . . Yes. I'm sure that there are things that could have theoretically happened that would have made it turn out differently, but I'm . . . the more I think about it, the more what I did seems in line with my character. Then . . . so I don't know if, practically speaking, I could have done anything else. I don't know how much weight to put on the word "could" in there but . . . .

PB: Did you report the incident . . . . Well, do you think that if you laid down on the floor he would have raped you, or he would have like changed his mind and left?

S: I think that if I had been very compliant . . . victim . . . that he would have *tried* to rape me. I'm not sure if he would have succeeded under even the best of circumstances . . . you know, best for him, but . . . yeah . . . that certainly seemed on his mind.

PB: Now, you did call the police. Did you tell anyone . . . how did the police know you knew self-defense, by the way?

S: Oh, because they'd asked me what had happened. They wanted the story and . . . I told them . . . I perhaps . . . I didn't mention this that when I had pushed him back, I told him "There's a _____ by the door," my karate _____ was standing right at the door. And I said, "And I know karate and I will kill a rapist." I did tell him I knew karate. That was it. And . . . so when the police heard that, you know, I mean it was just food for, you know, "Razz her!"

PB: The woman down in Hyde Park is wonderful . . . . the policewoman down there . . . .

S: Well the two police officers that came to my apartment—there were four initially, then two went out and got_____, the guy, the assaulter. But the other two were just . . . they were, by far and away, the least pleasant to deal with, out of the whole crew, and it was really . . . and I was feeling just the most vulnerable then . . . But they even gave me the line of, "Do you always let men into your apartment?"

PB: You know, and just last night, I'm telling this commander what's-his-name that the police have improved.

S: Well, after that, after those two, the rest were very nice, you know, and I even mentioned to subsequent officers that the first two had told me that.

PB: I have been informed to report to (whatever his name is) . . . I told him . . . . What were the names of the people who were obnoxious? If you want to tell me . . . .

S: I can't remember. You know, in fact, later, in the police car, when we were going down there, that line was still burning in my ears, and I said, "Boy, I'd always been told that police officers ask, 'Do you always let men into your apartment?' and I'm so disappointed to find out it's true." The officer said, "I didn't say that!" So it wouldn't do any good, at this point, to report his name.' But I really don't remember it.

PB: O.K. Did you tell anyone else?

S: Subsequently, yes. I told, you know, several people . . . family and friends and stuff.

PB: What was their reaction?

S: They were generally very supportive . . . very supportive.

PB: Was there any difference between the response of men and the response of women?

S: My father, bless his heart, felt . . . uhm . . . compelled to remind me that not all men are like that!

Tape 1, Side 2

PB: O.K., we were talking about gender differences in response and you told me that your father and told me that there really wasn't any other (men) and that you had mainly told women. Was it that you didn't find many differences because you just told very selected men or because, in fact, there weren't differences, or . . . .

S: Well, I would say that any differences in response would be characteristic of the differences in the friendships I had with the two. I mean that my closest friends were women and so, of course, the response was more extensive there. And the men who knew, you know, could have been people I work with, you know, I wasn't . . . Over my numerous court dates the story came out . . . "Where's she today? "Oh she's down at court again," you know . . . So there were several people at work who knew about it. But, you know, I don't interact as much with the men at work as I do with my women friends, so, there would be a difference there.

PB: O.K. I asked you what your idea was about what being raped would be like before . . . and . . . have your general ideas about rape changed from your own experience, or do you just think this particular rapist was not the way you imagine rape?

S: Well, my general ideas about rape are probably pretty much as they were before. It's not that I see this as a striking exception, it's just that — or this rapist as a striking exception — but . . . my own situation takes on more dimension . . . the general view, you know . . . it's . . . no, I wouldn't say that I . . .

PB: Well I think . . . I'm trying to remember what you said, I have it written down because it wasn't on this part of the tape but I asked you . . . you said you thought it would be . . . it would be a less personal kind of a thing and you still think of rape essentially as an impersonal thing?

S: Well . . . I think of it . . . I think what struck me as unusual about this is that . . . uhm . . . that the assaulter did come to see me as a person enough to respect my ground, you know. That's what strikes me as unusual. Maybe that's exactly why the situation diffused, you know, I don't know, but I think of rape as being, that that doesn't happen, that the assaulter never does see the woman as a person.

PB: Now, I do not mean to be contentious, but you said that he respected your ground, he did drop his hands, but then he started again.

S: Yeah, right.

PB: So, it didn't seem to have a lasting (effect) unless I'm misperceiving what you told me.

S: Well, what I meant is that he did leave, without assaulting me . . . well, he did assault me, but he didn't . . . .

PB: I know what you mean. Where did you get your ideas about rape?

S: Initially . . . initially my ideas were . . . uhm . . . from childhood horror stories more or less. And they very much followed the stereotypes about rape, that it happened in dark alleys and so on like that. They were drastically revised through my work at _____ and reading, such as Brownmiller's book and reading on the politics of rape and so on.

PB: How did you feel about the man at the time of the assault?

S: . . . . Uhm . . . Initially, I was surprised, stunned and afraid. As the scene went on and as it ended, I just felt . . . real . . . boy I hate to use this word — pity. I mean, "pity" sounds so condescending, but I think that's even what I felt . . . my heart went out to him. He just seemed to be such an incredibly incompetent character, but it wasn't sympathy, it was a pity.

PB: Yeah, pity not sympathy — that's interesting. Now, I'm going to talk about stages. One of my consultants said I should talk about stages in the analysis because it's real hard to analyze what happened and you specifically talk about stages, so I just want to note that we an use your data in terms of stages.

How do you fell about the man now?

S: Sad . . . I feel sad about him. Pity, still, I would say.

PB: Is he in prison now?

S: Allegedly. I haven't followed it up, but he got five years . . . he was sentenced . . . it was last spring, so he should still be in prison.

PB: How did you know to go to _____, or did they tell you?

S: _____ called when I was at the police station and it was . . . it was really very nice that I had gotten down there and was talking to a number of detectives and the University had sent down the "Duty Dean."

PB: Oh, yeah . . . they don't like their women to be messed with.

S: Well, he was very nice, you know, just a very pleasant person and no sooner had he arrived then she was on the phone, too and she wanted to know if I wanted her to come down and would I have any trouble identifying, and so she kept in constant contact with me and we went to court together, six of the times I had to go.

PB: Six continuances?

S: No, not all continuances. He didn't show up for the first two, and they finally got him — he didn't show up for the first three it was . . . once he . . . he was there and got out on bond, and then he skipped bond, then he was in the hospital, then they couldn't get him from the prison to the courtroom that one day, and they didn't do it the next day . . .

PB: He was in prison that whole . . .

S: Well he was on and off. After he had forfeited bond . . .

PB: Yeah . . . you said that at work they would say things like, "Oh _____ going to court again." Did you have any trouble getting the time off from work?

S: No, there wasn't any problem. It's pretty flexible, you know.

PB: You know, because like some people can't and some people can, you know.

S: Yeah, I thought it was, you know, a tremendous amount of effort to expand on this one case, but . . .

PB: Do you think if _____ hadn't been there that you would have gone through with it?

S: She was certainly a help, and I don't mean to undermine her role at all, but, yes I would have . . . I was pretty . . . because I didn't know there was even such a person when I decided to go through with it and to have quit at any point after that decision would have seemed like a cop-out to me.

PB: That's interesting. It's just a very difficult thing to go through the whole court procedure, and I'm trying to figure out — although that is not the purpose of this research — the decision, the factors that go into _____ that's all.

S: Well, parenthetically, if I had felt uncomfortable about the experience, — or more uncomfortable or something — I don't think it would have been such a certain decision.

PB: Do you think that your experience working with crisis helped you, you know, deal with the whole thing?

S: Yeah. I didn't actually do rape counseling myself, but worked with them when I was writing a directory for women for the city that I was living in.

PB: You wrote a directory for women?

S: Yes. I don't know that they've ever published it yet, but (when I left) the work was still incomplete and I don't know if the women's center took it over or not. I was very sad about that because I never saw it materialized, but I did do the section on rape and so I worked with the women, but I wasn't actually on the hot lines myself, you know.

PB: O.K., now that's the whole situational thing and we are now going to background . . . .

O.K., now has a man ever tried to attack you before.

S: Yes.

PB: O.K., tell me about it.

S: This was when I was 14-15, and it was at a New Year's Eve party and we had gone out for beer. I was accompanying him on this beer run, and when we got into the car, he leaned over to molest me and it was a very frightening scene, I was terrified. He seemed suddenly enormous, you know, and I was just . . . I didn't know what to do.

PB: Was he your age?

S: He was, I think, 19 or so.

PB: So he was quite a bit older, from 15 to 19.

S: Right, right. It was a real disparity.

PB: And what did you do?

S: Again, I wanted out of the situation as quickly and cleanly as possible and I was so . . . so . . . thoroughly confused and frightened by it that I was kind of panicky, and he had reached around and locked the door (beside) me. And . . . he wasn't threatening me in the way that _____ was, in the sense of "Be nice. Act like a lady." kind of thing. But this was, I guess, standard practice kind of thing, like "You fool, what did you think was going to happen when we got out to the car," you know, which made me feel even worse, you know. And I remember, "I'm not going to have sex with you, I can't have sex with you," you know, "Blah, blah, blah, blah."

PB: You were thinking or saying?

S: I was saying these things. And pushing him back, he had pushed me back down on the seat and he wanted me to perform oral sex. And . . . I just . . . I just couldn't . . . you know, it was just a . . . a . . . a really rotten scene.

PB: And, so how did you end up? Did you end up performing any sexual acts with him?

S: Well, he pushed my head down into his lap, you know, and kind of kept it down there . . . and . . . I just started kind of muffled screaming and he let me up.

PB: He let you up.

S: Yeah, and . . . we . . . I don't remember any of the conversation or anything really that was going on here . . . but . . . we went back into the party after that, and it kind of just diffused at that point, and that was . . .

PB: What do you think made him decide not to force you?

S: Maybe he lost his erection at that point, you know . . . It's probably much foggier in my memory than . . .

PB: Do you think what happened to you then had any effect on you later on in terms of your interest in rape, or your taking self-defense?

S: Not consciously, but I'm sure, in retrospect, that has. I'm very sure it has. It's certainly changed my subsequent actions with young men, you know. I think that I was a) much less trusting and b) (I guess this goes hand in hand) much more suspicious and much more wary.

PB: Has a man ever been physical . . . has any other man tried to attack you before?

S: No.

PB: Has a man ever been physically violent to you?

S: I was hit once, yeah. But that was . . . not in anger so much as to "show you who's boss" kind of thing by a guy who was at a restaurant that I once worked at. It was just a . . . but that's . . .

PB: Was he your supervisor, or . . .

S: No, he was a customer.

PB: And what happened? What was your response to that?

S: I walked away, you know; it wasn't a situation I had a stand at, but that . . .

PB: Were you ever molested as a child by a stranger, neighbor, teacher or relative?

S: No.

PB: O.K., these are some vignettes. You see smoke coming out of a broiler, you open it and there's a grease fire inside, what would you do?

S: Put baking soda on it. I can't believe I said that!

PB: Well, that's exactly what you do.

S: Well, O.K . . . .

PB: Well, I just don't . . .

S: Because I know that's what you do to a grease fire, you know . . . and . . .

PB: Has it ever happened to you?

S: No.

PB: You're driving along and your car suddenly stops. What do you do?

S: Get out and open the engine.

PB: And check it out and, you know, get back in your car, or what?

S: Well, seeing how this has happened to me before, see if the gas line is clogged or . . . maybe check the terminals in the battery, but that wouldn't tend to happen, not with driving. I don't know a lot about cars, but I would do my level best to look around.

PB: Have you ever taken any car repair courses?

S: No. I hate working on my car. I worked on it, you know, I get the idiot book out and I look at it, but, no, I've never . . .

PB: Do you know how to change tires?

S: Yeah, except on my car, you can never get the _____ off, but, yes, I know how to change tires.

PB: O.K., so you know something about the car, but you just don't like to do it. O.K. You are late for an appointment and you realize that you're lost. What do you do?

S: Try to get my bearings again, quickly. I would move as quickly as possible.

PB: (Do you have a map?)/(Did you have a map?)

S: Yeah, in my . . . I'm not sure if you meant lost in the city, lost in a building, lost . . .

PB: In the city, essentially.

S: If I were in my car, I might be inclined to pull out the map and take a quick look at it. If I were walking, I would try to find the nearest landmarks, as we were talking about before, to try to reget my bearings.

PB: O.K. You're taking care of a child who cuts her-/himself and is bleeding severely. What do you do?

S: I would run it under cold water and put ice on it until I could see how large the cut was and either take the child to the hospital or just keep it bound until the bleeding stopped if it wasn't too serious.

PB: Do you know first-aid?

S: No, _____

PB: Do you know what to do if somebody has suffered from a burn?

S: I've heard, again, that cold water is the best thing to do. If the burn isn't too serious.

PB: Sprained ankle?

S: In karate (I've had lots of experience!). If you can get at it right away, soaking it can keep the swelling down, but if you don't, then—if you bandage it right away, then the swelling can stay down—but if you don't, then you just have to let the swelling go down.

PB: Electric shock?

S: What to do for it?

PB: If somebody is shocked.

S: I wouldn't know. I wouldn't know what to do.

PB: Did you ever have a child cut himself or herself or, you know, anybody, where you had to deal with that situation. Did you ever have that experience?

S: No, only myself. Do I count as a child?

PB: Is that what you did?

S: Yeah.

PB: O.K., I've noticed that you lived alone. How long have you lived alone?

S: Since I moved here last fall.

PB: Do you like living alone?

S: Yeah.

PB: Why?

S: I really enjoy the quiet time. I find the time I have with my friends is all the more richer, and I don't have to vie for time alone. I like to be at liberty to carry out my idiosyncratic habits like, you know, Beethoven at 5:00 in the morning, and that's something that, out of courtesy to roommates, I could never do.

PB: Did you have roommates before you moved here?

S: Yeah. I lived with—and in fact that was a really close situation, and I so much appreciated it and it's almost in honor of that that I don't think I would even attempt another situation.

PB: Were those women roommates?

S: Yeah, there were two women I lived with and the three of us were very close, and it was really nice.

PB: When did you begin self-defense?

S: Self-defense . . . about two and a half years ago. And I started karate about two years ago. A little bit more than that.

PB: What is the difference between self-defense and karate. I mean, I know there's a difference, but I want to know what . . .

S: Well, the self-defense was more of a clinic kind of thing . . . several Saturdays kind of . . . and it was dirty fighting. It was just to give one suggestions of seeing yourself in action upon being attacked . . . go for the eyes or the jugular or if you're grabbed in this position how to get out of it, or, you know . . . just practicing, you know, with another woman and . . . The teacher for the self-defense was also the karate teacher eventually and I started studying under her a few months later in karate.

PB: Why did you begin . . . why did you decide to learn self-defense?

S: Well, I had gone to a conference that — for women, which was at one of the clinics that you could go to and broke down into smaller seminars in the afternoon — and I just went to it to see what it was like more than anything else. I mean, I knew I would be interested in learning some self-defense — didn't think I would be *that* interested! — but I was . . . I had heard about the teacher, and had heard that she was a marvelous woman and I wanted to meet her, and so . . .

PB: Did you ever take assertiveness training?

S: No.

PB: Do you know how to use any weapons? Guns or knives?

S: No.

PB: What words would you have used to describe yourself as you were three years ago?

S: Three years ago would be, you know, junior year of college and . . . I was . . . generally very angry and tired . . . very tired . . . and . . . busy. That was really a low point, I would say, in my life, altogether . . . confused would also fit in there, and radically feminist, and spreading myself thin.

PB: And, do you think about yourself the same way today?

S: No, I don't.

PB: How do you think . . . are you still as angry?

S: No.

PB: Are you still tired?

S: No.

PB: Are you still busy?

S: Yes.

PB: Are you still confused?

S: No. Much less so, I mean, I don't feel I've arrived at the golden answer, but . . . .

PB: Are you still radically feminist?

S: I am still feminist . . . I won't say that's radically so, in spirit, but my goal is to be much more productive in my actualization of that, whereas I wasn't so much before, I was really very much running on anger before and when the anger would dissipate, the energy would, too, which was a problem I kept running into.

PB: Oh, I see.

S: I feel in general much more . . . loving now . . . I can't quite . . . that's not a good word to use because it's used so often, but . . . .

PB: Loving towards women or loving towards men or humanity?

S: Humanity, I would say. Not that I . . . not that I feel less loving towards women, but I feel more that my . . . I see that the goals I hope for with women are inherently locked up with humanity. I'm not making that terrifically clear.

PB: I know what you mean. Are you still spreading yourself thin?

S: Yes! I would say so! Not as thin, maybe, but . . .

PB: Are you still in school?

S: Yes, I'm still in school and I'm in a hard science program.

PB: Is there anything else that you could add about yourself now that was not on the list?

S: I'm much more energetic and a lot happier.

PB: Now, did your response to sexual assault affect your self-image in any way?

S: No, if anything, I would say it was in line with my character. It didn't . . . I was a bit surprised, as I mentioned, about my telling someone I would kill them because I'd never said that to somebody before and that *surprised* me, but I won't say it made some glaring . . . impression.

PB: O.K., how old are your brothers and sisters?

S: I have an older sister and younger brother, older by three years and younger by seven.

PB: O.K., Did you ever live in a bad neighborhood, I mean, where there's a lot of crime?

S: Does Hyde Park count?

PB: Where did you grow up?

S: I grew up in a northern suburb of a large midwestern city. That was not considered a bad neighborhood. The nearby university was unfortunately notorious for high rape statistics, but it was not in general considered a bad neighborhood, which was one thing that made it so dangerous. No, I would say, not until I moved here . . . to the more dangerous aspects of life.

PB: What words would you use to describe your mother?

S: I get one word, huh?

PB: No, *words*.

S: Well . . . she is . . . the two words that come to mind are so contradictory that they demand more. They were "frail" and "strong." But that is very much how she is . . .

PB: Is it situational, that is in some situations she's strong and in other situations she's frail?

S: Yeah, very much so.

PB: Under what circumstances is she strong?

S: As she pursues her will . . . as she strives for something important to her. She is also . . . can be very strong when somebody needs her . . . a child . . . one of her kids.

PB: How was she about the rape?

S: She was very supportive. In fact, she's generally very supportive about my life altogether, and when she heard of that, she . . . just . . . was . . . you know, she thought it was tremendous how I handled it kind of thing.

PB: Was that being supportive, or was that ———— ?

S: Yeah, supportive.

PB: How about your father? What words would you use to describe him?

S: He's . . . extremely friendly and gregarious, outgoing . . . but — what is the word? — I can't put this into one word, maybe a phrase would do. He tends to sweep a lot of things under the carpet.

PB: Psychoanalytically speaking, would you say (he generally used) denial?

S: Yeah, O.K.

PB: When you (were home) did you and your brother and sister quarrel?

S: Well, that's two separate questions. My sister and I, no. We were very close. My brother and I are also very close, but because of the age gap, when we were growing up, I was more in a baby-sitting role and so there was all a discipline kind of thing, but it wasn't quarreling at the same level, but . . .

PB: So you were sort of in charge of disciplining him and taking care of him . . .

S: Right.

PB: And did you use physical force?

S: I'm sure I've hit him . . . yes.

PB: Who usually won these encounters?

S: Oh, I did! Seven years is a big gap! For a long time I could never understand how he could possibly love me, in fact I had tremendous guilt when I first started college that I had permanently ruined our relationship.

PB: How did your parents feel about the way you were disciplining him, or your direction, or if you were fighting with him?

S: They . . . they always thought I was fair . . . they always supported me, you know, and . . .

PB: Did they punish him?

S: Well, quite often the plan was I wasn't to do anything, and just tell them about it. Yes, so in those cases that was what happened.

PB: Did you and your schoolmates and neighborhood children quarrel?

S: No.

PB: Did you usually try to avoid fighting with other children?

S: Yes! Not only other children but other adults. It was a long-standing pattern.

PB: (Why did you enroll in) self-defense?

S: To avoid fighting other people.

PB: To avoid fighting other people.

S: I would say that motivations could be a little bit (separate), but . . . maybe . . . I do tend to avoid an argument at any cost, you know, I mean I just will . . . will back down very quickly, but . . . I don't know, I've never thought about that before. I don't think I've ever really examined deeply the reasons for getting into karate. I always thought it was "I want more autonomy," you know. I wanted to feel safe. Now I'm sure that's in there, but . . . then _____ the confidence that it would confer. Yes, it also does give me the liberty to avoid fights, that's true.

PB: Are you still taking it?

S: Karate? Yeah. When I'm not injured. It tends to amplify injuries. My back is one of nature's little mistakes.

PB: Did you usually threaten to tell adults in order to avoid a fight with other children?

S: I don't remember a situation in which I did that, but it would be in line with how I think of myself at that time, if you follow my meaning. Yes, that would make sense. I would do something like that.

PB: That's comfortable. Possible or probable?

S: I'd say probable.

PB: How did your parents generally advise you to react to expressions of aggression from other children?

S: I don't remember any advice given to that effect.

PB: When you were a child, did you enjoy roughhousing with other children?

S: Yeah. My brother. With him in particular. We used to play a lot . . . I guess there was little age difference there!

PB: You had the responsibility for taking care of your brother, you told me. Your sister didn't?

S: She . . . did . . . in part, but it seemed that somehow the responsibility was more on my shoulders than on hers. Maybe it was because when he was born, I was still into dolls—you know, I was seven or something like that—and maybe it was just that—Wow!—I know that it was pointed out to me many times that I really took to him quickly and that there was a closeness between he and I that there wasn't between him and my sister and maybe that kind of stayed with us, but I – and I think anyone in the family would generally concur with this – that I was principally in charge of him.

PB: Did you have other responsibilities for the house, too?

S: Yeah.

PB: What kind of responsibilities did you have for the house?

S: Cleaning and laundry and cooking . . .

PB: . . . what age?

S: Well, we had a sitter. My mother worked full-time. We had a sitter from when I was four till I was about 12. And I started working for a woman down the block who had just gone through a divorce, and I was taking care of her house for about two years and then I came and did it at our house from about 14 up.

PB: When you had problems as a teenager, to whom did you turn for advice?

S: Do I get choices?

PB: Yeah, you can have more than one.

S: Uhm . . . for advice . . .

PB: What did you do when you had problems, O.K.?

S: When I was a freshman in high school, I was really going through . . . I was really very distraught . . . and I was in . . . seeing a psychiatrist for a while, who was . . . I guess the whole family's had _____ with doctors. I _____ for mental problems initially, and then my mother was in therapy for a long time, and so when I was expressing anxieties, it was suggested that I go see Dr. _____ and that's who I saw for a while. But, I decided after about a month or two that I was miracley (sic) cured, and that I wasn't going to see him any more! And . . . and, subsequently I mostly didn't go to people with problems. I found some, you know, comfort in friends and stuff, but as I think back to high school, the overwhelming problem was I was just feeling very lonely and there was no one to talk to about feeling lonely, I mean, in its very nature, so I'd say generally no one.

PB: I'll put down "no one." I'm not sure you're really telling me you *solved* them by yourself. I think what you're saying is you *dealt* with them by yourself.

S: Yeah . . . "dealt with" would be better in that . . . yeah, it wasn't as though there was a particular crisis that I had to get an answer to, it was just a kind of ongoing thing.

PB: Why do you think you felt so lonely and, you know, it seems to me that you have a very, you know, nice self presentation and you have the kinds of attributes that make for having friends and not being lonely and this is just a question out of curiosity because . . . Was it that you were so smart and you were interested in physics and things like that that girls weren't, or . . . ?

S: I had . . . I had . . . friends, and there was usually, at any point in high school, a closest friend, a best friend kind of thing. I think that the loneliness I was feeling more than anything was that I wasn't going out on dates. And I wasn't going to the . . . I wasn't a part of the gang that could have fun at school parties and dances . . . .

PB: Was that because you were smart?

S: Like anyone that gets good grades and takes accelerated classes, I was classed as a "brain," you know . . .

PB: When you were growing up, what did you think life would be like when you were grown up?

S: Easier! I also had this notion – I think this only crosses my mind because I have thought of it lately – that one stopped growing at 18. That there was a phase of growth that one went through when young that one ceases to do when older.

PB: And did you have any fantasy about what your life would be like other than "easier," I mean, some concrete image or fantasy?

S: I used to always imagine my house, what my house would be like. And . . . curiously enough, I was always alone in the house. It was *my* house, you know.

PB: O.K., so it wasn't a house with a husband coming home . . . ?

S: No.

PB: Did you (have) the idea a man would take care of you when you grew up?

S: No.

PB: Before you were 12 or 13, how often did you play with dolls? Often? Occasionally? Once or twice?

S: Occasionally.

PB: How often did you read?

S: At what age are we talking?

PB: Well, you can specify, if you want, the ages.

S: I did not do outside, pleasure-type reading mostly in high school. Younger than that, I did a great deal. But, once into high school . . .

PB: Why not high school?

S: The phrase sticks in my mind . . . I was rather work-obsessed!

PB: O.K., play softball, except when required in school?

S: There was a time when I did, but not consistently. Fifth grade. I remember finding, to my surprise — my shock — that I really enjoyed it, so I guess we might say occasionally.

PB: Football?

S: The same thing: occasionally and . . .

PB: Why did you stop?

S: Well, it was just that I played it with the neighborhood kids kind of thing and so when the team got together, we played, but eventually the team just kind of quit getting together, you know.

PB: Would you say you were a tomboy when you were growing up?

S: No, not exactly. I was . . . far from dainty! I was *not* dainty! But . . . I usually associate "tomboy" with someone who climbs trees a lot and I, I mean, I was not . . .

PB: You say, you weren't "dainty," would you say you were like a traditional girl?

S: . . . uhm . . . I would say yeah . . . it didn't strike me that if there was anything . . .

PB: Now, were you ever told to hide showing how smart you were?

S: Two answers. From the parents, no. The suggestion was generally that one of these days, the boys will go for the smart girl. You know, it doesn't pay off yet, but it will. You know, this kind of thing. However, I did have a grandmother who . . . I guess the grandparents were a bit more vocal on this. One side was encouraging as the other side was discouraging. The discouraging was to the effect of they were sure I'd get a brain tumor from studying so hard and it was made very explicit, "You'll never get a man that way."

PB: O.K. Did you ever hide how smart you were?

S: Yes.

PB: When did you used to hide how smart you were? In high school, college?

S: I'll put it this way. I don't like to make people feel uncomfortable, you know, and I don't . . . I still . . . One of my favorite places to go is to the northern woods. There's a little town up there that I've gone every year since (I/it) was just an idea, and I enjoy the people up there, but even now when I go up there I make a point of literally not talking over heads.

PB: O.K., did you ever hide how smart you were so that boys would like you?
S: Yeah, I did that, too. And that would be high school. Yes.
PB: Did your parents want you to have a career, marry, or both?
S: Both.
PB: What kind of combination of the two did they have in mind?
S: I think that . . . I get the impression that that changed. When I was really young, I wanted to be an astronaut. I was caught up in the space age of the '60s and they were gung ho for that, I mean, they just thought that was terrific, you know. As it got closer to looking like it might happen . . . They never de-emphasized career at all, it's just that I started realizing more and more pressure as I got older that, "You will get married someday, won't you?" And that still goes on.
PB: Do you think you will get married someday?
S: I have my doubts. I know never to say never, but I really can't imagine it.
PB: How much schooling did your parents think you should have?
S: My father thought I should go through college and was dismayed when I went to grad school . . . not dismayed, but he quite assured me that GM would be glad to take me. And my mother was a bit more open ended on it: as much as I wanted would be fine.
PB: And how much did you want?
S: Well, I'm still wanting. She's still emotionally . . . well, my father is, too. They know that I want this and . . .
PB: When you were making career plans, did you always . . . well, you wanted to be an astronaut . . . did you think in terms of graduate work . . . ?
S: Well, the astronaut phase was junior high school. Into high school, I started thinking more science and went to undergrad school as a science major. And then . . . I knew I wanted to go to grad school. I knew I wanted my Ph.D. I thought that I'd do it in science, though, and . . . I guess in high school I decided I'd be going to grad school and . . . Then when I picked up the philosophy, they really were shocked!
PB: Well, did they actually think you would get married and then you'd stop your career, or did they think that you would have both simultaneously . . . ?
S: I don't think that they thought about it . . . I never had it worked out. I don't think they did either.
PB: Do you think if you were a boy they would have expected more from you in school?
S: No.
PB: How much education do your other siblings have?
S: My older sister went to college for two years and she is now a commercial artist. And my brother is tending toward more vocational lines.
PB: O.K. These are questions about you in the present. Do you engage in sports regularly?
S: Yes.
PB: What do you do besides karate?
S: Weight-lifting
PB: What other kinds of sports?
S: Well, I'm taking up handball, but I'm not very good at it. It's just beginning.
PB: What do you do when people irritate you mildly? Like if a woman pushed in front of you in line at a supermarket?
S: That really depends on my mood, but my tendency would be to be gracious.
PB: O.K., what if it were a man?
S: The same.

PB: What women in public or private life do you admire and why?

S: Oh, dear! The women that I have known well enough to really admire closely would be in private life, and . . . I'm very close to one of my grandmothers, whom I admire a great deal. The overall characteristic across the board is love and strength. Just an ongoing, you know . . . a caring, and a pushing forth of ideas and actualizations of things important to them . . . Across the board, from former karate instructors to professors that I really enjoyed . . . and women who work in women's issues . . . .

PB: I'm just curious, which ones?

S: Did I really come to admire?

PB: Yeah.

S: A professor in the Philosophy Department there . . . it was just . . . she's tremendously courageous . . . she's so open with her life and the style she chooses to live it and it's meeting with a lot of resistance in the department.

PB: She's chair of women's studies now.

S: Yeah. Tremendous! Oh, tremendous! She also has an overwhelming amount of strength and just a gentleness that I really admire. But she can also be very anger-driven, too. That's why I said, "for slightly different reasons," because I'd characterize as love and strength, and while she can be very loving, I know that there's also . . . very . . . an angrier side that I've seen on one occasion. I didn't know her as well, but also _____.

PB: In terms of precautions to avoid being in potentially dangerous situations, what kinds of restrictions did you place on your life before you were assaulted?

S: Since moving to Chicago, I have made — I don't really see the assault so much as a breaking point as I've gotten progressively more paranoid and more cautious.

PB: Could you operationalize that for me.

S: When I first moved here, I was looking for an apartment, and I sauntered up and down street after street after street in areas I would not walk now . . . in the middle of the day . . . in the Hyde Park area. And then, as I started to get to know the area better, I would walk less at night and if I had to walk some-where, stay on the main streets and walk very quickly. I tend to get my key ready before going out to my car. Just things like that. A constant kind of . . . Make a bee-line between cars and doors that I have to get to . . . .

PB: What kind of mechanical precautions did you have in your apartment when you moved in?

S: In terms of locks on doors, or . . . ?

PB: Peepholes, locks, etc.

S: I don't have a peephole, but there's a chain over the door. There's, you know, dibolt locks and then . . . .

PB: Does dibolt mean you have to unlock it to get . . . .

S: Right.

PB: What about to get into the house? Do you have to buzz to get in?

S: Yeah, down in the lobby, for every apartment you have to buzz to get in, but you can't see who's down there . . . at all . . . and you can't talk to them, so you buzz them . . . . The suggestion that I had gotten when I moved in there is that you buzz them in and then answer your door with the chain over it, because if you go down there, they could have buzzed someone else earlier and then be holding the door open and you go down to open it and they . . .

PB: Did you add any security devices when you moved in?

S: No.

PB: What floor did you live on?

S: I live on the first floor, but it's not a ground level, it's . . .

PB: When you move, do you try not to be on the ground floor?

S: Yes. But most of the apartments in Hyde Park are built so that they aren't on ground level.

PB: Do you ever get angry and yell at your friends or lovers or whatever?

S: I don't like to say "never," but, no.

PB: Think back to the last time you were angry. Do you remember the last time you were angry?

S: At a particular person or over a course of events?

PB: Think back to the last time you were angry at a person.

S: You mean angry, not just mildly irritated? It's just that it's a problem in my case, because I really hesitate to even admit to myself that I'm angry. I much prefer saying that, you know, I'm disturbed about this or, I just have to let this be for a while, or something, but to actually say I'm really pissed off at so-and-so seems to be a tough thing for me to say, but . . . yeah, o.k., I'll pinpoint an incident.

PB: O.K., what did you do?

S: Nothing.

PB: How did you feel?

S: Really hurt, just . . .

PB: Is that pretty much the way you ordinarily handle anger?

S: Yeah.

PB: O.K. Now, this isn't (on this), but it's something I have been trying to figure out in interviewing you and, you know as I said with your mother, people do not have to be consistent, but on the one hand you cannot remember being angry, you let people get ahead of you in supermarket lines, you do all this very nonassertive behavior. On the other hand, you did this terribly effective thing with the rapist, you learned karate and continue to take it, you're a radical feminist and still . . . you're more loving now, but . . . I do believe that behavior can be situation-specific, but what I'm trying to find out in my head is this apparent disparity between this one dimension, as I've said, the karate, and your other behavior and your self-image and your attitudes and everything about anger. And do you have any—you don't have to explain it—I mean, but I just wondered if you can see any way out of this *apparent* contradiction.

S: Well, the (part) that I was thinking about when I was explaining about (how) I really don't like to admit that I'm really angry at somebody is that—I was thinking it and I should have continued it and—because it forces me to have to do something about it. To actually admit that I was angry at somebody, I have to take some action. Either I have to sweep it under a carpet, or I have to confront them with it or I have to somehow work it out, you know.

PB: So you don't like to admit it because you feel if you admitted it, you would have to do something about it.

S: O.K., what I'm saying is that I think that I can roll with the _____, so to speak, up to a point, and then there's a certain threshold beyond which I move to action. And I think it's the physics coming out, a phase transition. I find it much easier on myself, if it's a small situation, a trivial situation, to let it go. Don't hang onto the anger, don't hang onto the . . . I know that anger can tear me apart. I've watched it do that before, and . . .

PB: You mean when you were in _____ ?

S: Yeah. I've watched it really rip me up, and before. And I know there are some things worth getting angry about and worth taking action on and other things that, at least in my case, it's much better not to. Maybe my threshold is . . . puts me in the marshmallow range, and it wouldn't surprise me, I mean, I probably might do very well with a bit of assertiveness training, but still . . . I can reach a point and do reach points when . . . I will take action when I'm pushed to a threshold and certainly when it comes to, you know, self-respect and/in _____ space, you know. If somebody nudges in front of me in a supermarket, you know, if I'm really having a rough day, I might say something . . .

PB: What if somebody started molesting you on public transportation?

S: That again is the space problem, and I would definitely do something.

PB: So that seems to be the area in which you will . . .

S: If there's something obscene done somewhere else that I feel I really have to do something . . . I would definitely want to do something, if there's something that really strikes me as an injustice . . . just a human dignity kind of thing. That puts me over the threshold. But, I guess what I would call "lesser offences" I'd much prefer letting them go.

PB: No, that's O.K. it makes sense; there was no contradiction at all . . . . What do you think . . . in order to protect themselves from rape, what kind of advice would you give to other women?

S: Just a general, overall . . . advice would be to . . . This is tough in the abstract. It's much easier in a more concrete situation. The transition to take care of themselves in a sense of first being able to think of themselves in motion, being able to think of themselves as taking action, of taking their own life into their own hands and being able to . . . take . . . to think highly enough of themselves that they realize . . . By no means am I suggesting that women who do not avoid rape do not think highly of themselves. That's not my point. But . . .

PB: We may find that out. We don't know what we're going to find out.

S: Well, no, I don't want to suggest that there's something wrong with them, at all, but if they can see the potential for . . . One real danger with really . . . and I know that I still feel the danger . . . and in a sense feel very vulnerable is that I do really feel a sense of my own space and stuff and I know that as long as I hold very dear to that, that if it's violated, I could be really crushed. And I don't care how much karate I know, if I'm attacked by enough people, with tough enough weapons, there's nothing I can do. And the dearer you hold that, the more you stand to lose. And I think that's really maybe one reason why women hesitate on feeling that good about themselves and about their bodies and about their strengths because then . . . then . . . that makes them . . . more vulnerable in some respects to assaults and that . . .

PB: Are there any kinds of specific precautions you think women should take?

S: Well, I think it would be terrific if women would learn and could learn effective means of self defense, but what it really boils down to — at least it's been my experience — is that, in talking with women who've taken self-defense clinics and stuff like this that the general, over-riding feeling is "This is all very nice and it's tricky, but what if the guy isn't in this kind of position or what if the situation isn't just like this?" The overall thing would just be to get the idea of being in motion, of being able to handle a situation, and that's an attitudinal change as much as any kind of physical preparation, you know. And that's what I have felt more in karate than the physical strength that it has conferred has been the mental, the attitude about taking care of oneself, and I don't know that there's a recipe for taking that, you know, maybe some women who could become very good with knives or guns would say that's a much better way. But certainly a way of being able to defend their space, so they feel good about having it, kind of thing would be . . . .

PB: And anything else in terms of precautions?

S: I always cringe at the suggestion that women have to be . . . their (attitude) has to be curtailed because men can't be trusted, you know, that "Oh, anyone living in Hyde Park I would strongly advise against walking at night." Stuff like that, including myself!

PB: What do you think are effective means of avoiding rape once a man accosts a woman?

S: Showing any sign of resistance.

PB: What methods do you think are ineffective?

S: Compliance to . . . well . . . yeah, compliance to the rapist's orders or . . . .

PB: Are there any other methods that you might do that you think wouldn't work?

S: I was thinking that I was very fortunate in my case that the assaulter was not armed. I would think that showing some kind of threatening physical violence against an armed assaulter could be potentially very dangerous. It's not that I'd say, "Don't do it," but I could see where the anger could even rile the assaulter up more. However, if he was an armed assaulter, it doesn't look so good for you anyway, so . . . .

PB: O.K. You said that you didn't change your behavior since this attack; you changed your behavior, though, since your first attack.

S: Well, it's hard to know because that was when I was 15 and a lot of my behavior, especially relating to being street-wise and relations with men and stuff, just hadn't formed before then, you know, at all. So, yes, it's certainly changed since then and I think that that probably had a gross effect on subsequent attitudes, but I can't really assess it too well.

PB: I know that you did say that the assault did not . . . that your behavior basically changed when you moved into Hyde Park and learned about Hyde Park. Would you say that you changed your behavior at all since your assault, though? The recent assault.

S: The recent assault. Yeah.

PB: How?

S: When the door buzzes and I'm not expecting anybody, I don't answer it. If it buzzes a second time, then I will cautiously buzz the person up and answer with the chain over it, but I do not take the chain off the door. For any reason.

PB: (Why do you think) rape occurs?

S: I think that the thing that perpetuates rape is generally still a popular culture, I mean the kind of . . . a kind of attitude about sex roles that perhaps we don't consciously observe but it's kind of in our bones, I mean, in talking about degrees of rape, and in the lower, the lesser degrees of rape, it's starting to look more like that altogether too romanticized interlude in which the woman is taken, you know, this kind of thing. I think we just . . . in the popular culture, across the board, we tend to carry around attitudes that . . . that . . . perpetuate the kind of fertile soil for rape. Now, at the individual level, why a particular man would go out and rape a woman, I would think as a kind of grasping for power . . . a grasping . . . I do mean a *grasping*, because it always seems at an individual level to be kind of a desperate attempt. I shouldn't say that . . . I don't know if it always seems to be that way, but . . . .

PB: Now, the first thing you talked about was society. The second thing you talked about (was) in terms of an individual man. Now, in terms of the individual male grasping for power, would you say that is because of his own individual background or society or the woman or whatever.

S: Well . . . I would imagine it has considerable amounts to do with his background, his particular background. I also think, though, that society makes a fertile soil for it in that, for example, the courts have always been much more preoccupied with making sure the innocent man isn't falsely accused of rape than assuring the rights of the victim. I mean, and also the ongoing attitude that the woman must have somehow provoked it, you know, that somehow it's still her fault, or something. It all makes . . . .

PB: (If you could have) a line, with individual background and societal contributions and zero to a hundred — it's clear that there are both factors — but where on this continuum, from 0 to 100, would you put society?

S: O.K . . . . I would tend to put it around 60 percent society. More than half, I would think. What I'm saying is that the attitudes are really . . . .

PB: You've been around here how long?

S: In Chicago? Since last September.

PB: O.K., so you didn't see the ads, that's why you didn't show up in the study before, because like I did blanket the city looking for subjects.

S: I seem to recall "Looking for Subjects," that somebody was looking for subjects and I imagined, after hearing about you, that it was you. But when I saw the signs it was before I was assaulted.

PB: So you were assaulted in March and I was looking for subjects . . . yeah . . . And why did you volunteer to be in the study?

S: Because although it's not clear to me exactly how you plan to use the information, if it could anyway improve the condition of rape or the understanding of rape or the . . . hopefully prevention of it, then I would like to contribute to that.

PB: How do you feel about the interview? Were important things left uncovered?

S: Well, you're delightful to speak with. I very much enjoyed it. I wondered at the relevance of some of the questions about childhood, in particular, and some of the situations "What would you do if . . . ?" and such and such . . .

PB: Why did you become a feminist? Do you know?

S: The answer that popped into my head is that I have no choice! What I mean is that _____ just attitudes about . . . feminist-type attitudes, but I was unable to call myself a feminist for quite a while until I knew what it meant. What really, I think, tipped the balance and I realized, "Yep, I'm a feminist," I think was a course that I took in college. (It filled out) the philosophical aspects of feminism and that's when I did a lot of heavy-duty thinking about some of these questions and reviewing some of these attitudes, and it started all coming (around) . . .

GAP IN TAPE (very slight, only a second.)

S: I'm thinking, in response to stressful situations that I think that my response to this particular stressful situation . . . this particular assault was greatly effected . . . that, I mean, one thing that was really helpful was the previous experience with thinking about rape and working, reviewing rape laws and working with rape counseling . . . and that this particular stressful situation was different from others in that I had been primed for this, where I'm not primed for grease fires . . .

PB: You knew what to do.

  S: Yes. My point is that my immediately prior background of the past couple of years made a lot of difference in the way that I . . . .

PB: Do you think it would be useful for other women to learn more about rape?

  S: Yes. Yes. Very much so.

PB: O.K.

END OF TAPE

Bibliography

Abrahamsen, David. 1960. *Psychology of crime.* New York: Columbia University Press.

Albin, Rochelle. 1977. Psychological studies of rape. *Signs* 3:423–435.

Anderson, Mary Pennington. 1980. Personal communication.

Bart, Pauline B. 1967. Depression in middle-aged women: Some socio-cultural factors. Ph.D. dissertation, University of California at Los Angeles. Dissertation abstracts 28:475–18 (University Microfilms No. 08-7452).

———. 1968. Social structure and vocabularies of discomfort: What happened to female hysteria. *Journal of Health and Social Behavior* 9:188–193.

———. 1970. Portnoy's mother's complaint. *Trans-Action* 7(13):69–74.

———. 1971. Depression in middle-aged women. In *Women in sexist society*, edited by Vivian Gornick and Barbara K. Moran. 84–117. New York: Basic Books.

———. 1975. Rape doesn't end with a kiss. *Viva* 11(9):39–41, cont. 100–101.

———. 1976. From those wonderful people that brought you the vaginal orgasm: Sex education for medical students. Paper presented at the annual meeting of the American Sociological Association.

———. 1979a. Rape as a paradigm of sexism in society. *Women's Studies International Quarterly* 2(3):347–357.

———. 1979b. Victimization and its discontents. Paper presented at the annual meetings of the American Psychiatric Association.

———. 1981. A study of women who both were raped and avoided rape. *Journal of Social Issues* 37(4):123–137.

Bart, Pauline B., Linda Freeman, and Peter Kimball. 1985. The different worlds of women and men: Attitudes toward pornography and responses to "Not a love story — a film about pornography." Paper presented at the Second International Interdisciplinary Conference on Women, Groningen, The Netherlands. *Women's Studies International Forum* 8(1):67–82.

Bart, Pauline B., and Margaret Josza. 1980. Dirty books, dirty films and dirty data: Observations on pornography research. In *Take back the night*, edited by Laura Lederer. 204–217. New York: Thomas Morrow.

Bart, Pauline B., and Patricia O'Brien. 1980. How to say no to Storaska and survive. Paper presented at the annual meeting of the American Sociological Association.

———. 1984. Stopping rape: Effective avoidance strategies. *Signs* 10(1):83–101.

Bart Pauline B., and Kim Lane Scheppele. 1980. There ought to be a law: Self definitions and legal definitions of sexual assault. Presented at the annual meeting of the American Sociological Association, August.

Block, Richard, and Wesley C. Skogan. 1982. Resistance and outcome in robbery and rape: Nonfatal stranger to stranger violence. Unpublished paper, Center for Urban Affairs and Policy Research, Northwestern University.

Bradley, Marion Z. 1976. *Shattered chain*. New York: DAW Books.

Brooks, Andree. 1981. Helping the short child cope, *The New York Times*, November 30, Section 2, p. 16.

——. 1984. Birth rank. Effects on personality. *The New York Times*, March 26, p. 17.

Brownmiller, Susan. 1975. *Against our will: Men, women and rape*. New York: Simon and Schuster.

Burgess, Ann Wolbert, and Lynda L. Holmstrum. 1974. The rape trauma syndrome. *The American Journal of Psychiatry* 131:981–986.

Carruthers, Iva E. 1979. War on African familyhood. In *Sturdy black bridges,* edited by Roseann P. Bell, Bettye J. Parker, and Beverly Guy-Sheftall. 8–17. Garden City, NY: Anchor Press.

Chicago/Cook County Criminal Justice Commission. *Rape be aware*. A pamphlet distributed by numerous Cook County agencies.

Clark, Lorenne, and Debra Lewis. 1977. *Rape: The price of coercive sexuality*. Toronto, Canada: The Women's Press.

Cohn, E., L. H. Kidder, and J. Harvey. 1981. Criminal prevention vs. victimization prevention: The psychology of different reactions. *Victimology: An International Journal* 3:285–296.

Davis, Angela. 1983. *Women, race and class*. New York: Random House.

Dejanikus, Tacie. 1981. New studies support active resistance to rape. *off our backs* (February):9–23.

Dixon, Marlene. 1983. *The future of women*. San Francisco: Synthesis Publications.

Dobash, R. Emerson, and Russell Dobash. 1979. *Violence against wives: A case against the patriarchy*. New York: The Free Press.

Donnerstein, Edward, and Daniel Linz. 1984. Sexual violence in the media: A warning. *Psychology Today* 18 (January):14–15.

Eichelberger, Brenda. 1981. Personal communication.

Erikson, Erik H. 1953. *Childhood and society*. New York: Norton.

Ferree, Myra Marx. 1976. Working-class jobs: Housework and paid work as sources of satisfaction. *Social Problems* 23(4):431–441.

——. 1981. Personal communication.

——. 1983. Personal communication.

Finkelhor, David. 1979. *Sexually victimized children*. New York: The Free Press.

Fitzgerald-Richards, Dell. 1974. *The rape journal*. Oakland, CA: Women's Press Collective.

Fox, Greer Litton. 1977. Nice girl: Social control of women through a value construct. *Signs* 2(4):805–817.

Freeman, Linda. 1982. Personal communication.

Frieze, Irene Hanson. 1983. Investigating the causes and consequences of marital rape. *Signs* 8(3):532–553.

Frieze, Irene Hanson, Jaime Knoble, Carol Washburn, and Gretchen Zomnir. 1979. Psychological factors in violent marriages. Unpublished paper.

Gearheart, Sally. 1979. *The wanderground—Stories of the hill women*. Watertown, MA: Persephone Press.

Giarrusso, R., P. Johnson, J. Goodchilds, and G. Zellman. 1979. Adolescents' cues and signals: Sex and assault. Paper presented at the annual meeting of the Western Psychological Association, San Diego, California, April.

Gilman, Charlotte Perkins. 1979. *Herland*. New York: Pantheon Press.

Goldberg, Steven. 1974. *The inevitability of patriarchy*. New York: William Morrow and Co.

Griffin, Susan. 1971. Rape: The all-American crime. *Ramparts* 10:26–35.

Groth, A. Nicholas. 1979. *Men who rape: The psychology of the offender*. New York: Plenum Press.

Heath, Linda, Margaret T. Gordon, Stephanie R. Riger, and Robert LeBailey. 1979. What newspapers tell us (and don't tell us) about rape. Presented at the meetings of the American Psychology Association, New York, September.

Henley, Nancy. 1977. *Body politics: Power, sex and non-verbal communications*. New York: Prentice-Hall.

Herman, Judith L. with Lisa Herschman. 1981. *Father-daughter incest*. Cambridge, MA: Harvard University Press.

Janoff-Bulman, Ronnie. 1979. Characterological versus behavioral self-blame: Inquiries in depression and rape. *Journal of Personality and Social Psychology* 37:1798–1809.

Kanter, Rosabeth Moss. 1977. *Men and women of the corporation*. New York: Basic Books.

Kanter, Rosabeth Moss. 1978. Personal correspondence.

Kantor, Glenda, and Gail Weinberger. 1979. Women and anger. Unpublished paper. University of Illinois at Chicago, Department of Sociology.

Kaye, Melanie, and Michaela Uccella. 1981. Survival as an act of resistance. In *Fight Back*, edited by Frederique Delacoste and Felice Newman. 14–25. Minneapolis, MN: Cleis Press.

Komarovsky, Mirra. 1962. *Blue collar marriage*. New York: Random House.

Kidder, Louise H., Joanne L. Boell, and Marilyn M. Moyer. 1983. Rights consciousness and victimization prevention: Personal defense and assertiveness training. *Journal of Social Issues* 39(2):155–170.

Ladner, Joyce A. 1971. *Tomorrow's tomorrow: The black woman*. Garden City, NY: Doubleday and Co.

LaFree, Gary. 1980a. The effect of sexual stratification by race on official reactions to rape. *American Sociological Review* 45:824–854.

———. 1980b. Assessing official reactions to rape: A multivariate analysis of the police response. Paper presented at the annual meetings of American Sociological Association.

Lederer, Laura. ed. 1980. *Take back the night: Women on pornography*. New York: Thomas Morrow.

LeGrand, Camille E. 1973. Rape and rape laws: Sexism in society and law. *California Law Review* 61:919–941.

Le Guin, Ursula. 1980. *The left hand of darkness*. New York: Harper & Row.

Lichtenstein, Grace. 1981. The wooing of women athletes. *New York Times Magazine* 130 (Feb. 8):26.

MacKinnon, Catharine A. 1979. *Sexual harassment and working women*. New Haven, CT: Yale University Press.

———. 1981a. In-class lecture at Stanford (California) University Law School.

———. 1981b. Personal communication.

———. 1983. Feminism, marxism, method and the state: Toward feminist jurisprudence. *Signs* 8(4):635–658.

Malamuth, N. 1981. Rape proclivity among males. *Journal of Social Issues* 37(4):138–157.

Malamuth, N., and Edward Donnerstein. 1984. *Pornography and sexual aggression*. New York: Academic Press.

Margolis, Marvin O. 1977. Mother-son incest. *Annual of Psychoanalysis* 5:267–293.

Marolla, J., and Diana Scully. 1979. Rape and psychiatric vocabularies of motive. In *Gender and disordered behavior: Sex differences in psychopathology*, edited by E. Gomberg and V. Franks. New York: Brunner/Mazel.

McDermott, Joan. 1979. *Rape victimization in 26 American cities*. Washington, DC: U.S. Department of Justice.

McIntyre, Jennie J. 1980. Victim response to rape: Alternative outcomes. Final report of grant MH 29045, National Institute of Mental Health.

Miller, P. Y. 1979. Female delinquency: Fact and fiction. In *Female Adolescent Development*, edited by Max Sugar. 115–140. New York: Brunner/Mazel.

Morris, Jan. 1974. *Conundrum*. New York: Harcourt Brace Jovanovich.

Naylor, Gloria. 1983. *The women of Brewster Place*. New York: Viking.

Near, Holly. 1978. Fight back. On *Imagine My Surprise* album. Redwood Records, Oakland, California.

Neudel, Marian Henriques. 1980. Personal correspondence.

Peterson, Susan Rae. 1977. Coercion and rape: The state as a male protection racket. In *Feminism and philosophy*, edited by Mary Vetterling-Braggin, Frederick A. Elliston, and Jane English. 360–371. Totowa, NJ: Littlefield, Adams & Co.

Piercy, Marge. 1976. *Woman at the edge of time*. New York: Knopf.

Pleck, Joseph H. 1981. *The myth of masculinity*. Cambridge, MA: MIT Press.

Queen's Bench Foundation. 1976. *Rape prevention and resistance*. San Francisco, California.

Riger, Stephanie, and Margaret T. Gordon. 1981. The fear of rape: A study in social control. *Journal of Social Issues* 34(4):71–92.

Rondini, Denise. 1982. Personal communication.

Rush, Florence. 1980. *The best kept secret: Sexual abuse of children*. Englewood Cliffs, NJ: Prentice-Hall.

Russell, Diana E. H. 1975. *The politics of rape*. New York: Stein and Day.

——. 1980. Pornography and violence: What does the new research say? In *Take back the night: Women on pornography*, edited by Laura Lederer. 218–238. New York: Thomas Morrow.

——. 1982. *Rape in marriage*. New York: MacMillan.

Russell, Diana E. H., and Nancy Howell. 1983. The prevalence of rape in the United States revisited. *Signs* 8(4):688–695.

Sanders, William B. 1980. *Rape and woman's identity*. Beverly Hills, CA: Sage Publications.

Scheppele, Kim L., and Pauline B. Bart. 1983. Through women's eyes: Defining danger in the wake of sexual assault. *Journal of Social Issues* 39(2):63–80.

Schwendinger, Herman, and Julia Schwendinger. 1974. Rape myths: In legal, theoretical and everyday practice. *Crime and Social Justice: A Journal of Radical Criminology* 1 (Spring-Summer):80.

Scully, Diana H. 1981. Personal communication.

Scully, Diana, and Pauline Bart. 1973. A funny thing happened on the way to the orifice: Women in gynecology texts. *American Journal of Sociology* 78: 1045–1051.

Scully, Diana, and Joseph Marolla. 1981. Convicted rapists' attitudes towards women and rape. Paper presented at the First International, Interdisciplinary Congress on Women, University of Haifa, Israel, Dec. 28, 1981–Jan. 1, 1982.

——. 1984. Convicted rapists' vocabulary of motive: Excuses and justifications. *Social Problems* 41(4).

————. "Riding the bull at Gilly's": Convicted rapists describe the rewards of rape. 1985. *Social Problems.*

Sennett, Richard, and Jonathan Cobb. 1972. *The hidden injuries of class.* New York: Vantage Books.

Shange, Ntozake. 1977. *For colored girls who have considered suicide and for whom the rainbow is not enuf.* New York: Macmillan.

Smith, Don. 1976. Sexual aggression in American pornography: The stereotype of rape. Presented at the annual meetings of the American Sociological Association, New York.

Smithyman, Samuel David. 1978. The undetected rapist. Claremont Graduate School. Unpublished dissertation.

Star, Susan Leigh. 1978. The politics of wholeness, II. *Sinister Wisdom* (5):82–105.

Statistical Analysis Version of Department of Law Enforcement Supplementary Homicide Report. 1981. Table: Total rape homicide offenses in Chicago Standard Metropolitan Statistical Area: 1976–1980 by victim and offender race.

Statistical Analysis Center Edition of the Illinois Crime Report Data. 1981. Table: Rape and attempted rape offenses in Chicago Standard Metropolitan Statistical Area: 1972–1980.

Storaska, Frederick. 1975. *How to say no to a rapist and survive.* New York: Random House.

Sykes, Gresham M., and David Matza. 1957. Techniques of neutralization: A theory of delinquency. *American Sociological Review* 22:664–669.

Veevers, Jean E., and Susan M. Adams. 1982. Bringing bodies back in: The neglect of sex differences in size and strength. Paper presented to the Canadian Sociology and Anthropology Association, Ottawa, Ontario, Canada, June.

Walker, Alice. 1982. *The color purple.* New York: Harcourt Brace Jovanovich.

Wolfgang, Marvin E., and Marc Reidel. 1977. Patterns of criminal homicide. In *Forcible Rape,* edited by Duncan Chappell, Robley Geis, and Gilbert Geis. 115–128. New York: Columbia University Press.

Zillman, Dolf, and Jennings Bryant. 1982. Pornography, sexual callousness, and the trivialization of rape. *Journal of Communication* 32(4):10–21.

Case Index

Subject Index

About the Authors

Pauline B. Bart, a leading voice in the women's movement since the 1960s, is a professor of sociology in the departments of psychiatry and sociology at the University of Illinois at Chicago. She has been a visiting professor/ scholar at Harvard, University of California at Los Angeles, University of California at Santa Barbara, and San Diego State University. Professor Bart received her PhD in 1967, writing about depressed middle-aged women. Her research has always been relevant to women's condition, holding true to her belief that the purpose of feminist scholarship is to demystify the world of women. She is both a mother and a grandmother — her son is a lawyer and her daughter is a social worker. Some of the books for which Professor Bart is known are *A Funny Thing Happened on the Way to the Orifice, Taking the Men Out of Menopause* and *The Loneliness of the Long Distance Mother.*

Patricia H. O'Brien, a doctoral candidate at the University of Illinois at Chicago and an instructor at several area colleges, has been active in researching women's issues for ten years. She is known throughout the Chicago metropolitan area for her work with rape victims. Professor O'Brien clinically applies her research knowledge to her role as Board President at Rainbow House/Arco Iris shelter for battered women, a position she has held for over two years.